D1590462

Praise for TONY ALLEN

"There would be no Afrobeat without Tony Allen."
— **FELA ANIKULAPO-KUTI**

"The greatest living drummer as far as I'm concerned."
— **BRIAN ENO**

"There is no question that Tony Allen is a genius, one of the greatest percussionists in the history of popular music."
— **ROBIN DENSELOW**, *The Guardian*

"When Tony Allen and Afrika 70 play, the funk really does seem like it could go on forever."
— **PAT BLASHILL**, *Rolling Stone*

"In the 1970s Mr. Allen's drumming put the central beat in Fela's Afrobeat. With off beats on the bass drum and accents staggered between hi-hat cymbal and snare drum, his splintered but forceful mid-tempo strut was part parade, part shuffle, and part funk."
— **JON PARELES**, *The New York Times*

"Tony Allen, who along with vocalist/activist Fela Kuti created one of groove music's most glorious subgenres, Afrobeat, deserves a place on the list of greatest funk drummers of all time. For more than forty years he has been honing a distinctive style that crackles with vitality, pulsates with rhythmic wit, and pushes audiences into dance-party ecstasy."
— *Modern Drummer* magazine

"Tony Allen is best known as the hands and feet behind Fela Kuti's explosive Afrobeat, and his playing is both fabulously propulsive and melodic, in a way that might seem paradoxical, but makes perfect sense once you've got your feet in motion. . . . Simultaneously breaking up the rhythms and reassembling them in one loose-limbed, easy rocking motion, his playing is at once apparently effortless and breathtaking."
— **MARK HUDSON,** *The Daily Telegraph*

"Were someone to lend me a time-machine to catch great bands of the past, Fela and Allen's Afrika 70 band in Lagos circa 1972 would be one of the first stops. It was then [that] Bootsy Collins, James Brown's bass player, went backstage and told [band members that] they were 'the funkiest cats on the planet' and Paul McCartney, in Lagos to record *Band on the Run*, said they were the best live band he'd ever seen."
— **PETER CULSHAW,** *The Observer*

"An octopus-like polyrhythmic machine, Allen was to Fela and Afrobeat what Melvin Parker/Jabo Starks/Clyde Stubblefield were to James Brown and funk: These drummers simply deepened and changed the pocket of popular music forever."
— **MATT ROGERS,** *The Village Voice*

"Few percussionists . . . can claim to have invented a rhythm — but that's what Allen did when he added his propulsive rhythms to the music of Kuti and together they created the sound the world came to know as Afrobeat."
— **NIGEL WILLIAMSON,** *The Independent*

TONY ALLEN

TONY ALLEN

An Autobiography of the
MASTER DRUMMER
OF AFROBEAT

TONY ALLEN *with* **MICHAEL E. VEAL**

Duke University Press
Durham and London 2013

Library of Congress Cataloging-in-Publication Data
Allen, Tony, 1940–
Tony Allen : an autobiography of the master drummer
of afrobeat / Tony Allen ; with Michael E. Veal.
pages cm
Includes bibliographical references and index.
ISBN 978-0-8223-5577-9 (cloth : alk. paper)
ISBN 978-0-8223-5591-5 (pbk. : alk. paper)
1. Allen, Tony, 1940– 2. Drummers (Musicians)—
Nigeria—Biography. 3. Afrobeat—Biography.
I. Veal, Michael E., 1963– II. Title.
ML399.A455A3 2013
786.9092—dc23 [B]
2013013821

Tony Allen

*I would like to dedicate this book to my parents,
Mr. James Alabi Allen and Mrs. Prudentia Anna Allen.*

Michael E. Veal

*I would like to dedicate this book to the memory
of my father, Mr. Henry Veal (1925–2011),
a great man and great father who will always be
the most important drummer in my life.*

contents

acknowledgments

TONY ALLEN: I would like to thank God, my wife Silvie, my first wife Ibilola, all of my children, Damon Albarn, Benson Idonije, Tunji Braithwaite, Shina Abiodun, James Abayomi ("Kosygin"), King Sunny Ade, Martin Meissonnier, Awa Ba, and Dr. Pierre Nicollet.

MICHAEL VEAL: I would like to thank Tony and Silvie Allen and family, M & m, Mom and Dad, all of my friends and family, Eric Trosset, Aida at Le Khelkoum, Nazaire Bello, Marlene Boulad, Bruno Blum, Elizabeth Calleo, Nils and Heather Chaplet, Abayomi Gbolagunte, Taïna Grastilleur, Jean-Marc Laouenan, Gerwine Bayo-Martins, Martin Meissonnier, Cyrille Nnakoum, Max Reinhardt, Nadia Saddok, Usman at Porokhane, Sammy at Le Relais Afro Star, and all the members of the reading group at the Columbia University Center for Jazz Studies. I would also like to acknowledge the following people: Ken Wissoker at Duke University Press for his long-standing faith in this project; the Yale University Griswold Fund, which funded research trips to France in 2006, 2008, and 2011; and my assistants, who helped transcribe many hours of interviews: Anna Pelczer, Henry Trotter, Nancy Steadle, and Singto Saro-Wiwa. Finally, I would like to thank those readers who gave valuable feedback during the writing process or were helpful in other ways: Kofi Agawu, Franya Berkman, Eric Charry, John Miller Chernoff, Kwami Coleman, Manthia Diawara, William Glasspiegel, Alex Kennedy-Grant, Rachel Lears, and the anonymous reviewers for Duke University Press.

introduction

MICHAEL E. VEAL

In this era when the art of drumming is being challenged by the art of digital drum programming, the masters of drum set playing are more valuable to us than ever. Their ability to manipulate the human nervous system into ecstasy by segmenting perception into a matrix of clashing and interlocking rhythms ensures that no matter how much their work is digitally sampled, looped, or chopped, the sonic power of their real-time rhythm remains unparalleled and undiminished. This sonic power is crucial for us because it also contains a social power. In the decades immediately following World War II, for example, the bebop and postbop drumming innovations of Max Roach, Philly Joe Jones, Elvin Jones, Tony Williams, and Art Blakey helped bolster modern jazz's cultural demand for recognition as a high-intensity African American art music of the postwar American metropolis. In the 1960s, the syncopated funk rhythms of drummers such as Clyde Stubble-field, Jabo Starks, and Ziggy Modeliste helped bolster a revo-lution in political and cultural consciousness by reasserting a sonic image of "Africa" into the African American cultural equa-tion. In Jamaica, the cultural imperatives of Rastafari-influenced roots reggae were voiced upon a foundation laid by drummers such as Carlton Barrett, Leroy "Horsemouth" Wallace, Carlton "Santa" Davis, Lowell "Sly" Dunbar, and others. In Nigeria, Tony Allen is another master of the drum set whose rhythmic inno-vations with Afrobeat legend Fela Anikulapo-Kuti helped power a critique of cultural attitudes that resonated across postcolonial Africa and beyond. As dance music producers around the world look toward Africa for compelling rhythms, as jazz drummers continue to absorb the influence of world percussion traditions, and as the power of rhythm continues to give dancers a glimpse of liberation and of joy, it is time for Tony Oladipo Allen to be recognized for his major contribution to the world of drumming and to contemporary African music.

It has been an honor for me to participate in that recognition by co-authoring *Tony Allen: An Autobiography of the Master Drummer of Afrobeat*. Tony and I first met in New York City in 2000, and, based on my previous work on Fela Kuti, he asked me to help write his autobiography.[1] The process has been an adventure, on many levels. Most of the formal interviewing for this book took place intermittently between 2004 and 2011, mainly in Tony's home in the Parisian suburb of Courbevoie. But the book also chronicles informal conversations we had elsewhere — in moving cars, on the Paris Metro, and backstage in dressing rooms across Europe. Many West Africans are naturally gifted storytellers — experts at instilling dramatic tension into even the most mundane anecdotes — and Tony is no different. The recollections and insights in this book, however, are anything but mundane; Tony's story is fascinating, providing insight into the man many consider Africa's greatest drum set player.

Tony's journey is a complex one that transcends many boundaries and subverts simplistic and essentialized ideas about African culture and identity. From the beginning, he was a nonconformist who instinctively rejected many of the strict formalities associated with traditional Yoruba culture. He grew up in Lagos as the oldest child of a Protestant, Nigerian, Yoruba father and a Catholic, Ghanaian, Ewe mother, his paternal family name long ago Anglicized by Christian missionaries and slave traders. Despite being repeatedly warned about the risks of an artistic lifestyle, Tony — like most other musicians — simply *had* to play music, but, unusually for African families, his parents were ultimately supportive of his musical inclinations despite their own doubts, giving him the space to "find his own way." Tony, then, is a twentieth-century, urban African modernist, and his life story should be understood as reflecting the complexities of his time.

This is the story of a musician — both a human story and a musical story, told on the rhetorical turf of a musician and a musician-academic. On his own terms and in its own language, Tony's story provides many angles on the proverbial broader picture. It is a glimpse into the musical worlds of post–World War II Nigeria and Ghana of the 1950s and 1960s—the "Golden Age" of West African highlife—a crucial yet under-documented period of Africa's musical history—and it offers a colorful articulation of many themes central to the history of African popular music. Tony's early travails as a freelance musician in Nigeria drama-tize the difficulty of keeping bands together amid jealousy, intrigue, the trials and tribulations of patronage, and intense competition for meager resources. We see musicians striving for status in a strongly hierarchical society that has not typically accorded musicians a great amount of social prestige. We see the enormous power that words of praise or insult hold in West Africa. We see music used as a powerful agent of both social co-hesion and social (especially ethnic) division. We witness an entire post-war generation of innovative music sprout on the wings of Pan-Africanist cultural currents, and with music as a medium of both cross-cultural understanding and misunderstanding, we see the peoples of Africa and the African diaspora reencounter each other after centuries of separation due to slavery and colonization. We see successive trends in West Afri-can popular music as it is impacted by popular genres from around the African diaspora, such as jazz, son, calypso, mambo, soul, funk, reggae, dub, and hip-hop. Finally, we see the advent of "world beat," and of ex-patriate African musicians making careers for themselves outside their native countries in the context of globalization, and in the wake of col-lapsed and formerly viable national music industries in Africa. In the big picture, Tony's story parallels the history of Nigeria in the second half of the twentieth century, as the country progressed from the last decades of colonization, to national independence and civil war in the 1960s, to the oil boom and its radically destabilizing social effects in the 1970s, and on to the military dictatorships of the 1980s and 1990s and the uncertainties of the new century. Other themes might be thought of as more specific to Tony's particular story: the drum set as a symbol of African musical modernity; the challenge of surviving as an African musician in Europe and as an English-speaking musician in France; and an intimate view of the inner world of Fela Kuti's Koola Lobitos and Africa 70—two of the greatest bands to ever play African popular music.

Why has a musician of Tony's power and artistry remained underacknowledged for so long? The most obvious answer is that in general the contribution of drummers is not widely recognized. It is a oft-repeated truism among musicians that "a great drummer can make any band sound great," but this sentiment is not widely understood by the general public, who—for obvious reasons—are much more inclined to focus on lead vocalists and flashy front-line soloists than they are on the musician powering the band from beneath a halo of cymbals. This may explain why to date there are so few biographies of any of the masters of the drum set.

Another, more subtle factor is one that Tony himself alludes to in this text. It is often the case that outside Africa, "African drumming" is stereotypically understood to mean "hand drumming." In fact, Tony is just one of several excellent African drum set players—including Paco Sery, Kofi Ghanaba (Guy Warren), and Remi Kabaka—whose contributions have been marginalized in the primitivist/exoticist discourse around African drumming that prevails in the West. This is particularly ironic given that a number of the great American jazz drummers have expressed their admiration for Tony's playing.[2] In the biggest picture, the marginalization of African drum set players reflects the West's ongoing reluctance to acknowledge Africa's contribution to modernity in *any* field of endeavor.

A third reason is that Tony's best-known work was created in the employ of Fela Anikulapo-Kuti (1938–1997), a bandleader not always known for his generosity in promoting or acknowledging his sidemen. In all fairness, Fela was not unique among African bandleaders in this regard. The greatness of African popular music is fundamentally predicated on communal creation, but the flow of power, compensation and recognition in most bands is almost invariably top-down and pyramidally shaped. Very few individual African musicians have been able to carve out names for themselves outside the bands with which they are associated, regardless of their talent. This was even more the case in Fela's bands given that all of the music was composed and arranged solely by him, and because so much of his presentation was based around his personality.

Tony was an official member of Fela's band for fifteen years, but their de facto professional and personal association spanned three and a half turbulent decades. These constitute what were arguably the most exciting and cutting-edge decades in the history of West African popular music, and they were decades during which Fela was one of the central figures. But this book is not a mere filling-in of the gaps in Fela's story, given how central Tony was to his music. In the same way that the achievements of John Coltrane would have been unthinkable without the contributions of Elvin Jones and Rashied Ali, the achievements of Miles Davis unthinkable without the contributions of Philly Joe Jones, Tony

Williams, and Jack DeJohnette, the achievements of Ornette Coleman unthinkable without the contributions of Ed Blackwell and Billy Higgins, and the achievements of James Brown unthinkable without the contributions of Clyde Stubbefield and John "Jabo" Starks, the achievements of Fela would have been unthinkable without the contributions of Tony Allen. It is worth noting that of all these drummers, Tony is the only one to date who is the subject of a full-length biography or autobiography.[3] His name might not be as widely known as Fela's, but the truth is that few substantive articles about Fela fail to mention Tony's contribution to the development of Afrobeat, and everyone agrees that Fela's music lost a substantial amount of its power and dynamism after Tony's departure in 1978. Some even go as far as to periodize Fela's music according to the designations "With Tony Allen" and "After Tony Allen." Fela went on to write many more brilliant compositions between Allen's departure and his own death in 1997, but in general they lacked rhythmic dynamism that Tony had added to his greatest music. As Tony has often noted, his parts were the only ones in the band that were not precomposed by Fela. Comparing Tony's "No Accommodation" (recorded with Africa 70 in 1979) with Fela's 1982 track "Original Sufferhead" (both songs are built from similar drum set patterns) makes clear just what and how much Fela lost when he lost Tony.[4] Nevertheless, Tony's influence remained fundamental to Fela's music and the Afrobeat patterns he composed with Fela in the 1970s were used as generic patterns by all of Fela's later drummers, including Adebiyi Ajayi, Ogbona Alphonso, "Moustique," Masefswe Anam, Nicholas "Ringo" Avom, Benjamin (Ola) Ijagun, and many others. Tony acknowledges Fela's genius throughout this story, but Fela's greatest music would have had much less of its lasting power had Tony not made such a seminal contribution to it.

Tony was at the epicenter of Fela's music, from their mutual fascination with straight-ahead jazz in the early 1960s, through the swinging, good-time days of dance-band highlife in postindependence Ghana and Nigeria at mid-decade, through the funk and Black Power epiphanies in Los Angeles at decade's end, to Fela's countercultural "Kalakuta Republic" in the 1970s, and into the early years of African music's global presence in the "world beat" market of the 1980s and 1990s. Their story began as one of friendship and collaboration, and later degenerated through a series of misunderstandings that provided yet another vivid example of the destructive impact of fame and the sobering effects of personal tragedy. In terms of social background, Tony was neither a poor

Lagosian nor a member of the educated elite, but a member of the Lagos Island middle class. As such, he would have reasonably expected that Fela, from the highly respected Ransome-Kuti family, would act in accordance with the traditional Yoruba ideal of the *gbajumon*—the "big man" of wealth and achievement who consolidates his social status by redistributing his largesse among those in his social network who have shown him dedication and loyalty.[5] But the world of Fela Kuti—especially as it increasingly became his own highly idiosyncratic creation—was not a world particularly steeped in tradition. It was the world of an African pop star whose entire engagement with the world was predicated on rebellion and the flouting of convention. The hazier things got in the course of Fela's growing fame, the easier it was for more fundamental and reasonable considerations to slide. In this sense, Allen was not alone in feeling underacknowledged and undercompensated. What remains in the end, however, is a moving story of two musicians forever linked—despite it all—because of the brilliant music they created together. In the long run, I believe historical accounts will list as one of their most significant achievements the creation of a "national" style. Despite the scores of innovative musicians in their country, it is Afrobeat that has gradually become recognized as the sonic signature of "Nigeria" in the global sphere, much like the role of *reggae* in Jamaica, *calypso* and *soca* in Trinidad, and *mbaqanga* and *isicathamiya* in South Africa.

It is also notable that, aside from Fela's musician sons Femi and Seun, Tony is the only member of Fela's entourage to make a substantial name for himself outside Fela's context. Despite the magnetic pull Fela clearly had on many people (including many musicians who stayed with him for decades), Tony alone seems to have possessed the clarity, inner strength, and ingenuity to reinvent himself and create a new and successful life for himself away from the brilliance and madness of Fela's world and of Nigeria. Tony left Nigeria at a time when a sharp rise in violent crime, a succession of military dictatorships, an austere economic climate, and a culture of corruption had choked much of the life force out of the local music industry. He successfully established a life for himself in Paris during a period in which—although conditions were relatively favorable for African popular musicians—it was extremely difficult for Africans in general to do so because of a sharply rising tide of anti-immigrant hostility. He could easily have built a prosperous career for himself by playing Fela's classic songs—songs that Fela himself resolutely refused to perform once he had recorded them—for nostalgic Nigerian expatriates and curious Europeans and Americans. He chose instead to carve out his own identity within the Afrobeat genre and to build his own audience from the ground up. Tony's early solo years were marked by notable collaborations with other Afropop innovators, such as Nigeria's King Sunny Ade and Zaire's Ray Lema, and since the 1980s he has released a score of well-received albums of his own material, while fruitfully interfacing with a variety of currents in jazz, electronica, experimental music, British pop, and hip-hop. Now a dual Nigerian and French citizen, he lives in the suburbs of Paris with his wife and their three sons, enjoying a stability that is highly uncommon among immigrant African musicians in Europe.

Because of the musical, thematic, and cultural overlaps that define Tony's history, I have tried to shape this book according to the conventions of autobiographical writing in both jazz and African music. There are numerous examples of autobiographical writing in jazz, with which *Tony Allen: An Autobiography of the Master Drummer of Afrobeat* shares a number of themes. It is a survivor's tale, like Art Pepper's *Straight Life*;[6] and much like Miles Davis and Quincy Troupe's *Miles: The Autobiography*[7] or Hampton Hawes's *Raise Up Off of Me*,[8] it presents a warts-and-all self-portrait. Like Louis Armstrong's *Satchmo: My Life in New Orleans*[9] or Sidney Bechet's *Treat It Gentle*,[10] it is a colorful evocation of a bygone era. And like virtually all musical autobiographies, such as Duke Ellington's *Music Is My Mistress*,[11] Jimmy Heath's *I Walked with Giants*,[12] or Horace Silver's *Let's Get to the Nitty Gritty*,[13] it is a story in which other great musicians make cameo appearances at various times: Louis Armstrong, Dizzy Gillespie, Wayne Shorter, Sunny Ade, Bootsy Collins, Stevie Wonder, Victor Olaiya, Frank Sinatra, Randy Weston, Julius Araba, Ginger Baker, and Frank Butler, among many others.

But the overall tone here is fairly specific to three genres. The first is African musical autobiography, of which there are not many written in English; to date, the best-known would include Fela Kuti and Carlos Moore's *Fela, Fela: This Bitch of a Life*,[14] Manu Dibango's *Three Kilos of Coffee*,[15] Miriam Makeba and Nomsa Mwamuka's *Makeba*,[16] and Hugh Masekela and D. Michael Cheers's *Still Grazin'*.[17] Despite differences in musical tradition, gender, location, or personality, the narrative ethos that unites these works is a particular mix of the euphoric highs of artistic creation and the excitement of the creative lifestyle, against a backdrop of political turmoil, social change, economic hardship, and exile.[18]

The second subgenre to which this book belongs is the classic "sideman narrative," of which Fred Wesley's *Hit Me, Fred!* is an excellent recent example—a tale of a sideman struggling for recognition while laboring under autocratic and egotistical bandleaders.[19] The third is the ongoing literature on what might be called "musical Pan-Africanism," of which Steven Feld's *Jazz Cosmopolitanism in Accra*, Robin D. G. Kelley's *Africa Speaks, America Answers*, and Ingrid Monson's *Freedom Sounds* are three recent and notable examples.[20] Ultimately, *Tony Allen* is a portrait of a tenacious human being who has been able to maintain and even prosper within these varying circumstances, due to abundant talent, resourcefulness, and the personal and spiritual power to renew himself and his life. In this sense, it shares most—narratively and rhetorically—with the autobiographies of Dibango, Masekela, and Makeba, on the one hand, and Wesley, on the other.

While this book is not, strictly speaking, an academic work, I believe it will nevertheless make a contribution to the growing field that might be called "African cultural studies"—studies that may have their various disciplinary roots in cultural anthropology, ethnomusicology, music history/theory, cultural studies, or other disciplines but are united by their focus on African popular or mass cultural forms.

Tony's story also has much in common with the stories of other individual artists in postcolonial Africa, beyond the specific sphere of music. In particular, I found it inspiring to write this introduction at the same time that I read Henry Glassie's revealing biography of the influential Yoruba visual artist Twins Seven Seven.[21] It was fascinating to compare and contrast the way that two Yoruba modernists—one a visual artist from a traditional rural background in Oshogbo, the other a musician from an urban, cosmopolitan background in Lagos—projected the vitality of Yoruba artistic creativity out into the world in two very different yet equally dynamic ways.

Broader issues aside, this book would not have been written in the first place were it not for Tony's contribution as a drummer. Readers of this book should keep in mind that the concept of a drum kit was a new and novel one in Tony's world of mid-twentieth-century West African percussion, where the tradition had been (and largely continues to be) ensembles comprised of several musicians playing individual parts. The polyrhythmic complexity that we typically associate with West African percussion music is a direct result of the combination of these individual parts into complex composite structures ("hocketing"). From its roots in the vaudeville era of the late nineteenth and early twentieth centuries, by contrast, the drum set ("drum kit," "trap drums") was conceived as a deliberate miniaturization of the percussion section—an economical solution to both spatial and financial constraints. Its use allowed multiple percussion instruments to be accommodated in the smaller performing spaces of the vaudevillian theater, and because it centralized multiple instruments under the control of a single musician, it was a more economical way of employing a percussion section.[22] Thus it is not surprising that, when Tony and other African musicians first heard the sound of the drum set via jazz recordings that had made their way to Africa, they assumed they were hearing several musicians playing individual percussion instruments. The irony, of course, is that the jazz drummers had worked hard to master the technique of independent coordination, precisely so they could execute a core Africanist principle in the context of African American music—that of improvising against a steady, ongoing groove pattern. It was Tony's embrace of the challenge of independent coordination—starting with independent movement of his hi-hat cymbals and eventually developing over the entire drum kit—that set him apart from other highlife drummers and established him as a master percussionist by the time Fela's Koola Lobitos highlife band morphed into the Afrobeat outfit Africa 70 in the early 1970s.

At several points in the text, in fact, Tony emphasizes the significance of his independent use of the hi-hat cymbals. This might seem a relatively minor point to most drummers, until they realize that the tradition in Nigerian and Ghanaian highlife was to use both hands on the snare drum (a technique derived from both indigenous traditions and British military drumming), while using the other drums for occasional accents. The hi-hat cymbals were rarely used by highlife drummers. When Tony integrated the hi-hat cymbal, it allowed him to maintain a continuous, jazz-derived offbeat in counterpoint to the rhythms he was playing with his other limbs, and it also allowed him to integrate the innovations of the rhythm & blues and funk drummers who used their hi-hats in a variety of dynamic ways.

From the very first moment that I heard Tony's recorded performances with Africa 70—such as "Question Jam Answer" (1972); "Confusion," "Unnecessary Begging," "Alagbon Close," and "Water No Get Enemy" (all 1975); "Yellow Fever" (1976); and "Shuffering and Shmiling" (1978)—I knew I was listening to one of the world's great drummers. In terms of technique and style, Tony's sound is most accurately described as a jazz- and funk-inflected rearticulation of rhythms drawn from local Nigerian and West African genres such as highlife, *apala*, and Nigerian mambo. He is not a powerhouse fusion drummer on the order of Billy Cobham or Dennis Chambers, nor is he a heavy "fatback" drummer on the order of Parliament-Funkadelic's Jerome Brailey or James Brown's John "Jabo" Starks. His goal is not to awe the listener with virtuosic displays and flashy solos. With a light, jazzy touch on the instrument, a very poly-rhythmic concept of groove playing, and an arsenal of subtle inflections, Tony's philosophy of drumming privileges dynamic flow, propulsion, and ongoing conversation with the other members of the percussion section. In this sense, he adheres to core social and philosophical principles articulated by West African traditional drummers, many of whom shun virtuosic displays in their performances in order to more effectively ground themselves within a dynamic musical conversation that is itself part of a broader and ongoing social interaction.[23] On one hand, Tony's playing can be understood in the context of the small-band jazz drummers who inspired him, such as Max Roach, Philly Joe Jones, and Art Blakey. On the other, he can be compared with other innovative drummers of his generation from around the African diaspora, who helped tease new vocabularies of dance music drumming out of jazz by fusing it with various local idioms, such as Carlton Barrett, Sly Dunbar, and Leroy "Horse-mouth" Wallace in reggae, or Ziggy Modeliste, David Garibaldi, and Clyde Stubblefield in funk. In the broadest view, Tony's playing can be placed in the lineage of drummers in local traditional and popular Nigerian genres such as apala and highlife, who formed the stylistic context for his emergence. In a more abstract sense, he can also be placed in the lineage of Ghana's Kofi Ghanaba (1923–2008), one of the progenitors of "Afro-Jazz" and the acknowledged "father" of African drum set playing, whose American sojourn in the 1950s (which included musical encounters with Duke Ellington, Charlie Parker, and Max Roach) helped him revolutionize the role of the drum set in West African music.[24] The fact that Tony has recently begun performing on a custom drum set crafted for him by the artisans at the Arts Center in Accra, Ghana (a set that features hand-carved traditional African drums rack-mounted in place of Western tom-toms) suggests that, in a sense, he has come full circle from the days when he admired pioneers of the African drum set such as Ghanaba and Rim Obeng.

"Fefe Naa Efe" (from Fela and Africa 70's 1973 album *Gentleman*) is not one of Fela's better-known songs. But for listeners whose ears are attuned to the language of drumming, it is one that makes clear how crucial Tony was to Fela's project of developing Afrobeat out of highlife by drawing on the structural innovations of funk and the harmonic innovations of modal jazz. The steadily chirping soundstream of hand percussion instruments—clefs (claves), shekere (beaded gourd rattle), and congas—reflect the highlife influence in Fela's Afrobeat and provide a perfect web of sound for Allen to play within and against. Like the great jazz drummers, he keeps a steady conversation with the other instruments, particularly the soloists, advancing to the front of the ensemble by playing the ride cymbal for thematic passages and then dropping back into line with the percussion to support the ensemble. Like a great boxer, he knows when to jab with his bass drum in order to punctuate a soloist's line, when to momentarily scatter and reconsolidate the flow with a hi-hat flourish, when to stoke the tension by laying deeply into the groove, and when to break and restart that tension by interjecting a crackling snare accent on the downbeat. In terms of his solo work, on the other hand, Tony's solo on Fela's "Open and Close" (1973) seems to place him most directly in the lineage of Max Roach in terms of structure, phrasing, and sound. This solo, in fact, compares closely with Roach's own solo on recordings such as Sonny Rollins's seminal "St. Thomas" (1956).[25]

For many years there was no extant footage of Africa 70 in performance, and as a result I often had to imagine Tony's body language while playing. When I finally saw him play in 2000, my mental image was confirmed: he played with a very still, centered torso, allowing each limb to work independently. This orientation is helped by his slim, compact build and medium height, which brings the top of his head to the approximate level of his mounted cymbals. It is this compact sphere of motion that allows him to play so fluidly and polyrhythmically.

Tony's playing has evolved over the decades. With Fela's Koola Lobitos, he drew on the legacy of big band jazz drumming as it was reflected in dance-band highlife, playing aggressively with the front-line horns. During the early "Afro-rock" years of 1970–71 and songs such as "Chop and Quench" and "Beautiful Dancer," his sound was choppy and aggressive, a jazz-inspired fusion of highlife and rhythm & blues drumming that blended with Fela's choppy, James Brown–inspired guitar and bass patterns. At mid-decade, he was playing highly syncopated, funky patterns such as those on "Kalakuta Show" or "Alagbon Close," which blend funk and highlife in a way that build polyrhythmic tension to the breaking point. Even after the infamous and devastating army attack on Fela's "Kalakuta Republic" in early 1977, the musical chemistry between Fela and Tony remained unbroken, as reflected in the somber, funkified clock rhythms of "Sorrow Tears and Blood" (1977). By the time Africa 70 cut "Shuffering and Shmiling" and "Vagabonds in Power" the following year, Allen's drumming had become smoother and more jazzy, cutting through the Afro-funk like a sharp knife. In this last phase of the Africa 70 band, he began to compose terse, minimalist funk patterns for tracks like "Fear Not for Man" and "No Agreement." Since the 1980s, Tony has gradually tended toward an equally polyrhythmic but less interactive approach, given that his playing has increasingly provided a foundation for a soundscape production style inspired by dub-influenced electronica on albums such as *Black Voices* (1999).[26] But regardless of how his playing has evolved, he has never lost the groove, keeping the time as steady as a drum machine, and simultaneously as loose, fluid, and subtle as a jazz drummer.

Fela's Afrobeat can be viewed from one angle as the final innovation in the evolution of dance-band highlife; from a different angle as the most sophisticated African variant on the early, polyrhythmic style of funk music as it was developed by James Brown and his musicians between 1964 and 1971; and from a third angle as a brilliant indigenization of jazz drumming (a tradition that, for obvious reasons, is itself historically rooted in several core Africanist principles). In this light, it is interesting to note that many of Tony's most fruitful collaborations have taken place with American funk and jazz musicians, including former Brown band members trombonist/arranger Fred Wesley and saxophonist/arranger Alfred "Pee Wee" Ellis, as well as with vocalists Michael "Clip" Payne and Gary "Mudbone" Cooper and keyboardist Joseph "Amp Fiddler," all from George Clinton's Parliament-Funkadelic orbit. The story of Afrobeat is foremost an African story but secondarily one that is very much about cultural interplay and about the centrality of the African diaspora in formulations of contemporary African music. That Tony's breakthrough moment as a drummer came as a result of his encounter with one of John Coltrane's drummers is a vivid testimony to the way some of the strongest currents in postwar black music intersected and nourished each other despite historical, cultural, and geographic distances.

An autobiography is an act of self-invention and self-creation and, in this "as told to" format, equally an act of collaboration. My goal was for the book to feel like a continuous, relaxed session of Tony telling stories. This was essentially how we conducted the interviews, and this is the kind of narrative flow I have tried to preserve here. As always, however, transforming raw conversation—no matter how captivating—into a narrative that is simultaneously an authentic representation of the subject and compelling on the page is the major challenge in this kind of writing. The goal is to make the pages "speak" to the reader, and I would like to think that my knowledge of African music, jazz, and African culture in general helped me interact with Tony in ways that resulted in the richest and most revealing narrative. Given that Nigeria is officially an English-speaking country and that English is one of Tony's native languages, his speaking voice during our interviews was pretty much standard English with an idiomatically Nigerian slant. For the most part, he did not speak in deep pidgin English or Lagos slang. In editing these conversations into a coherent written narrative I occasionally "smoothed out" some grammatical anomalies, but overall few adjustments were necessary in the area of language, and I feel that the tone and flavor of Tony's voice have been accurately reproduced here.

What does it mean for an African American to coauthor an autobiography of an African musician living in France? For me, it meant first of all the honor and pleasure of playing saxophone with Tony's band around Europe, a musical opening that in turn provided other professional openings for me in Europe. Second, it allowed me to discover Tony's skills as an excellent chef of Nigerian food. From him I learned to cook a variety of savory stews such as groundnut stew, *egusi* stew, and pepper soup, as well as staples such as pounded yam (*fufu*) and *gari*. And I'll also admit that without the "culinary incentives" emanating from Tony's kitchen as we worked, the tone of this book might have turned out very differently!

Working on this book also meant having the opportunity to spend extended time in Paris, one of the world's great cities. Anyone who has spent time in Paris can immediately sense the reason that artistically and intellectually inclined people have always gravitated to the city. Its unique ambience results partially from pragmatic urban planning and construction decisions made long ago—the city is planned as a spiral (which tends to yield adventure), and buildings are built to human as opposed to corporate scale (which allows the lives lived within to feel meaningful and poetic). The ambience obviously also results from a characteristically French emphasis on cultivating the senses through a variety of pursuits which, for a musician, are magnified by the social respect and admiration given to artists and art forms of all kinds. Even though it lies on the opposite side of the city from Tony's home, I adopted the area around Belleville-Menilmontant (i.e., the 19th and 20th arrondissements) as my "second space" away from New York City, due to its hilly topography, cultural diversity, beautiful parks (Le Parc de Belleville, Le Parc de Buttes Chaumont), storied history (Père Lachaise cemetery, the Paris Commune, etc.), wide boulevards, and overall arty atmosphere.

As richly chronicled by Tyler Stovall in his 1998 book *Paris Noir*, the relationship between African Americans and Parisians has historical roots in the Jazz Age that followed the First World War, a period when many African American jazz musicians settled in areas such as Paris's famed Montmartre district.[27] This cultural presence was rearticulated in the decades following World War II by expatriate literary figures such as Richard Wright, James Baldwin, and Chester Himes and was later given an experimental inflection by avant-garde jazz musicians (such as those associated with the AACM and BAG collectives) who made the city their temporary home in the late 1960s and early 1970s.[28] Given this, it is safe to say that African American artists and intellectuals have generally found a sympathetic atmosphere and some of their most receptive and appreciative audiences in France, and as such it is unsurprising that a sizable percentage of the canonical works of African American art (especially literary works) have been created there. And even though the actual *African* presence was still relatively small at midcentury, African culture was gradually asserting itself in the sphere of visual art, with Paris-based artists such as Pablo Picasso and Georges Braque raiding traditional African figural art traditions for their unique formal and conceptual qualities.

However, the France of Jacques Chirac and Nikolas Sarkozy was by no means the same Paris as that of the Jazz Age or Cold War years. Similar to the political predicament in which James Baldwin and Angela Davis gradually found themselves in the 1960s,[29] most African Americans visiting Paris today would probably find themselves acutely sensitive to the complexities of race in France during the era of "Fortress Europe." Emigration of both North and sub-Saharan Africans to France has increased dramatically since World War II, but these immigrants are largely marginalized in mainstream French discourses. A mere glance would reveal that virtually everyone cleaning the Parisian Metro seems to be of African descent; that black people have a minimal presence in the mass media (the exceptions being football players); that the stations of the Paris Metro are used as de facto immigration checkpoints for Africans and so-called "Arabs" (actually North Africans) and that there is growing unrest in the *banlieues* (suburbs) surrounding the major cities that has much to do with issues of race, ethnicity, religion, and culture. A more studied glance would reveal the social effects of a wave of anti-immigrant sentiment that began to mount around the time Tony emigrated to France in the mid-1980s, symbolized by highly publicized and controversial events such as the struggles of the *sans-papiers*, the discriminatory Pasqua laws passed in the late 1980s, and the emergence of right-wing politicians such as Jean-Marie Le Pen and his Front National party.[30] The most fitting soundtrack to what I observed (and occasionally experienced) seemed to be neither the "hot" jazz of Django Rheinhardt, the hallowed voice of Edith Piaf, nor the moody 1960s pop of singers such as Serge Gainsbourg or Françoise Hardy. Nor was it the traditional music of African immigrants, such as the Malian *ngoni* player or the Muslim calls to prayer that could be heard emanating from a *foyer* close to my apartment. Rather, it was French hip-hop, a medium that seemed the truest reflection of all of the tensions of immigration, globalization, and cultural adjustment symbolized by the substantial African presence in France. In all fairness, these social tensions are related to the broader encounter of differing cultures and are to be expected given that France is home to Western Europe's largest immigrant (and Muslim) population, by far. Hopefully this wave of social tension will gradually resolve through France's gradual fashioning of a new, twenty-first century vision of itself.

All of this is relevant to Tony's story insofar as it is the environment in which he has lived, worked, and raised a family for the past twenty-five years. He might be hailed as a master percussionist by night, but by day he faces many of the same challenges as other African immigrants to France and, indeed, in Europe in general. One evening, as we glanced out of his apartment window toward the monumental Grande Arche de La Défense, our conversation drifted into diffuse and philosophical areas.[31] Tony remarked to me, "Back in the '60s and '70s, we were playing for the love and joy of it. Today we're playing for survival." I don't believe his comment referred simply to the issue of money or even recognition. Tony emerged during a period in which black musicians—whether in Africa, Afro-America, or the Caribbean—were cultural heroes riding a wave of national independence and cultural nationalism, and the cultural assumptions of Pan-Africanism were driving forces behind some of the era's greatest musical achievements. Much of his most enduring work was created during that period in which post–World War II economic prosperity provided the material foundations for social optimism and social change. That is surely a different world from that of the expatriate African musician of the twenty-first century, his native country perpetually on the brink of chaos, trying to make it within the tightening gates of Fortress Europe.[32] More than money, Tony's comment reflected profound changes in the existential state of musicians like himself, not to mention the general place of musicians in contemporary society. Which is to say that sometimes one has to do what one does not only to survive, but also to remember and reaffirm who one believes oneself to be.

But this is much more a narrative of cosmopolitanism than it is of exile. Not only have these challenges failed to erode Tony's creativity, but his music has taken him places in the world that neither Fela nor any of his other former employers in Nigeria had the opportunity to see — places such as Brazil, Israel, Japan, Iceland, Dubai, and La Reunion, to name just a few. Night after night, it was heartening to see him receive extended ovations at the end of his shows around Europe and the United States. The audiences were not only acknowledging the presence of a living legend, a pillar of Afrobeat, and a survivor, but also the more immediate fact that they had just been funked-up for two hours by the virtuoso drumming of a musician who, at seventy years old, shows no signs of slowing down. Without question, Tony's work in the decades since 2000 has been much more varied than his earlier years, with him having diversified his activities and become a global ambassador of Afrobeat. Arguably, he has done more than any other musician to blend Afrobeat with a variety of other musical genres. If the funky, dubbed-out Afrobeat-electronica of his own recordings such as *Black Voices* and *Home Cooking* set the perfect mood for the coffeehouse scene in Amsterdam, the *Inspiration/Information* collaborations with Jimi Tenor are a perfect fit for London's hip neo-jazz scene. Tony's collaboration with Damon Albarn's band The Good, the Bad and the Queen has projected his unique sound to the global pop audience, while the collaborations with Jamaican guitarist Ernest Ranglin have helped solidify his credentials in the sphere of "world jazz." Meanwhile, Tony's own recent albums such as *Lagos: No Shaking* and *Secret Agent*, with their roots in classic Afrobeat and highlife, are true to the classic Afrobeat aesthetic. Despite all of the changes that both he, his music, and the world have been through since the end of World War II, Tony stands as a model of remarkable consistency at seventy years old. In many ways, he is currently enjoying the best years of his career. From the party times of Nigerian highlife, through the tense cultural warfare of Fela's Kalakuta Republic, to the dubbed-out ambiguities of his expat Afrobeat-electronica, Tony Allen's groove has remained as fluid as a stream and as steady as a rock. No matter how much reality itself has been sampled, looped, or chopped in our age of virtuality and information overload, he has never lost his head in the midst of headiness. After more than a half century behind the drums, he is still providing a funky pulse that helps us make sense of our worlds.

NOTES

1. See Michael E. Veal, *Fela: The Life and Times of an African Musical Icon* (Philadelphia: Temple University Press, 2000).
2. One such admirer was Max Roach, who unfortunately passed away before I could ask him to contribute a blurb for the back cover of this book.
3. An exception to this is Leslie Gourse, *Art Blakey: Jazz Messenger* (New York: Schirmer, 2002).
4. Allen's "No Accommodation" can be found on the reissue compilation *Afro Disco Beat* (Vampi Soul 090), and "Original Sufferhead" can be found on Fela's CD of the same name (MCA/Universal 314-547-382-2).
5. Christopher Waterman, *Juju: A Social History and Ethnography of an African Popular Music* (Chicago: University of Chicago Press, 1990). See chapter 5, "The Social Organization and Contexts of Juju Performance in Ibadan," for a discussion of the *gbajumon*.
6. Art Pepper and Laurie Pepper, *Straight Life: The Story of Art Pepper* (New York: Da Capo, 1994).
7. Miles Davis with Quincy Troupe, *Miles: The Autobiography* (New York: Simon & Schuster, 1990).
8. Hampton Hawes and Don Asher, *Raise Up Off of Me* (New York: Thunder's Mouth Press, 1974).
9. Louis Armstrong, *Satchmo: My Life in New Orleans* (New York: Da Capo, 1986).
10. Sidney Bechet, *Treat It Gentle* (New York: Da Capo, 1978).
11. Edward Kennedy "Duke" Ellington, *Music Is My Mistress* (New York: Da Capo, 1973).
12. Jimmy Heath and Joseph McLaren, *I Walked with Giants: The Autobiography of Jimmy Heath* (Philadelphia: Temple University Press, 2010).
13. Horace Silver with Phil Pastras, *Let's Get to the Nitty Gritty: The Autobiography of Horace Silver* (Berkeley: University of California Press, 2006).
14. Carlos Moore, *Fela, Fela: This Bitch of a Life* (Chicago: Lawrence Hill, 1982).
15. Manu Dibango in collaboration with Danielle Rouard, *Three Kilos of Coffee: An Autobiography* (Chicago: University of Chicago Press, 1994).

16. Miriam Makeba in conversation with Nomsa Mwamuka, *Makeba: The Miriam Makeba Story* (Johannesburg: STE, 2004).

17. Hugh Masekela and D. Michael Cheers, *Still Grazin': The Musical Journey of Hugh Masekela* (New York: Three Rivers, 2004).

18. There have also been a number of musical autobiographies published locally in Nigeria, though these tend to be a bit narrower in thematic scope. For example, see Sunny Ade with Clement Ige and Femi Abulude, *Hooked to Music: An Autobiography* (Ibadan: Distinct Publications, 1996). See also Ebenezer Obey in collaboration with Mike Awoyinfa, *Ebenezer Obey: The Legend's Own Story* (Ibadan: Egret Books, 1992).

19. Fred Wesley Jr., *Hit Me, Fred: Recollections of a Sideman* (Durham, NC: Duke University Press, 2005).

20. See Steven Feld, *Jazz Cosmopolitanism in Accra: Five Musical Years in Ghana* (Durham, NC: Duke University Press, 2012); Robin D. G. Kelley, *Africa Speaks, America Answers: Modern Jazz in Revolutionary Times* (Cambridge, MA: Harvard University Press, 2012); and Ingrid Monson, *Freedom Sounds: Civil Rights Call Out to Jazz and Africa* (Oxford: Oxford University Press, 2007).

21. Henry H. Glassie, *Prince Twins Seven Seven: His Art, His Life in Nigeria, His Exile in America* (Bloomington: Indiana University Press, 2010).

22. See, for example, Paul William Schmidt, *History of the Ludwig Drum Company* (Milwaukee: Centerstream, 1991).

23. One of the most valuable contributions of John Miller Chernoff's *African Rhythm and African Sensibility* (Chicago: University of Chicago Press, 1979) is the author's comprehensive explication of this core philosophical tenet of West African drumming, exemplified by the following passage: "A musician's creative contribution will stem from his continuing reflection on the progress of the situation as both a musical and social event . . . The drummer must integrate the social situation into his music" (p. 67).

24. Ghanaba was known as Guy Warren until he Africanized his name in the 1960s. For more information, see Feld, *Jazz Cosmopolitanism in Accra*; Kelley, *Africa Speaks, America Answers*; and the chapter "The Original Cross-Overs" from John Collins, *West African Pop Roots* (Philadelphia: Temple University Press, 1992).

25. "St. Thomas" can be found on Sonny Rollins, *Saxophone Colossus*, Prestige OJCCD-291-2 (1959).

26. Tony Allen, *Black Voices*, Comet 005 (1999).

27. Tyler Stovall, *Paris Noir: African-Americans in the City of Lights* (New York: Mariner, 1996).

28. See the chapter "Americans in Paris" from George Lewis, *A Power Stronger Than Itself: The AACM and American Experimental Music* (Chicago: University of Chicago Press, 2008). See also the chapter "Points of Departure: European Interludes" from Ben Looker, *The Point at Which Creation Begins: The Black Artists' Group of St. Louis* (St. Louis: Missouri Historical Society Press, 2004).

29. See for example Baldwin's essay "Take Me to the Water" from *No Name on the Street* (New York: Vintage, 2007) or Alice Kaplan's profile of Davis's Paris years in *Dreaming in French* (Chicago: University of Chicago Press, 2012).

30. Manthia Diawara's *We Won't Budge* (New York: Basic Civitas, 2003) does an ex-

cellent and artful job of surveying the convergence and divergence of African and African American attitudes during this period.

31. Conceived as a monument to France's humanitarian ideals, the Grand Arche de La Défense was completed in 1989. See François Chaslin and Virginie Picon-Lefebvre, *La Grande Arche de La Défense* (Paris: Electa-Moniteur, 1989).

32. James Winders's *Paris Africain* (New York: Palgrave, 2006) is an excellent survey of the complexities of the African musical presence in France since the 1980s.

RIGHT IN THE CENTER OF LAGOS

1 I was born Tony Oladipo Allen in Lagos on July 20, 1940, and I grew up in the area called Lafiaji, right in the center of Lagos Island. My family lived at number 15, Okusuna Street. Lafiaji was a good area. It was very near to what we called the Race Course in those days. Today they call it Tafewa Balewa Square. King's College is in that area, too. Later on, my family moved to Ebute-Metta, on the mainland.

My father's name was James Alabi Allen. He was a Nigerian, a Yoruba from Abeokuta. We don't exactly know how the name "Allen" came into my father's family, but it's probably a slaver's name. It must have come either from my great-grandfather or from his own father, because one of them was among those people rescued by the British slave patrols in Sierra Leone. Many of the slaves that were taken from Nigeria and rescued by the slave patrols—especially the Egbas that were taken from Abeokuta—they would drop them in Sierra Leone. That's why today my father's family still has a place in Sierra Leone. I remember that once when I was arriving in Britain, the immigration officer looked at me suspiciously and asked where I got the name "Allen." I just looked at him and laughed and told him, "I wish I could know my real name. Because the name 'Allen' is coming from you guys. You gave me my name, historically, so why are you asking me where I got this name from?" He kept his mouth shut after that.

My father's father, Adolphus Allen, was a prominent man in Lagos. Allen Avenue in Ikeja is named after him. I don't know too much about him because I was only two years old when he died. What I do know is that he was a clergyman who founded a church called Bethel Cathedral, which is on Broad Street on Lagos Island. Before that he was a policeman, and he must have passed through some hard things working with the white guys back then, because it was his will that none of his children would become policemen, and none of them did. My grandfather also owned a big piece of farmland in Ikeja, on the outskirts of Lagos. That land was later sold by my father and his brothers to the Lagos State government, and the government built the Airport Hotel on it. It was also part of that land, but on the other side of Obafemi Awolowo Way, that my father sold to Fela years later. In the old times, that was the smaller part of the farm.

My mother's name was Prudentia Anna Mettle. She was born in Lagos as one of the daughters of the Ghanaian settlers in those days. Her parents and grandparents had settled in Nigeria way back, probably in the 1800s. My mother's mother was from Keta, Ghana. So my mother spoke Ga and Ewe, and believe it or not, she could even speak Yoruba better than my father! As for me, I grew up in Lagos speaking Ga, Ewe, and Yoruba. In those times, most of the Ghanaian settlers were fishermen, and they lived on Victoria Island. Back in the old days, Victoria Island was a real fishermen's village. Think about environments like Hawaii with all the beaches and fishermen's huts—that is what Victoria Island was like before they developed it into what it is today.

There were six of us children in all, and I am the oldest one. The one right under me is my brother Adebisi. He's an aeronautics engineer, working for British Airways in London and Lagos. The next one after him is my brother Olatunji, who is a civil servant in London. After him is my brother Olukunmi, who is a doctor in London. After Olukunmi is my sister Jumoke, who is a head nurse in Boston, in the United States. And the baby of us all is my sister Enitan, who is a trader in Lagos, in the market. I also have a half-brother from my father. He's called Tunde and he's a mechanic in Germany. Since I myself have been in Paris for twenty-five years, you can see that we have all spread out from Nigeria, across the world.

We all have Yoruba names, but since our mother was from Ghana, we each have a Ghanaian name too. For example, my brother Adebisi is also called Kofi, and my sister Enitan is also called Afi. As for me, there are people in Lagos today who still know me as Kwame, because I was born on a Saturday and that's the customary name in Ghana if you were born on that day. My family on my mother's side all call me Kwame.

Maybe being a "dual breed" like that is why I've always done my own thing. I've always been independent. Like when it comes to clothes, I'm somebody that always liked dressing casually, ever since I was young. I simply like casual dressing. But it was the pride of all my colleagues I was growing up with to have these fancy Yoruba attires, these big *agbadas* and all that stuff. If you want to talk about our own traditional Yoruba clothing, you have to have about three layers to put on, maybe four. First you put on the normal singlet (sleeveless undershirt) underneath, for the perspiration. Then you put on the one called *buba*. That's the one with short sleeves. After that you put *dansiki* on top, which is the third layer. And still, you must put *agbada* on top of that. Then it's complete. And some people can even put some lighter materials on top of that! That's the tradition. Even all of my brothers love it. But for me, I prefer to pick what I like, dress casually, and go by my own style. I mean, dressing is not really part of what I think about. I can dress elegantly if I want to. But I'm not really putting a lot of energy into styles and all that. I just want to be comfortable, that's all.

But the Yorubas are really into conformity. For example, every time when there is any occasion, like a funeral or whatever, they have to celebrate and throw a big party. And every group at the party has to have very specific garments. Like maybe this side is the mother's side of family. The family will tell them that they should dress in a certain style. And then on the father's side, they will tell them to choose another style. The family will bring the sample cloth out to the family and tell you, "This is what we are choosing for the occasion and this is how much it costs." It's not like here in the West, where you can just put on a regular suit for any occasion. You have to have the garments made in a certain style, and every section of the family has to wear the same stuff. That means it's gonna cost you to be at that party, because you have to get this stuff made. And then you only use it that one time. For a different occasion, you have to get a whole new set of clothes made. If it's not a funeral, it's a newborn baby. If it's not a newborn baby, it's a wedding. If it's not a wedding, it's the opening of a new house. And some people don't even have all this fucking money! They have to go borrow this money, just to be part of this occasion. I never played this game, man. It's one game I detested completely from home.

In the old days, I always preferred to go for the normal English suit, without the tie. And after a while, even the suit itself became a big problem for me, because it was becoming too heavy in the climate. It was like punishment for me in that climate. You know what I mean? I felt like I couldn't handle that. That's why back in the '70s, I was dressing with the jeans with the short cutoff vest. Sometimes I would come into Fela's house and he would look at me and say, "Allenko, you know what you look like? You look like those ones in the North that drive the cows. Like a cowboy! It's the cowboys that dress like this." He was trying to tell me that I looked "bush." And I would tell him, "Well, as long as it looks nice on me, I don't care. I love it like this!" It's just that I always had my own outlook, even before I got into music. That's my basic personality. I like to be myself. And I wouldn't have made my own way in life if I wasn't like that.

I grew up fast because I was the oldest one. I took care of all my brothers and sisters, especially the two right behind me. My mother let me do that from the age of about eight. Sometimes I used to sit in the kitchen with her and the other housewives from the neighborhood, and I would cook right along with them. The other housewives were a little jealous of that. They always used to tell my mother that she was spoiling me and that I wouldn't respect women in the future if I could do their work for them. But it was good for me because I've always been a good cook and have always been able to take care of myself. I wasn't really brought up with Nigerian cooking, because I was brought up by a Ghanaian mother. On the other hand, my father was a Nigerian, a Yoruba guy from Abeokuta, and he had his own way of eating, which he could have preferred. But my mother did the cooking, and she had to satisfy my father. He must be able to enjoy his dinner, and I never heard him complain a day in his life. That tells you something about my mother's cooking! And that's why for me, I am cooking more on the Ghanaian side than the Nigerian side. The Ghanaians have their own approach to recipes, which is different from the Nigerians. Different ingredients. So if I say I want to cook African food, you'll really be having two things in one — part Nigerian, part Ghanaian.

When I was eighteen, my mother left and went to Ghana for a while, and took Jumoke and Olukunmi with her. That left me to take care of the house and the rest of the kids. I was cooking for everybody, even my father. He used to go to work and leave money for me to buy food, because he couldn't even fry an egg! So I did everything around the house for a year and a half, until my mother came back.

I was even driving from around the age of thirteen. But the way I started is a real story! You see, my father specialized in automobiles, and he used to have jobs at home sometimes, because people would bring their cars to him instead of taking them to the workshop, where they knew they would be charged much more for the workmanship and the materials. So this particular day, one guy was supposed to come and collect his car while my father was at work. And because the kids were on midterm holidays, I was at home. My father gave me the keys to the car and told me that if this guy came, I should give him the keys so he could take his car.

On that particular day the car was right in front of the house, and the sun was really hot. But there was a big tree right across the street, in front of the Catholic school. So this guy from the neighborhood who was kind of like a big brother to me — I was thirteen and this guy was maybe like twenty-five — he came to tell me that there was too much sun on the car and that I should move the car under the tree. I didn't know anything about driving cars, nothing at all. But since he was a grown-up and I was only thirteen, I couldn't think quickly for myself to ask, "What the fuck is this guy telling me? The car is not suffering!"

So I just took the key and opened the door to the car. I thought I would start it and then try to put it in gear. But it was already in gear! The car took off, and there was no way I could control anything. I was just lucky that there was no oncoming car. I was able to cross to the other side of the street, but the trunk of that tree was right in front of a gutter, and I went toward there. I meant to stop under the tree, but — no way. And at the same time, there was a woman with a baby coming out of the maternity hospital that was just down the road. I brushed the woman with the car, and she fell into the open gutter with the baby in her hands. And the baby was just one week old!

Luckily for me, there was this guy pushing a hand truck or street cart, what we call *omolanke*. They used to use it to carry heavy loads on the road. The guy took off running, but he left his omolanke sitting there, and when I hit it, that was what stopped the car. Meanwhile, the woman was lying in the gutter with a one-week-old baby and a broken leg. They called for an ambulance and took her to the hospital. And then they called the traffic police. And of course the guy who told me to move the car had disappeared completely, and he didn't come back to the house until twelve o'clock in the night! The police came, parked the car properly, took me to the police station, and phoned my father. They couldn't put me in the cell because I was too young, so they put me behind the counter. When my father came they gave me bail and released me with him, but a court case was on now because that woman with the baby had been admitted into the hospital.

At the end of the day it was a Yoruba thing, and my father wanted to settle the police matter through the back door. But it took time on the police side, because it was a case for them. The charge was driving without a license, and reckless endangerment. They told my father that I should appear in the police station every morning before going to school. And this went on and on. Even after the holidays it continued. We even went there on Saturdays. It was really just a matter of corruption, because my father had to pay them some money every time we went.

My father was trying to pay to scrap the case, but it wasn't that easy because the big guys there were white men and you couldn't just scrap a court case like that. On the other hand, if they found out that I drove a car, I might have ended up in welfare (i.e., child services). Finally, the police told us that we had to see the inspector, who was an Igbo guy. My father gave money to this inspector, and they still didn't scrap the case. They were still making us come every morning, and my father was still paying. And we weren't even going to the station anymore, but to the house of the inspector in the barracks!

Luckily for us, this white sergeant came in one day and said, "I see these people here every day—what is the problem? What are the charges against them?" The inspector told him that I had pushed an omolanke into a woman and the woman fell into a gutter. He said it like that because he wanted to keep taking money from us every day, but if he told them I drove a car they might take me and put me into welfare. So the sergeant said, "This boy pushed a hand truck? What the hell is he doing here!?" And he told my father that from then on, we shouldn't come back there anymore. So, luckily for me, I got out of that one!

This was one time that I thought my father was coming to eliminate me completely. I thought I'd be dead! But he never touched me! I think it was because he never looked at it like something normal that I would do on my own, 'cause I had explained everything to him. I was not even thinking that the car was in the sun. This guy came to put it in my head and I fell for it because I didn't have my own thinking cap in order at that time. And the day that all this shit happened, they were looking for the guy 'til about midnight. He never even came back home to his own family to eat. Everybody was waiting for him, so he came back in the middle of the night and he had to face his own family that were asking him, "What the fuck have you done!?" My father understood what was going on. He was not a wicked guy, he was a very nice guy. He would never think to beat us unless our mother reported us to him.

My mother was Catholic and very, very religious. When I was very young she sent me to a Catholic school called St. Paul's, in Ebute-Metta. I was serving on the altar with the reverend fathers every Sunday, and it seemed like I was bowing to everything. But as soon as I left school, that was it. I seldom go to church as an adult, and if I do decide to go, I might fall asleep in the middle of the mass, because I probably will have just finished playing in a club on Saturday night and gone to church directly from there. It's not that I don't believe in God. I believe in God, but I rarely go to church.

So I must be a bit like my father. He was a Protestant, but this is a guy that I never saw put his feet in the church. My mother was the only one going to church. I remember that when I was six, the reverend fathers and reverend sisters came to our house to preach to my father. Even if he wouldn't convert, they were preaching to him that he should come and marry my mother in the Catholic church. It took some time, but later he agreed to do it. That was the only day I ever saw his feet in a church.

But he was a guy who prayed every day. He had a Bible and he used to wake us up to pray the Psalms every morning before he went to work. It was just that he didn't want to deal with all the politics of the church. If you're not attending church regularly and you die, they won't bury you, but he used to say he didn't give a shit about that. He always told us that when he died, we should just throw his body onto the street because we would just be dealing with the body, not the real him! That was always his joke. And years later, when he died, we did have to go and wrestle with the church and pay a certain amount for all his back dues so that he could get a proper burial.

My mother didn't play any instruments, but my father played guitar and mandolin as a hobby, so we had instruments at home when I was growing up. My father never played professionally, but he had friends who were musicians, and he kept those guitars so he could play with them. In the evening when he wanted to entertain us, he gave his friends the guitars and he picked up the mandolin so they could play as a trio. At that time, the *juju* music was starting to develop among the Christian Yorubas. What my father was playing with his friends was like an early juju type of thing, the kind of juju that doesn't have electric guitar or bass or keyboard. Just acoustic guitar or mandolin or banjo, and somebody would just play a bottle and another one would play the percussion.

J. O. Oyesiku was one of the musicians who used to come by. He was a good friend of the family. Sometimes on the weekends I would go with my brothers to visit him, and his wife would cook for us. Oyesiku was a soldier in the army, but he didn't live in the barracks. After he retired he moved to Ibadan, and that's when he really had time to follow up with his musical career. Another one of our family friends was Julius O. Araba. His profession, really, was as a draftsman, working for the Nigerian Railways. He did music as a hobby, but his music was strong and he was much more popular for his music than for his drafting!

Besides myself, my brother Olukunmi was the only one of us who tried to follow up on the music thing. He was good guitarist, and he had a band when he was studying medicine in the university, called the Clinics! As a matter of fact, when I started my own band years later and my guitarist was not going to be around, I would go meet him on the campus and give him a cassette and say, "Listen to this—four days from now you'll be onstage with me!" And he would come and play as my guitarist, just like that. We spent four years that way. But he never wanted to play professionally. When they finished as medical students, the Clinics all went their separate ways. Nowadays, Kunmi just has a guitar at home to amuse himself.

When we were growing up we also used to listen to a thing we called mambo that was happening at that time. I'm not talking about the Cuban mambo. This one was like a percussion and fanfare style, like parade music. You had different percussion instruments with the bass drum played with the one-sided beater, and the kind of snare drum that you hang around the neck. And then you had trumpets and maybe trombone, or sometimes tuba. It was most common on Christmas Day, among the Ewes in Lagos. It was really the Christian Ewes that got this mambo thing going in Lagos, so every Christmas Day, we would see that on the street. That was the vogue. Apart from that, if you were having a party, then you could hire a mambo band for the party. That's when you could watch the band sitting down and playing instead of parading through the streets.

At the same time, on the Muslim Yoruba side, there was *apala* and *sakara*. Those were just drums and voices, plus in apala they use the *agidigbo* (bass thumb piano), and in sakara they use the *goje*, which is kind of like a native violin. I myself used to play the agidigbo as a child, too. One of our neighbors used to love it when we boys would gather ourselves together at night and do our apala thing with agidigbo, bottle, maybe some tin cans, and we would sing too. In fact, she liked it so much that she even gave us money to buy our own agidigbo. When you're talking about apala, Haruna Ishola was really the master, man. It's like classical music for us. The lyrics of this guy are incredible. If you could only understand what that guy was singing about, man—too many things! Things about life, like proverbs. Apart from the singing, when you check the way this guy composes the rhythmical language, it's flowing because the instruments are not all playing the same thing there. It's a kind of interwoven language, so it's very interesting. It's like a conversation. But when we were doing those things, I never thought in my life that I would turn out to be a musician. I didn't want to be one of these agidigbo guys, playing apala and all that. It was just a question of having kicks imitating those guys and trying to sing like them. But I did really love drumming. At home, I used to set chairs up and play on them, just kind of amusing myself. And from my elementary school days at St. Paul's, I used to play snare drum in the school marching band. I held onto that for as long I was in elementary school. But I finished primary school when I was twelve, and then I forgot about music completely. That was around 1953.

After that, I went to secondary school to study. But by my third year, it was too tough for me. To be honest, I wasn't ready for it. I was tired of learning all these things that didn't seem relevant. I couldn't see what I was going to do with Latin and all those things. And the teacher was really becoming a pain in the neck, man. That's the way I was looking at it at that time. In fact, I went to my father one day and said, "I am going to beat up the teacher." And my father said, "No, you *cannot* do that!" So I went back, but one day I just said, "No more." That was in 1957. Then my father asked me, "What is it that you want to do now?" I told him I wanted to be an automobile mechanic. I wanted to be under the cars, working with the engines. That's what my father did, and that's what I wanted to do. But he told me, "You—no, never!" He didn't think I was built to deal with those heavy engines. He thought I would have been a painter, like an artist, because I used to draw a lot in my spare time. He thought I would be doing that. I didn't want to go that direction, but I thought, maybe I'll be an architectural draftsman, like Araba. So my parents sent me to school with a private teacher who had eight students.

I had been going to this school for about six months, and I was progressing, drawing nicely. Then one day, I noticed that there was an electrical switch on the wall. It was completely broken, and it was dangerous. You know, in my childhood I used to play around with electricity — fixing wires and batteries and light bulbs. So I had different components at home, and I told my teacher that I had a brand-new switch that I could install for him, and it was only going to cost him two shillings and six pence. In those days my tuition fee was one pound, and one pound was equal to twenty shillings. This was before Nigeria switched to the naira currency. So I got my switch and I fixed the problem, and I wanted him to pay me. He kept telling me, "I'll get it to you," but he never paid me. Every day he says he'll give me the money. I said nothing.

At the end of the month, my father gave me the money to pay for the next month, because you have to pay in advance. So what I did was take the one-pound note and change the money, and I deducted my two shillings and six pence and I gave my teacher the rest. And he flipped out completely! He said, "Hey, what's this?" I said, "I just took my money out of the one pound." He shouted, "*No!* You can never do that! You have to give me my one pound for the month! I told you, I will give you your money." I said, "But it's over one month now since I put this switch in." The teacher said he was not gonna accept that. So I said okay, and I gave him his full pound. And then I took my screwdriver out and I took off my switch and I put it in my box and that was it. He saw this and he said, "What?!" Because this guy was running the school in his own home, his parents and grandparents were there. He started yelling, "Mommy, mommy, mommy — come and look at this! Come and look at what Allen has done!" So I left the fucking switch like that, and I told him, "Now you're gonna buy the switch, the electrician is gonna fix it, and you're gonna pay for *both*." I did it like that diplomatically, because I didn't want to fight the guy. And I took my bag and walked out. So that was the end of drafting school.

I went back home and narrated the whole story to my father. And he said, "Okay. What next?" He asked if I wanted to look for another drafting school. I thought about it and told him that I wanted to go to an electronics school. So I had to start all over again, reading a whole new type of literature and taking notes for the exams — first for the theory and then for the practical. I studied for about one year and a half and then I got a job. My uncle I. K. Mettle was the chief engineer of a German radio company called Witt & Busch, and he got me employment there. So I worked as a radio technician for about four years. We were building amplifiers—six-valve, heavy-output amplifiers. Right now I could coolly build a six-valve amplifier myself, no problem. That took me right up to the end of 1960.

At the same time that I was doing the electronics work, I started going out a lot at night, crawl-ing the pubs. I was making some money of my own, and at that time, man, Lagos was swinging! There were so many clubs and great bands around in those times, and they were all going twenty-four hours. On Saturdays especially, nobody slept. We had the White Horse, the Lido, and the Western Top on Agege Motor Road. The Empire Hotel was also on Agege Motor Road, and that's where Fela later made the Afrika Shrine in the 1970s. We had the Ambassador and the Gondola in Yaba. There was Bobby Benson's Caban Bamboo on Ikorodu Road. Then we had the Central Hotel and the Kakadu on Herbert Macauley Road in Alagomeji. The Kakadu was where Fela later made the Afro-Spot during the Koola Lobitos times in the '60s. I myself might crawl three or four pubs in the night, just checking out the bands, because Lagos was full of great bands! They were all playing highlife, but playing it in different styles. The big bandleaders at that time were Victor Olaiya, Cardinal Rex Lawson, E. C. Arinze, Steven Amaechi, Eddie Okonta, Agu Norris, Eric Onuha, and Bill Friday. Those were the bands ruling the country back then.

You might not believe this, but Nigerians used to go to school in those days to learn ballroom dancing. When they finished with work, they went to learn quickstep, tango, waltz, foxtrot, and all those dances. And then there was the highlife, of course. Highlife is in straight meter, meaning it's in 4/4. And everybody responds to 4/4 beats quickly. If it was a slow one, the couple would dance close together. If it was a fast one, the women would stick their bottoms out and shake them, while the guys behind were caressing it slowly. That is why the bands had to know how to play all of these styles. And the people would be dressed in evening clothes—men were wearing suits and ties and women were wearing dresses. I my-self had to dress that way, with a suit and tie. It's totally different compared to what we have there now, a completely different world.

During the time that I was working with my uncle, I also did some dee-jaying for parties and private affairs. If you want to deejay, you have to buy records, and you have to be a record lover yourself. My uncle had a lot of highlife records from Ghana, and also a lot of Latin American music on those labels like GV and HMV. But he wasn't going to be deejaying anywhere. He would just drive me there with the equipment and everything, and pick me up afterwards. So I had something to do every weekend because I worked on Saturdays and Sundays. I was mainly playing Ghanaian highlifes, like E. T. Mensah, the Ramblers, and the Stargazers. Those were deep, deep records — wicked records — and they were very popular. And I was playing Nigerian highlifes like Bobby Benson, Victor Olaiya, and Cardinal Rex Lawson.

I'm telling you — it was fantastic, man! Complete enjoyment! They would booze me up completely at these parties. I would be drunk even before finishing the party! You cannot compare those parties with what they call "parties" here in Europe. Because in Lagos we used to have outdoor parties, and they could go from one night to the next morning. We were playing music out there with all the neighbors around, but nobody was going to complain because they too were enjoying what's going on. Even if they were asleep, they were enjoying the music in their sleep! They would never have said that it was noisy. But you could not do that here in Paris. Try to set up a band or a deejay out here in front of this apartment building, and everybody would be in jail — you wouldn't even get through one tune! So you can see the enjoyment of what we had there in Nigeria. It was really like a paradise! My prayer is to see Lagos back like it was then. Even if we can get back just one-quarter of what we had in those times, I think I will go back.

Through going around to all the clubs and playing those records at parties, I was just checking out the music thing. And when I started taking up an instrument, the first one was the guitar. The second one was the fiddle bass, the upright. And the third one was tenor sax. But I got discouraged. My fingers were swelling up with blisters. And with the sax, my lips got cut up by the reed. It wasn't comfortable at all.

Actually, the drum set was my aim. I wasn't playing yet, but I was already checking out all the highlife drummers. At that time, I really admired those guys like James Meneh, Oje Neke, John Bull, and Femi Bankole. It was their dexterity that I admired. There was also a drummer that used to play with Bill Friday who was called Anex, who had very good technique. He was a real tight drummer who could make you dance, and you could even dance to his solos. I used to love to watch Anex play with Bill on Sundays at the Teatime Dance, which was at the Ambassador Hotel.

So I wanted to play the drums, but it wasn't easy to just sit down at anybody's drum set. No way, man. You had to have some kind of connection to be able to reach those drums! So I decided to use the radio as my connection, since I was known as a radio technician. One day I met a guy named Akanni Pereira, who bought a radio at the place I was working. He asked me if I would come and fix the antenna for him in his home. He gave me the address and I walked to his house after work. I was just trying to make some extra money in my spare time. When I got to his compound, I found out that he was a musician. In fact, he was one of the best guitarists in town. He was playing with Victor Olaiya and the Cool Cats, and the band was residing in Olaiya's compound, which was like a hostel for the musicians — not all of them, but the important ones, the giants of the band, like Akanni; Tex Oluwa, who was the bassist; and Sivor Lawson, who played the saxophone. All the instruments were there as well. At night, they were playing at the Cool Cats Inn on Abule-Nla Road off Apapa Road, in Ebute-Metta. It was run by a guy named Mr. Biney, who was a lawyer and who also owned the only zoo in Lagos.

So Olaiya comes in, and by the time I finished my work, the entire band had arrived for rehearsal and the music started. Boom — I became a spectator right away! I had finished up my work, but I was obliged to stay all the way to the end of the rehearsal. I was watching the entire band, but I was *really* looking at the drummer. He was a guy called Osho, and he was one of the best drummers at that time. So at the end of the rehearsal I asked Akanni to introduce me to this drummer because I would like to learn how to play the drums. And he did. I asked Osho if he would teach me how to play the drums and if we could discuss a tuition fee. He told me that I had to pay him ten pounds for the studies. So the bread I was taking from Akanni for the job I came to do, I asked him to give that money to Osho for me.

We arranged for the lessons to start, and Osho told me to buy my own drumsticks. So when I was coming back from work the next day I went to Kingsway department store on Broad Street on Lagos Island and bought my first drumsticks. Then I went back to Akanni's compound and waited for them to finish their rehearsal. And when they finished the rehearsal I took my first lesson. Osho's setup was kick, snare, toms, and ride cymbals. I had to train my muscles because it was painful at first — my leg muscles got kind of stiff.

The first thing Osho taught me was how to play the highlife, which is mainly played on the snare, with accents and rolls, and sometimes the kick or the tom-toms. Then the second lesson was a rumba, and the third was the waltz, in slow time. But suddenly Osho stopped showing up for my lessons. What could I do? One day Olaiya's saxophonist, Peter King, walked in and he said, "Ah, Allen. Every day I come and you keep repeating the same things." And I told him that Osho never showed up for any more of my lessons. So Peter said, "Let me teach you to play the mambo, just so you can progress." And he sat on the drums and he showed me how to play mambo. We're talking about the Cuban mambo now. And so now I had four rhythms—mambo, waltz, highlife, and rumba.

I was learning quickly, but like I said, Osho never came to teach me again. I would wait and wait, but since I was living with my parents, they used to get mad when I stayed out too long. There wasn't any telephone there, and they got worried. I had just a few lessons, and then that was it. So I became discouraged, and I went back to my job. But then Olaiya himself gave me a part-time job playing clefs for the Cool Cats at night. He liked me a lot because I'd been introduced by Akanni, plus I used to repair his own radio for him too. So he just said, "Come and play with us, man, and earn some extra bread." I did it for maybe six months, but it was fucking tough. Because we would finish playing like two o'clock in the night on Lagos Island, but my family had moved to Ebute-Metta on the mainland by this time. By the time everything was completely finished, I usually arrived back home like five o'clock. Then I had to be back at my job at eight o'clock. I found myself falling asleep at work with the soldering iron in my hand, and one day I dropped it on myself. I realized that this was becoming too much for me—I couldn't keep doing it. It's nothing to play clefs in a band, anyway. It's like the lowest position in a band. I wouldn't quit my job to play clefs. So I went to Olaiya and told him nicely that it was too tough for me because I wasn't getting any sleep. He understood. I gave them back my uniform and we all stayed friends. I stuck to my job working as a radio technician and going to the clubs at night.

But one day I became fed up with this job too, because of a German guy there who was my superior and who was always complaining about me to the boss. I put up with him for a long time, but he was getting on my nerves and I couldn't stand him anymore. The problem was that I ate in the same place where he ate, at Kingsway, where they had a restaurant inside that everyone would go to. Every time I was eating there he was coming in there and asking me what I was doing eating there. And so every time I arrived back at work, the big boss would always ask me if I went there to eat at worktime. I told him, "Yes, motherfucker—sometimes, because I don't eat normally like everybody. I have my own program inside me which means I don't have breakfast and I must have something inside me like snacks or something." That was because I always had a very sensitive stomach. But this German guy kept on me every time. One day it became physical, because I was reading an electronics book and he came from behind me, stood right behind me, and just grabbed the book from me. So when I got up from my chair I turned around and slammed him directly into the door, and he collapsed. I wanted to kill that guy that day. I knew that was the end for me there. So I took my leave and went back home and narrated the story to my father. This time he asked me, "What is it now? What is your next step going to be?" So I told him, "Music—that's all." This was sometime around 1959 or 1960.

This was very bad news for my parents, to hear that I'm quitting my job to go play music full time. As a matter of fact, I thought I would be going through some big shit with my parents. But that was the first time in my life that I saw my father not objecting to my decision. This was the first time he never said, "You are crazy!" He just asked me, "Why do you want to play music?" I said, "Well, I'm sick of those German guys. I'm tired of them. I just want to quit and I don't want to cause too much trouble. Let me just go play music. I'm not going to play free of charge. I'll earn a salary every month, so I'll still be able to pay my expenses." So he told me, "Alright, if that's what you have decided to do." He never came out and said it, but maybe he was thinking about the fact that he himself was talented and always wanted to play music professionally, which he never did. He might have thought that, as his first son, I was going to make use of what he never did. My mother was really sad. But he told my mother, "We'll let him go, and if it's no good for him, he'll come back. We're here and we'll rescue him."

2 My parents knew they could trust me because I had already been through a big shit with them about smoking grass. I've been smoking all my life, and I started at the age of fifteen. That is forbidden in Nigeria, like everyplace else. No parents want to see their children smoking grass, but as a teenager, you want to do everything that the others are doing. I remember the first time I smoked. It was Christmas Eve of 1955, and my mother had gone to church. And this neighbor of ours who was about seven years older than me came to me and said, "Let's try this stuff." He gave me some puffs and I noticed that it wasn't the same thing as smoking cigarettes. I felt something come over me in a wave and I went to sit down on the pavement in front of the church. This church had a very high steeple and I saw the steeple turning upside down. The whole church was floating. I told myself, no — this can't be real!

I enjoyed smoking that time, but what really made me go into it was that in my childhood, I wasn't a good eater. It was always a fight to make me eat, and my mother was always angry because once she made the food, I would disappear or even sneak and give the food to my friends sometimes. But I remember that the day I smoked, I came home and opened the cupboard, and I just couldn't stop eating. I ate so much that my stomach was bloated. When my mother came back and discovered that, she never believed that it was me that had eaten all this food. She thought I had given the food to my friends again. She asked me, "What happened to you to make you eat this food?" Of course, I couldn't tell her the real reason. And from that day, for the next five years, I was hiding my smoking from my parents.

But my mother started to attack me, because she would see my eyes when she came home, and she knew. She never said it to me, but she would always check my eyes and would report me to my father. And so my father put a curse on my smoking. He decided that he wasn't going to be trailing me and watching me and trying to catch me. You know how to put a spiritual curse? For Africans, a curse is like telling someone, "Even if nobody sees you, it will still be known. And if you are lying, certain negative things are gonna happen to you." He put that on me. And meanwhile I was just smoking and smoking. It took me five years, but after that I had to confront my parents. I told them that those five years I had been smoking grass. I had been denying it every time, but there was no point in denying anything anymore. Because in all these five years, I never did something like committing rape, I never went to go burgle anyone's house, and you never had to come bail me out at the police station. My father agreed with me about that. Then they asked me why I smoked grass. I told them that it made me feel better and that as a musician, one needs something to face the audience sometimes. You can't always face them in your normal head, because you might have stage fright. I told them it made me feel better than drinking. It also helped me creatively. In the middle of the night, I have different waves going through my head, and if I'm not receptive of what's passing through my head, spiritually and musically, I cannot utilize it. The smoke helps me make use of those things. Those were the things I told them at that time. My father thought about it and saw that it was true, that he never caught me involved in any bullshit. So he removed the curse and instead gave me his blessing, and I went on with my smoking.

It just so happened that at the time I decided to go into the music full time, Olaiya was disband-ing, and two new bands were forming from the old Cool Cats. The band split in half. Half went with Olaiya into his new band, and half went with the new Cool Cats band led by Sivor Lawson, the saxophonist in the old band. Osho went with Olaiya, so Lawson had to look for a drummer. And fortunately for me those guys playing with him were my friends, and they said, "Why don't you come and join us?" I told them I would like to play the drums, but I hadn't had enough experience yet. So they got another drummer for the time being and I went back on the clefs, so that I could assimilate the music properly. The other drummer was a half-caste guy from Ghana named Kofi Galland, who also sang. It was good, because it was a steady gig.

After two months, we developed a routine. Kofi used to sing three songs every night, and while he was up front singing, I would sit down and play the drums. At least I was playing the drums for three songs every night. Then after nine months, Kofi came to me and told me that he was leaving the band and he thought I should take over on the drums. But he never told Lawson he was leaving. He left in the middle of the night, and in the morning he was gone when they came to find him for rehearsal. So they had to look for a new drummer immediately, because there were gigs scheduled. But the guys told Lawson, "There's no point in looking for any drummer, because Allen is here." So instead they looked for somebody to take over from me on the clefs, and that's when Ojo Okeji came in. He came from Ifon in the West, and we became real good friends. (Ifon is the major town in Osun State in western Nigeria.) The bass player was a guy from Cameroon called Ngomalio. And while Ojo was playing the clefs, Ngomalio was teaching him to play the bass. So that was it — the gig with Lawson was really what started me off as a drummer, and that was the beginning of everything for me.

Playing with Lawson was a valuable experience for me because it was a very good band. The music was fantastic. We had a full house every weekend. In fact, we were so good that some reporters from the *Daily Times* came to interview the band and take pictures of all the members. That was the best newspaper in the country at that time. When it came to my turn, the reporter asked me, "How long have you been playing the drums?" and I told him eight months. He said, "Eight months — I don't believe it!" Then the guys all told him the same thing — that I had actually been playing for eight months. The reporter thought I had been playing for maybe five years. So you can see that I was developing rapidly.

Once we were even invited to open for Louis Armstrong, as part of the Nigerian Independence Day celebrations. This must have been around the end of 1960, and it was the same African tour that took him to Ghana, where he played with E. T. Mensah. Armstrong arrived and played at the National Stadium in Lagos, with Victor Olaiya's band opening for him. I missed him there. But then he played in Ibadan, which is where we opened for him, at Liberty Stadium. We traveled to Ibadan, and I remember that it was raining hard that day. But the stadium was completely full anyway because Louis Armstrong was a world-known musician. Everybody loved him in Nigeria and wanted to see him play.

I set up my drums, but the rain was destroying my snare, because it had a leather head. The water made the pitch go way down until the snare sounded like a tom-tom. I did everything I could to make it sound better. I even lit a newspaper and tried to dry the snare out a little bit, and we managed to play. Louis and his whole band were checking us out. We were playing highlife things. Louis was even dancing around a bit on the side of the stage — he seemed to enjoy the music.

After that, Louis's drummer came on. I can't remember his name, but he looked Chinese or Japanese to me. (Armstrong's drummer during this period was the Filipino American Danny Barcelona (1929–2007), whom he often referred to onstage as "The Little Hawaiian Boy.") He was a fucking good drummer, and his drums were sitting in the rain too. I told Sivor, "Look at the difference between the two snare drums — the water stays on top of his! His snare is like a pond!" That's because it had a plastic head. I thought it was going to be impossible to play. We didn't really have plastic drum heads in Nigeria at that time, so I didn't really understand how they worked. But then the road manager came and he simply took out a rag and cleaned the water off the top of the drum. And when the drummer played, the drum sounded great — completely different from the one with the skin head. Afterwards, I had a good discussion with this guy backstage and we had a good time together. I admired him, because he was good. Louis himself was a very jovial guy, always cracking jokes and making everybody laugh. We all admired him so much. Meeting Louis Armstrong was a great experience for me, and I hadn't even been playing one full year yet!

Within those eight months, we'd already gone on tour of Nigeria, throughout the East, West, and Midwest. That was another experience for me. If we played in a city like Warri or Benin, it was pretty much the same as in Lagos. But it was a whole different story when we had to go to the interior. First of all, there was no electricity. The only thing they might have had were gas lamps. Or maybe the village chief might have had a generator, but only for his compound. So we had to play with 12-volt batteries. We had a type of amplifier that was convertible to 12-volt batteries. That amplifier could only carry the microphones, but we also put the guitars through it, because there was no separate amplifier for the guitars. We made do and it sounded great. It was always a full house in the village and the people always enjoyed it. And when the concert finished, everybody went home in the darkness with torches or gas lamps for the road.

Most times we had to sleep in the club. Nobody was looking for beds or anything fancy like that. When the concert finished, I usually just put down a mat and slept next to my drums. Sometimes if we were lucky we could get a bed, but those beds were full up with bedbugs. When you awakened, you would be covered with bites, and there was nothing you could do about it! And some of these clubs were really in the bush, man, I mean in the jungle. When I would lie down to sleep I would hear all the animal noises on the other side of the fence and I would be praying that no animal jumped on me in the night!

In the larger towns, it could be different because they might have two things going on in the clubs. It might be the club on one side, and call girl business on the other side. That means they must have rooms there. So sometimes they can say, "Okay, two rooms for the band," and we would manage with that. Sometimes, if we were lucky, we could go and sleep with one of the girls and have a softer place to sleep. But the point is, we didn't sleep in hotels. If we had spent money on hotels, we would have gotten back to Lagos with no money, and the proprietor was there waiting for his bread so that he could take his cut and pay us our salaries.

But in the end we still arrived back with no money. What happened was that the band manager, whose name was George, was in charge of all the paperwork and the money. And while we were on tour some guys tricked George and Lawson through gambling. These guys knew how to play cards and they did that every night. They started in the middle of the night when we were asleep and when we woke up, they were still playing. They cleaned Lawson and George out, and they were gambling with the band's money! So when we got back to Lagos, there was nothing left.

The proprietor couldn't believe this, so he sent a different band out for the next tour, and he put us on hold. That band was led by a guy named Odiachi. When Odiachi came back with all the bread he was supposed to, the proprietor fired Lawson and the band dissolved. That was it. Altogether it was eighteen months of experience with Lawson — nine months of playing clefs and nine months of playing the drums — and the Cool Cats were finished. I didn't want to look for any other band. I had to change my mind about playing music full time. I told myself that I was *finished* with music. *Completely finished.* If that was the way this business worked, I wasn't touching this job anymore. I couldn't afford to be doing this type of job, because my father always told me, "Don't leave certainty for uncertainty." So I quit. This was around the middle of 1962.

I went back home to start studying again—this time, to pass my CTI guild exams in electronics. I had to do correspondence courses where I sent in the markings and they would send it back to me. It was like a one-year crash course. But after six months, the temptation came back for music. This time it was a band called Agu Norris and the Heatwaves. Norris was a trumpeter and singer from the East, but he made his living in Lagos. His gig was to play the third set at the Empire Hotel, after E. C. Arinze and Steven Amaechi had finished. They kept on coming to beg me. And I refused and refused. The contract was for just four Saturdays a month at the Premier Hotel in Ibadan. It was a good gig with a very good salary. The money was tempting, but we had to travel from Lagos to Ibadan every weekend. I told them I didn't want it, I didn't care about the money, and to please just leave me alone. But Norris kept on coming and also sending his people to me, telling me I shouldn't be talking like that, that the Cool Cats thing was just my first experience, that it wasn't the end of the road. So finally I said okay, let me try it again. I started with Norris at the end of 1962. And that was it—I have never stopped playing music, right up until today.

With Norris, we were playing copyrights, highlife, and everything else. Most of the bands just played copyrights in those days, which meant cover versions of popular songs, played like the original recording. This was because you had to play popular hits for the crowd, and also because not all the bandleaders knew how to compose. That's why you had to learn to play everything, because you might have to play a waltz, quick-step, rumba, mambo, or cha-cha-cha, you know. As a matter of fact, to become a musician in those days you had to know how to play all those styles. Any popular tune, you had to be able to play. Today it's completely different. One drummer doesn't even know what another is doing.

But with Norris, it was the same experience as with Sivor Lawson—meaning, more problems with the money. The deal was that Norris was supposed go to Ibadan to collect the money at the end of each month and come back to Lagos and pay everybody. But instead he collected the money and then sat down there with his friend Eddie Okonta. Okonta was a trumpeter and a bandleader from the Midwest. They would sit down together and drink the money away—the salary of the band. Then Norris would get back to Lagos and say he never received the money. It was always like this—he drank the money out every time. Until I said, "No! We have to go back home with money. We have to pay all our house rents." So one day we arrived there, and we had this Jewish club manager. We were eating, and this guy was telling us, "Time to go play." We said "Play? We ain't playing today!" He said, "Why?" and we said, "Where's our money—our salary, where is it?" The guy told us that we must be joking. He said, "I paid your money to Mr. Norris last week!" So he had to go check his guy Norris. He asked him, "Norris, what happened, where's the money? I need music. You signed a contract."

This manager was begging us now. He asked us, "Please just play, we'll work it out after the concert." We told him that if we played, it was just because we respected him, but if we didn't get our money we weren't going to leave and we were gonna to stay right there on the stage. And that's what happened. We finished playing and we never moved. It was Sunday morning and we were all still on the stage. It was like our protest, so they had to call a board meeting around eleven o'clock the next morning. A meeting of the whole Western Hotel company, along with Norris. And they told him, "Mr. Norris, this is what we're going to do. The first contract you signed is six months. This is the fourth month of the contract. So we are going to loan you one month in advance again, right now, to pay these guys. And then, you're going to have to work one month without pay." But after the first week, Norris tried to pay us half again, telling us he was gonna pay the rest the following week.

I was the only one among the guys that wanted to pull out when he came back with the half salary thing, because I had already secured a new band. The first gig of the new band was gonna be Saturday in Lagos, the same day that I was supposed to play in Ibadan with Norris. So I had to go to Ibadan pretending I was going to play, just try to grab the balance of my salary. It was kind of tricky, in a way. I told Norris that I wanted to do some shopping before the show, and I asked him to give me the money so I could go buy a few things. He asked me, "Why can't you wait until tomorrow, when we finish?" He told me he couldn't give it to me all at once, that he'd give it to me after the show. I asked him how much he had on him right then. He said half of the half—a quarter of what he owed me. So he gave it me and I flew out from the hotel, crossed the road, and took a taxi straight to the motorpark. And that was it. I left right away and went to play a gig with a new band in Lagos.

The new band was the Nigerian Messengers, led by Charles Wokoma, who was a saxophonist from Rivers State. He had just left Olaiya's band to start his own band. But then Agu Norris came to Lagos and said, "I'm going to take you to court!" I just laughed, you know. I said, "Court? I'm waiting for it! Because in the first place I never signed nothing with you. Everything was verbal. And furthermore you still owe me. If you didn't owe me I might never have thought of leaving like that. The point is we are responsible. We have kids. Don't keep fucking us up. So I'm waiting for the court case!"

You see, I just had my first wife then. She's called Ibilola Agbeni. We were married in Africa according to what they call "native law and custom." If you're having kids, it's automatic marriage for us sometimes. You become husband and wife just by having kids together. And then the time comes later when you want to go get it done officially. Like me personally, I was six years old when my father married my mother right in front of me. But the couple really forms before the marriage.

Ibilola and I had six children together, and they all still live in Nigeria. There's our son Adenike, who was born in 1965. The second one was our daughter Ibiwunmi, who was born in 1967. The third one was our daughter Abidemi, born in 1969. Then in 1972 we had twin girls, Kehinde and Taiwo. The youngest is our son Segun, who was born in 1980. They don't really do music too much, except maybe for singing in the church sometimes. But Nike and Kehinde are singing on my album *Home Cooking*.

Anyway, with Charles Wokoma it turned out to be the same blues. It's always the same shit. At the end of the month it's a struggle for your bread. I was barely managing with it until one of my friends came to tell me that Eddie Okonta had just left the Paradise Club in Ibadan. My friend's name was Yinka Roberts, a guitar player. We used to be in the Cool Cats together with Olaiya. And Yinka asked me if I wanted to form another group for the Paradise gig. I asked him who the bandleader was going to be, and he told me it was going to be a saxophonist named Sunny Lionheart, a Yoruba guy from Ijebu-Ode who had been playing with Eddie Okonta's band. He had a band called the Paradise Melody Angels.

That meant I had to leave Lagos now and move to Ibadan. Before, I was going once a week. But this time we were going to be playing every day in Ibadan. That meant I had to move house. This was serious. Since I was born, I had never left Lagos to go stay anywhere else. So for the first time in my life, I left. This was in 1963. I went to stay in Ibadan with my friend Ojo, who had been the clefs player with Sivor Lawson's Cool Cats when I was there. Since then he had learned to play the bass, and he was now playing with a highlife group in Ibadan led by a good trumpet player named Rex Williams. But Ojo always wanted to be in a band with me, so Sunny brought him into the band. There was also a singer in Ibadan named Adeolu Akinsanya, who was with Kehinde Adex's highlife band. Adex was a trumpet player from Ijebu-Epe, not far from Lagos. But we got Adeolu and Adex to join the Paradise Melody Angels, because Adeolu was a great singer and composer and Sunny needed lyrics and songs.

For the first month I was living with Ojo. Then when my first pay came, I rented a room for myself. It was a very small place because now I was paying rent for two houses — one in Ibadan and one in Lagos. But I couldn't afford to pay both, so I just told my parents to move all of my stuff out of the house in Lagos. My wife was still living with her parents anyway, and she started to come to Ibadan to stay with me for a few days, and then take the bus back to Lagos.

So that band was going on, but by the fifth month of living in Ibadan, I became fed up with the whole salary business again. I didn't want to play the same money game with Lionheart anymore, so at the end of the month, I just took my salary and split back to Lagos. There was no band for me to play with there, but I just wanted to go back home. Since I didn't have my own house anymore, I had to move in with my parents. Fortunately for me my brother's room was big enough for the two of us. At this time I was just turning twenty-three. And my wife always came to me to visit me at my parents' house, sleeping there for days sometimes. I wasn't wanting for anything and I wasn't looking for any bands.

This went on for about one month, when all of a sudden Adeolu and Kehinde showed up in Lagos. They were sick of Lionheart too, so they came to Lagos to form a house band in a hotel called the Western Hotel on Agege Motor Road in Idi-Oro. They were gonna call the band the Western Toppers. Actually, they brought a drummer with them from Ibadan, but they told me this boy was such a braggart and thought his playing was so great that they were already sick of him. And really, he couldn't play anything. Definitely, he couldn't play at my level. So their aim was to get me back on the drums. I asked them, "What about the bread? Because I'm not going to be earning less here than what I earned in Ibadan. We have to agree on my salary first." I asked them to pay me twenty-six pounds a month. That was a lot of money in those days. Even if it was a normal day job, you must have "read the book" (studied and passed your school exams) properly to get a monthly salary of twenty-six pounds. Because your house rent would only be about two pounds a month.

So they went to tell the proprietor that I was asking for twenty-six pounds a month. "What!?" The hotel proprietor there had never paid such amounts to any drummer before in his life. But they told him that if he wanted a band better than everyone else, Allen was the guy they needed. "No," he said, "I want to hear the guy." And so they called me and I went to meet the guy. He asked, "Is that you that said you wanted twenty-six pounds a month?" I said, "Yes sir, that's what I said." He said, "The maximum I ever paid a drummer is ten pounds. Let's just hear how well you play first." So that night I went with the band, and since they were gonna be playing a lot of stuff that we'd played before, in Ibadan, I knew the material. After I had finished, the proprietor came running: "Ah yes, yes, yes, yes! It is true—no drummer ever played like this before!" So he was convinced.

The key was that I had discovered a way to play my hi-hat cymbals. I never saw any other drummer opening and closing his hi-hats back then in highlife. Most of them were just playing on the open snare. If the hi-hats were there, they were played closed. But I had really worked on my hi-hats, and it changed my way of drumming completely. It kind of balanced my way of thinking because I could keep the snare and hi-hats going together. It was more polyrhythmic that way. After the show the proprietor came to tell me that he was just a struggling guy too, and couldn't we negotiate? He told me that he would give me a house, and he would give me eighteen pounds a month. And the house was very close by. Just two blocks across the railway line in Idi-Oro and I'm there. This sounded like a good offer. And this guy was a very nice guy, so I accepted, and the band sent that other drummer back to Ibadan.

The Western Toppers music was great, because Adeolu was a fucking good singer, a great composer, and I loved his way of composing in the Yoruba language. His melodies were super. I respected Adeolu from childhood because we used to play together as children in a little band we had called Rio Lindo. He used to sing and play the agidigbo in that band. So working with him was great. I played exactly one year with that band.

Playing in all those highlife bands and coming up under all of those tough bandleaders was good training for me because I learned how to demand respect for myself. But in my heart at that time, it was really jazz that I was aiming for. I have always listened to the great jazz drummers whenever I could. Listening to those guys made me understand the way the drum set should be played. In the beginning I was listening to Gene Krupa and I thought he was the greatest drummer in the world. But later when I started to hear others, like Philly Joe Jones, Elvin Jones, Art

Blakey, and Max Roach, it was like magic to me. "Ahh," I said to myself. "Fucking hell." This was serious. I wanted to play like all of them. All of these African American guys, I felt as if they were stomping on my face with their drumming, because they were so great. The way they were drumming, it had all the spirituality and all the celebration in it. It wasn't English. It wasn't Western. It wasn't what Gene Krupa was doing. It was a whole different language. We should have been playing the drum set like that in Nigeria. After all, it originally came from here. They took it, went there to the Americas, polished it, and sent it back to us in Africa.

I realized that the Gene Krupa style of playing had too much rolling for me. He was coming from more of a military style, and it was good—we all studied to get that and I wanted to get that myself. But people like Max Roach didn't solo with lots of continuous rolling. Guys like Max and Elvin and Blakey and Philly Joe, they were *telling a story* on the drums. Krupa wasn't doing that. These guys were telling a story by playing different rhythms, and they were doing it with independent coordination. That's the way the drums should be played, man. That's why jazz was a big discovery for me, a discovery that made me much better. And it was Fela Ransome-Kuti that gave me the opportunity to really play this music. After I met him, the whole game changed.

THE SKY WAS THE LIMIT

3 At this point it was 1963 and Fela had just arrived back from London and was working at the Nigerian Broadcasting Company (NBC). His job was presenter of jazz programs. He was playing jazz for thirty minutes on Friday nights, playing mainly Blue Note records. Fela spins nicely, man. Those thirty minutes, you were really going to enjoy them.

Fela was strictly a jazz man at that time. He was playing trumpet, and a little piano, too. And he eventually decided that, since he himself was a musician, why should he be promoting other people's music? So he decided to form a band called the Fela Ransome-Kuti Quartet with some musicians from the radio station and some outside help. But the NBC was mainly full of classical musicians. There was Fela Sowande, who was the boss, the composer, and the biggest of them all. He ran the whole NBC, all the radio stations in the country—North, South, East, West. He was the master. And then there was Tunde Oyesiku, who also played classical compositions at NBC. Fela himself had been studying classical music in London and had just come back to Lagos after receiving his diploma. But there were no musicians who really thought anything of him at that time, because he was just working as a deejay at the NBC. He wasn't really playing anything with anybody outside, or rubbing shoulders with the musicians around Lagos. And that's why, to do the jazz thing, he had to make use of the musicians they had there at the NBC. There was one staff member at the NBC named Kingsley Etuk who was a very good jazz pianist. Then they brought in Ngomalio, the bassist from my first band with Sivor Lawson.

Benson Idonije was Fela's friend and was working at the NBC with him as a broadcaster. Benson was the only one I saw who was really support-ive of Fela at that time, besides Fela's mother. Maybe the reason was that Fela's family had sent him to London to do medicine and he decided to do music instead. Even though he had followed it up with a diploma, they were still trying to advise him to do other things. But Benson believed in Fela as a musician and wanted to be his manager in the future if anything started to happen. And since Fela was from Abeokuta and didn't really know Lagos so much at that time, Benson was also showing him around town to help him get himself together musically.

Fela, Benson, Kingsley, and Ngomalio had been trying out different drummers. They started with a guy named John Bull. Then they brought in a guy named Femi Bankole. Fela thought Bankole was good and it looked like they finally had a band, but then the civil war was coming and that messed up many bands. Things were still in order in Nigeria for the first three years after independence. Then the politicians started their tribalism shit in 1964. They started their shit all around the country—North, South, East, and West. They started rigging elections, and the fighting began. We had been living together and getting along for years, so Nigerians were manipulated into that. It was around 1964 when we began to wake up in the morning, or come out of the club in the morn-ing after a gig, and see dead bodies piled up in the gutters. They had either been killed with bows and arrows or set on fire. It was Yorubas and Hausas fighting each other around Lagos. The politicians sparked this shit by starting to say, "This is Yoruba, that is Hausa." The Igbos weren't in this thing yet.

Then the actual war started because oil was in one state in the East and the people in that area, who were mainly Igbos, said they had to secede. That was the time of Colonel Odumegwu Ojukwu and Biafra, which was the nation they wanted to make. It's not possible! How can they secede like that? It's one country, run from all the resources of the country. Wherever it's coming from in the country, nobody cares. It should be for the nation. It's true that they were killing many Igbos in the North and in Lagos, too. But it wasn't a tribal thing. It was politics, with different parties using the tribal thing to manipulate Nigerian people. It was just madness, a war of total madness. All in the name of stupid *oil*. No war should have been fought in Nigeria because of oil. We never had oil before this time, and I never saw much poverty in Nigeria before the oil time. After the Second World War in the 1940s, I remember that I used to go with my mother to buy rations. But it wasn't a poverty thing—it was a matter of it being wartime. Some people were poor, but not to the extant that they are today. Today it is just about survival of the fittest. It was the oil that created that madness. Before the oil time, we were living on agriculture and different resources like tin, zinc, bauxite, gold in some places, food, cocoa, coffee, and cotton. We were living coolly at this time, and nobody was suffering. But today, you can see what oil has done to the country.

Because of the war, the Igbo musicians were all going back to the East, Ngomalio was going back to Cameroon, and many musicians were going into the army. Femi Bankole himself went into the army. Everyone wanted to get out of Lagos. But Ngomalio told Fela, "I will give you my student." His student was Ojo Okeji, who was playing with me in the Toppers. Ojo went to meet Fela, and Fela told him not to worry about reading, that they would just play a twelve-bar blues. Ojo did it, he played clean and tight. So that was it. Ojo was in. But they still had no drummer, and Fela, coming from the UK, had the attitude that there were no good jazz drummers in Lagos. There were lots of highlife drummers. But he was looking for someone who could really play jazz properly—someone who knew about playing sixteen-bar or thirty-two-bar songs and who knew the proper sequence of a jazz tune. Then Ojo told them, "I know a very good drummer that will play better than all these so-called drummers." Fela asked him, "Who is he?" And Ojo told him that the drummer's name was Tony Allen. So Fela told Ojo he wanted to see me the next morning.

Although I didn't know Fela personally at that time, I knew of him from his radio show and also because his house at Mosholasi (the one that later got burned down by the army) was not too far from my place. At that time, he was known by his family name, Fela Ransome-Kuti. I went to meet him at his house at Mosholasi in the morning. And the first thing he asked was "Are you the one who said that you are the best drummer in this country?" I laughed and told him, "I never said so." He asked me if I could play jazz and I said yes. He asked me if I could take solos and I said yes again. So he asked me to wait for him in the sitting room while he got dressed. Then we got into his car and drove straight to the NBC. The drum set was there in the studio, and the other musicians were waiting: it was Kingsley on the piano and Ojo on fiddle bass. Fela had his silver trumpet.

Fela just counted off "one-two-three-four" and we started a tune. He played the theme, and then I played a fill to let them know that we are going to the second cycle [chorus] again. And we went on into it. When that cycle finished, I injected another fill. On the third one, Fela stopped. And he looked at Benson and shouted, "Benson do you hear this?" Benson said, "Yes!" Fela said we should continue, that we're going to play some more and then end the tune by trading fours. We started, everybody played nicely for a few minutes, and then we started to trade fours. On my fourth solo he told everyone to stop again and he called out to Benson again: "Benson, did you hear that?" Then he turned to me and asked, "Have you studied in the States? Have you studied in London?" I said no. He then asked me, where did I get my own way of drumming? I said here — right here in Lagos. Ah, he said — he said he never thought he would ever find a good drummer, and that I had helped him observe every cycle. And he said that when we were trading fours, every one of my solos was unique — none resembled the other. So we just closed the day like that.

I still had my own gig, working six nights a week with the Toppers. But in between, I started to gig with Fela, playing jazz, like Art Blakey and the Jazz Messengers, Horace Silver, and those types of things. We would play for parties on the boats, sailing in the lagoon and on the sea, what we used to call *buka*. Sometimes I would have to fake sickness with the Toppers so that I could play with Fela. I loved this jazz music so much, and finally I had the opportunity to do it. That meant that I didn't have to play so much highlife. I didn't have to play so much cha-cha-cha, tango, or waltz. It was strictly jazz, for the first time in my life. So it was like the sky was the limit for me, and it made me practice more and to listen more closely to all those great jazz drummers.

All of those jazz drummers were my idols when I was in my twenties because at that time I thought they were doing something impossible. To me it was impossible that it was only one guy playing all this stuff; at least, I thought there had to be somebody extra playing the cymbal on top there. I thought it had to be two guys playing the drums. For example, Tony Williams was a killer, man — the intensity and the speed! That guy was a fucking good drummer, man! Listening to people like Tony Williams and Art Blakey, I knew it had to be *more* than two drummers! But I could only listen to the records because there was nothing like video back then. And I eventually found out that it was true — it was only one guy! So those were the things that really inspired me, and I just knew that if

I couldn't play this way, I shouldn't call myself a drummer. Jazz changed my way of drumming completely, because jazz solos are different from highlife solos, on the drums. When they start to play drum solos in high-life, the people dance to the solos. And the solo is like talking. Most of the drummers, they talk with the drums because that's what we do on our traditional drums. They make parables, and if you understand the language, you'll know what he's talking about. In those days that was vogue. I've done all that. I had to play like them first before any other thing. But it wasn't really what I was after. I was asking myself, "Where do we go next?" And that's when I realized that I had a job to do, man, and I have tried to do my job properly.

From the first day, Fela and I became close friends. From the jazz times all the way through the '60s, very good friends. There's nothing he wouldn't tell me. We'd hang out in the night and joke with each other. He'd ask me, "How many girls have you got tonight?" I'd say, "Two." Then he would say, "Two. Ah, I beat you now." I'd say, "How many?" He'd say he's on the fourth one. Four! Things like this, you know. Many times we talked when we had to travel somewhere ahead of the band, to get the gig and all the agreements together. We would drive there together and believe me, that wasn't easy because Fela should have been a Grand Prix driver. You would never sit down inside Fela's car, I'm sure. By the time he drives five kilometers, you would beg him to stop. You're talking about speed? He could have made a lot of money as a racer because he's really a fucking driver!

Often he would ask me to pick his kids up from school in the after-noon when he didn't feel like going. And sometimes I would even cook for them because I'm a good cook, and Remi, his wife, was coming from the UK. Remi couldn't really cook Nigerian food. She could only make something like tomato stew, so if she wanted another local dish like *egusi* or something like that, she would ask me to cook it, and when Fela tasted the food he would always say, "Remi, you never cooked this stew! Who cooked this?" And she would always have to say it was Allen! I really did a lot to help this guy out, but I did it out of friendship.

We went on with the jazz thing for about one year and a half, and then Fela suddenly decided he didn't want to have a jazz band anymore. The question was, "Where's the money?" Because many local bandleaders in the country were rich at that time — the highlife bandleaders, and some of the juju bandleaders, too. They were rich with houses, fleets of cars, and many wives. The public wasn't really seeing jazz as the music they loved to dance to—they were seeing it more as an educational thing. So we couldn't play it all the time. We were only playing on Thursdays for the boat parties. For me, I couldn't make it playing once in a week like this. And Fela himself had a family to support. He came back to Nigeria with two children, and his wife Remi was pregnant with the third one, which was born in Lagos.

So he decided that if he could not beat them, he would join them. He had to join up with the highlife people, and that was it. This was in 1965. Fela liked highlife anyway. After all, he was singing it with Victor Olaiya before he left for London, so why wouldn't he like it? Highlife was so sweet in those days, and the style coming from Ghana, man, you *know* it was great! E. T. Mensah, Ramblers, and all those great bands. Those records stormed Nigeria! So Fela decided to form a highlife band. But it wasn't going to be highlife like Rex Lawson would play, or like Olaiya would play. No—the style was going to be "highlife jazz." It was going to be like a combination of the two. He could still put all of his jazz stuff in there, but at least the people could dance to it.

Even though we were no longer playing straight jazz, the change didn't bother me at all. Sometimes the jazz didn't feel full enough for me, because jazz drumming doesn't have too much bass drum action. I mean, the kick is there, but it's just to accent every now and then, and you're playing most of your stuff on top, on the snare and cymbals. It's very much like floating, in a way. I like more bass drum in my own style. But I passed through the jazz thing, and thank God I got my experience from it. It enlightened me so much about how beautiful and enjoyable drumming could be when you know how to handle it. For Fela and me, that was our trip for one whole year, and I was able to bring all of the jazz into how I played in the new band. "Highlife," "jazz," African beats, call it anything—I combined them all together in my own style of playing.

With all the music business going on, Fela knew he wasn't going to last long with the NBC. He was going back and forth between the two jobs, and his superiors didn't like that. So he didn't wait for the sack—he just resigned himself after a couple of years. He knew it was coming. Benson also knew that he was risking his own job at the NBC, because sometimes he had to travel with us. People were always telling him, "Be careful, man, because if you follow a guy like Fela, you're going to lose your job." One night I was gigging with the Toppers around the end of 1965, and I happened to peep through the window of the club. I saw a brand-new white Opel Cadet caravan pulling up. And on the side it was written, in blue letters, "Fela Ransome-Kuti and his Koola Lobitos." Actually, Fela had a group in London before with the same name, just to try and make some bread and have fun while he was in school. But this was going to be a new group with totally new members.

Fela and Benson came into the club and told me that since they had discovered me to be so strong in the jazz thing, they would now like me to be the drummer in the highlife band. But Fela didn't really know how to talk to people, or how to approach them nicely. His way of talking was like, "Give me that. I want it." Not, "Excuse me, could you please give me that thing?" He was just like that, no manners. He wasn't polite. Totally different from his brothers Beko and Koye. That's why, when it came to business, Benson had to do the talking for him many times. So when they came to convince me to leave the Toppers, it was Benson that was doing most of the talking. Later, Fela even sent a messenger to a club where I was playing, saying that I should resign from the Toppers immediately. Resign like that, in the middle of the month? I told them no way! I told them that I would do that if they were really ready to get the band together, but I'd have to wait 'til the end of the month, when I got my salary. Then I'd resign. I had to think about it, too, because as I told you, my father always advised me, "Don't leave certainty for uncertainty." And several times in the past, I had already left certainty for uncertainty. With this Koola Lobitos thing too, it was kind of dangerous, because with the Toppers, at least I had some sort of umbrella. I even had a house with that deal. But Fela was telling me that when this thing takes off, he and I would be sharing the money like a partnership. That motivated me.

So it was destiny, you know. Everything in life is a risk, and I was gunning for something. And that's why at the end of the month, for the first time in my life, I submitted my resignation letters. One went to the proprietor of the hotel where the Toppers were playing. He gave me my salary and I gave him the letter. And the other I gave to Adeolu.

I knew that the proprietor was a worrier. He came to my house and asked me what had happened? Was it money? If it was about money, why couldn't I just tell him that I needed more money? He said he could even give me the salary I originally asked for—the twenty-six pounds—*and* that I could still keep the house. But I told him it wasn't a question of that. I told him that I liked everybody around the business, especially him, but I wanted to be somebody and to reach somewhere with this music thing. Everything was roses with the gig, but there was one thing that was lacking—I wasn't challenged by the music. It wasn't that the Toppers were not good. They were good. It's just that I was looking for a challenge, and to me, Fela's music was going to be a big challenge. So I told the proprietor that if was a matter of the house, just tell me how much I should pay, and I would pay it monthly. We worked all that out, and then I went to continue with Fela.

That's when the rehearsals started for Koola Lobitos. The core of the band was Fela, me, Ojo on bass, and Lekan Animashaun (Baba Ani) on baritone sax. Later we added Isaac Olasugba on alto, who had just arrived from Liberia, and Yinka Roberts on guitar. When Yinka left around 1968, we got Fred Lawal. And we had Eddie Ifayehun, who was the first trumpet player that stuck with us. When Eddie left, we got Tunde Williams around 1967. We later added Christopher Uwaifor on alto, also.

Fela wrote all the music in the band. Every fucking thing from the Koola Lobitos to the end of his life, he wrote and arranged everything except for my drum parts. Nobody ever came with his own ideas. And this is the way I think it should be. After all, he was the bandleader and the owner of the band, so he had to get his music together the way he wanted. At a certain point, though, Koola Lobitos was looking for a few outside songs, and Fela even asked me to invite Adeolu from the Western Toppers to come and give him some lyrics, since they were both from Abeokuta. But I told him that I myself knew this song "Yeshe" at that time—it was kind of an erotic song, but also a folkloric song. Fela didn't know it. So I told him, "Let's just sing 'Yeshe.'" He took it and arranged it in his own way and it became popular. Bands were even playing it in Ghana. That was the only time I ever contributed anything, songwise. But my drumming patterns were all my own. Fela left that completely up to me.

But believe me, man, those first auditions were something else! The musicians that we hired in those days had been playing with other highlife bands before and weren't prepared for Fela's music. The bunch that came for the first Koola Lobitos rehearsal never even came back the next day! They were complaining that what Fela was writing for them was impossible to play, that it was too weird for them. Sometimes for the horn players, Fela had to take his trumpet out and show the fingerings and the blowing techniques. He would show them by ear. As a matter of fact, he preferred for us to learn it by ear first because that way you really had it inside of you. Even if a musician could read the part in front of them, Fela would still play for it them, because they had never played the types of rhythms that he was writing.

Some of the musicians didn't like this. So a guy might pretend for the day until the rehearsal was finished, but the next day, when we would all be there waiting, you didn't see him. Okay, time to start all over again. That means the next day, we had to start looking for another trumpeter or saxophonist or guitarist. Many of the musicians even came to gigs, said they were going to piss, and then split and left their instrument on-stage, just before the gig started. It wasn't their instrument, anyway—it was Fela's, because in Nigeria at that time, the bandleaders owned all the band's instruments.

But really, it's not like we had many instruments when we started out. At the beginning, it was really a struggle for us to play on good instruments. Believe it or not, the first time Fela ever bought new instruments for the band was in 1971, when we went to London! All those years before that, we were just making do. When we started Koola Lobitos, Fela only had his trumpet, and his mother had bought him a bass to use in the band. Most of the other instruments, we had to rent from Bobby Benson. Bobby was one of the most famous highlife musicians, and he had his club called Caban Bamboo on Ikorodu Road. And since Bobby was always traveling back and forth outside the country and coming back with new instruments, he opened an instrument shop in the back of the club. Bobby was always rescuing us, and many times we had to rent from him at the last minute before a gig. Even I myself didn't have a regular drum set back then. There was a guy named Femi Asekun who was a drummer and a producer at NTA (Nigerian Television Authority) who gave me a set that I had to piece together myself. It only had bass drum, snare, one tom-tom, and a ride cymbal. No hi-hat. I did the best I could with it. The only time I sat down at a good set was when we played at Bobby's club, because they had a good set there that was used by his son Tony, who was also a drummer. Tony liked my playing, and one day he gave me a brand-new bass drum pedal as a gift. Another drummer who helped me out sometimes was my friend Bayo Martins. I think Bayo liked me for having a low profile compared to all the show-off musicians around Lagos. Bayo knew that my drums were always falling apart. He was married to a German woman named Gerwine and he had a set of drums that he brought back from Frankfurt that were fantastic, man! Bayo liked my playing and he told me, "Tony, you are a great drummer, so take my drums to use any time when you are playing with Fela." It was something that I really appreciated, because playing his drums was like driving a limousine for me! Meanwhile, I was taking care of the amplifiers when they were breaking down. I took care of all the electronics because I knew how to do that from my training.

I didn't really compare the other bandleaders with Fela. Those bandleaders were all richer than him, and their records were selling. But one had a lot more to learn from Fela, musically, than from the others. He wanted to make a mixture of things, which makes you gain more knowledge. It was a good flavor, musically. To me he was presenting a big challenge because anytime we were going to rehearse any new song, it was like we were going to the battlefield, man. You didn't know what was in the head of this guy, so you would be praying to handle it coolly because it wasn't so easy and nobody writes music like this guy, ever! Especially during the Koola Lobitos days. You were shaking already before you arrived there. So you had to have guts to play in that band.

And Fela fined you for every mistake. In fact, he had a whole system of fines. If you played the wrong note, you were fined. If you came late to a rehearsal or a gig, you were fined. Then there was what he called "first touch." The rule in the band was no physical fighting. But sometimes it happened, and whoever threw the first punch was fined. The fine system was another reason many of the musicians didn't stay. But we kept on going and going. We didn't get any rest, recruiting new musicians all the time. But with Fela, the music was always moving forward, to me. There were some nice tunes, like "Ololufe," "Oloruka," "Ako," and "Obe." Those were kicking tracks for me, and I can still imagine myself playing them, even today! I stayed with Fela for fifteen years because things were always moving forward, musically.

No drummer could play what I was playing with Koola Lobitos. My playing was more dynamic than the other drummers in the country. The basic style was still highlife, but with something extra. Fela wrote out the parts for everyone else in the band, but the only thing that he wrote for me — if he wanted to write anything — was the horn accents. It was magic to see me syncopating with the horns. I wasn't just playing it straight anymore, I was syncopating with the horns on the front line and then coming back to my groove again, playing like with a big band approach. Even with all that phrasing, I kept the groove going. Plus, we had added Isiaka on percussion, to keep the groove going straight.

We did our recording at Phillips Studio, in Ijora. But recording in studios at that time was just like playing live, because it was the old system of recording. No multitrack, just two tracks. You couldn't overdub anything, and you had to get everything right in one take. The whole band was recorded directly on two tracks and was mixed down immediately; there was no mixing afterwards. Most of the time that was no problem for us because we were a very tight band anyway. But with Fela being a perfectionist, one three-minute track could take only God knows how long in the studio. Sometimes six hours! Any small-small thing wrong, and he would say, "No!" If anybody made one small mistake, you had to start all over again because Fela wanted the record to sound perfect.

Koola Lobitos had a strong reputation and we sometimes even backed artists visiting from out of the country. The first one was a pop singer from England and Jamaica named Millicent Small, who had a very popular hit ska song called "My Boy Lollipop." The promoter Eddie Boma gave us the job that time. That was in '67. We played ska, just the way the record sounded. Since that tour was a success, a bigger promoter named Steve Rhodes brought Millie the second time, in 1968. This time, she was coming on a package with another Jamaican singer named Jackie Edwards. They sent all the scores in advance, and the music was ready for them by the time they arrived. Chubby Checker was also a guest with us, during the time of the Twist. Maybe it was around '68 or '69. A lot of accidents happened at the time of the Twist. Many people were twisting in Nigeria, and unfortunately, some twisted themselves to death. Some people really twisted their intestines on the dance floor, and then fell down with a cramp. By the time they got them to hospital, they were dead!

There was one night that the band almost died, too! We had gone to Ibadan to play, and we hired a Mercedes-Benz minibus. Fela was driving his own car and the whole band was in the minibus. We went to Ibadan and played, and then we had to head back to Lagos after the show. Fela stayed behind because he wanted to get some sleep. And I remember that after the concert, my stomach was feeling so bad that they gave me a seat for two people so that I could sleep while we were driving. Then we left for Lagos.

Near Lagos, at a place called Majidun, there is a bridge to Ikorodu with a river running underneath. It's just like forty miles to Lagos. I was in a deep sleep, and all of a sudden I felt tumbling. Everybody was screaming. Myself, I wasn't screaming. I just opened my eyes into darkness. I relaxed because I didn't know where I was. The driver had slept off and run off the road, man! Everything was broken. People were passing on top of me and mashing me down to climb out of the bus. And then I got up and realized that everything was upside down and I was walking on top of the ceiling.

But the thing is, we escaped the river! Because the driver had just crossed the bridge when this thing happened, so the river was behind us and we went rolling into the bush on the other side. And I thanked my God a million times because if that thing had happened just a few seconds before, we would have plunged into the river and that would have been it. Nobody would have survived.

They came to rescue us and bring us out. And all the musicians were broken completely. The nearest hospital was at Ikorodu and everybody was taken there. I got a broken ankle and shattered glass in my hands. Benson got broken ribs. Later they transferred us to the orthopedic hospital in Lagos. Fela's nurse sister Dolu came to see us and to give advice to doctors and all those things. Then we all went home. When Fela arrived in Lagos, he went to the Afro-Spot, because it was Sunday morning and we were supposed to be playing the Jump that afternoon. But he didn't see his musicians! That's when he was told that "all your musicians should have been dead! But they aren't dead!" So if you're still living, you should thank your God and pray that you still have a long way to go.

Those were minor problems, man, because the Civil War had started in Nigeria in late '66. But even with the war on, we were still able to travel around the country, at least for a while. We even went to the East, inside the war zone, a couple of times. We went to Calabar to play for the Nigerian army, because they had invited us. They brought us in from Lagos in one of their air force jets. There were no seats on the plane, so we sat on the floor. Another time, we were invited to play inside the war zone at Port Harcourt by Commander Benjamin Adekunle, who they used to call the "Black Scorpion." Adekunle met us at the airport in Port Harcourt with bundles and bundles of British pounds that he handed right over to Fela. Only God knows how much was there. Adekunle enjoyed the gig so much that when we finished, his colleague in Calabar wanted us to come back and play there as well. So Adekunle said we should go play in Calabar before we returned to Lagos, which we did. When we finished, it was around two thirty on a Sunday and we still had to make it back to Lagos to play the Sunday Jump at four thirty. And no plane had arrived to carry us. The air commanders told Adekunle that there were no planes available at that time. But at that moment there was a plane passing overhead, flying toward Kano. Adekunle radioed and told the pilot that on his way back from Kano, he should land in Calabar and pick us up. And that's what he did! He flew us to Lagos, and we were able to make the Sunday Jump.

Another time, we were attacked in Port Harcourt by some fans of Cardinal Rex Lawson. What happened was that back in Lagos, we had gone to do a music competition, and the four finalists were Fela, Roy Chicago, Rex Lawson, and Victor Olaiya. So we went to do the next round at the Federal Hotel, but that night Rex Lawson decided not to come to the competition. He decided to play at the Central Hotel in Yaba instead. And so Fela and Koola Lobitos won the cup that night and we took the trophy in a procession to where Rex was playing, because Fela and Rex were rivals. Fela was on top of the car holding the trophy. We arrived at the hotel and took the trophy inside to show Rex that we won the cup. He was onstage singing his songs, and we danced around with the trophy and after that we went back home. That trophy stayed in Fela's house until the house got burnt in 1977.

So when we went to play in Port Harcourt, we went to hear Rex play on our off night. There was a total blackout in the streets there because of the war, but there was a big crowd in the club because they had generators working. We were drinking and enjoying the music coolly until the end of the show. But outside the club, some of Lawson's fans came to pick a fight with us because of what happened back in Lagos at the competition. They just decided to show us what they could do on their turf, because Lawson himself was from the East—that was a part of it, too. Fela was the one they were going after because he was the leader and they wanted to get him. But Fela himself was not a fighter, so we were protecting him—it was me, Yinka Roberts, and Ojo Okeji. The fight went on for about one hour. But luckily we got out of that. Those were the kinds of experiences we had, trying to play music during the war.

The war was one reason we spent a lot of time in Ghana. Ghana was like our second home. I would have loved to stay there because Nkrumah was there at that time. Ghana was like the England of Africa to us. It was completely different from Lagos. Ghana was really swinging. There was more music in Ghana than in Lagos. More clubs, too. In fact, the idea of the "Afternoon Jump" is something we brought back from Ghana. They didn't do that much in Lagos before then, but they did it in Ghana a lot, having concerts on Sunday afternoons. Most of the concerts we played in Ghana were in the afternoon. We only really played a few at night. When we brought that to Lagos, everyone else started copying it. One reason it caught on in Lagos was because of the war. People were afraid to go out at night.

To us, Ghana was like a white man's land, in a way, because of the coolness of the country and how everything was so organized. There was no laziness there. There were no layabouts there. Nkrumah did that, there's no lying about that. In fact, many Nigerians were leaving Nigeria to come and live in Ghana and do their business there. They didn't even want to think about Nigeria anymore. At that time, whenever we went to Ghana, I myself never wanted to come back to Lagos. I felt like, why couldn't we stay where things were happening? But Fela couldn't do it, because for a while he still had the job at the NBC.

Ghana was full of great bands. The musicians were great because they had schools for everything there. Like music schools that you could go to even if you had no money; if you wanted it, it was there for you. And musicians were also being trained in the air force and in the army. So many great musicians were coming out of Ghana. The Stargazers band was there. There was Mack Tontoh, who later went on to form Osibisa. The Ramblers were there too; they were led by Jerry Hansen, and it was one of the most disciplined bands in Ghana, apart from E. T. Mensah's band. And then there was Uhuru Dance Band. Uhuru was one of those groups that played highlife, but sometimes they mixed it with the traditional drumming, like the traditional Ashanti drumming. Fantastic, man. I think they inspired some of those younger bands that were fusing the traditional music into the highlife in the 1970s, like Hedzolleh, Bunzu, and Basabasa Sounds. They were all doing the same kind of fusion. But this type of music has disappeared completely today, man.

Uhuru was one of the outstanding bands in West Africa at that time. It was a big band, about ten pieces, and the leader was Stan Plange. Stan also directed the big band at the television studio in Accra. They always bought their pieces from those jazz big bands in the States, and they played them note for note. Uhuru always had good singers, too, like Charlotte Dada. It was a band I loved to hear. I loved to sit down in front of them and listen and watch them.

Uhuru's drummer Rim Obeng was one of my idols. I already had a reputation as a killer drummer by that time, and I know Rim admired my style of playing. But the first time I saw him playing with Uhuru I said, "Wow, I still have work to do!" I never wanted to leave the place when he sat down at the drums. I just wanted to watch this guy play all night.

And the strange thing about it was that he was playing with curved sticks, like they use on traditional drums. He was using these curved sticks on a Western trap drum set, and the sound was so fucking good! After seeing Rim, I tried to adapt to those curved sticks too. I was trying to find out how he could use those sticks with so much flexibility. I played that way with Koola Lobitos for about three years. The only problem was that those sticks couldn't handle the cymbals. They broke very quickly.

Rim and a bunch of other musicians left Uhuru for the Ghana Armed Forces Band. That was another great band. They were as good as Uhuru and all the other highlife bands. Rim was there until he left to go to the States. He came to Lagos to stay with Fela for one or two weeks, then went on to the States, to Los Angeles. Then that was it. I never heard from him again. Another fantastic drummer in Ghana was Remi Kabaka, the founder of a band called Paramount Eight, who were a good strong band when it came to playing highlife and jazz covers. Remi had a style that reminded me of Art Blakey. It was Rim and Remi that were really keeping me on my toes as a drummer!

Koola Lobitos played a lot of gigs alongside all of those bands. They would play before us, or we would play before them. Since then, though, Ghana has gone down. Nkrumah really tried to help his people, but they didn't know what the plan of the guy was, and they fucked it up. It's not the same country now that it was then. They've closed most of the clubs now. The last time I was in Accra, all the old clubs had become churches. And they are not playing highlife anymore—they are playing what they call "gospel-highlife." Or they are making what they call "hip-life." They have gone through many things since the days of Nkrumah. They've just started coming up again, slowly, recently. But it's still much more stable than Nigeria, and it always was.

Back in Lagos, people were starting to change their minds about Koola Lobitos around 1968–69 because we were getting our shit together properly and we had our own fans. Around that time we were playing tunes like "Ololufe," "Laise," "Obe," and "Ako." Every week we played the Sunday Jump at the Kakadu Club, and the place was always full. After that we moved from the Kakadu to the Central Hotel, where Cardinal Rex Lawson was playing before he left for the East. We also did a thing called VC7 with Isaac Olasugba. It was really the Koola Lobitos band without Fela, and with Isaac leading. We recorded a song called "Eke" and another one called "Oritshe." That was great music.

It was around that time that Fela and our Ghanaian promoter Raymond Aziz came up with the name "Afrobeat." Raymond asked Fela if this "highlife-jazz" name really meant anything. He said, why not name this music "Afrobeat"? Everything was "Afro-this," "Afro-that" at the time. It was really just a name to help sell the music. It didn't mean anything special, at least not at that point. They just wanted to find a name that was catchy. And that is also the reason that when Fela went back to lease the Kakadu again, he renamed it "Afro-Spot." The Afro-Spot was on Herbert Macauley Street in Alagomeji. We played a lot of battles there against other bands. Young pop groups like the Cyclops, the Hykkers, and the Clusters were the three giants of the school bands, and they used to play at the Afro-Spot sometimes. Most of them played what we called "copyright music": covers of the Beatles, Rolling Stones, Elvis, everything. I admired them a lot, because they could interpret properly. They all had good singers. Stuff like Otis Redding, they could sing it note for note. Some of the Ghanaian bands used to come to Lagos and play with us too. It was always "Koola Lobitos versus the Ramblers International," "Koola Lobitos versus Uhuru Dance Band," and "Koola Lobitos versus the Black Santiagos" (they were from Togo). Those gigs were great, because we could watch each other and learn. For example, that's where Rim and I learned a lot from each other. That's what made the music so strong at that time — all of these bands were listening and learning from each other, and we had a ball, too.

The music was great in Koola Lobitos, but the musicians were always going zigzag. When you see musicians coming and going, why do you think they're leaving? After all, the gigs were steady, and the music was great for the ones who hung in there with us. If it was cool for them, do you think anybody would leave? They left because something was not happening. And that thing was the bread. When it comes to the bandleaders in Nigeria at that time, the bread was always a problem, and Fela was following the same system that was there before him. The bandleaders loved to spend all of their money, and then to spend the money of the musicians, too. And some of them, they didn't even want to part with any money at all, even though they were employing you. They preferred to have many girlfriends and to spend money like a big man. In most cases somebody will suffer for it, and it is the musicians that suffer. There was no chance to create perfection with the music, within this business of musicians and bandleaders. Especially under the bandleaders that owned all their own instruments, because the musicians don't even have their own instruments to play. They have to play in the band to even be able to touch an instrument. Sometimes, like in the case of Fela, all the music is his, too. You see, that's why the bandleaders always underestimate the musicians, because they feel like "I'm the one doing all the work anyway."

The typical salary system for musicians in Nigeria back then was that you got paid once a month. But the payment system in Fela's band, from Koola Lobitos all the way through Africa 70, was weekly payment. And this was because Fela could not handle money, and he knew it. He was very extravagant with money, and his way of life made the money disappear. If he had kept the money when we made it, he would have been able to pay it properly at the end of the month. But it was even a struggle to get the proper bread at the end of one week. For example, Sunday is the day we got our pay. But he was the first person to come knocking on my door on Monday morning, to borrow half of my money back. He just paid me six pounds yesterday, and he wants to borrow three pounds today! And because his house was so close to mine, he could just put his car in reverse and come to my door, borrow the money, and then take off.

He would say, "Lend it to me, and I'll pay you back tonight." Because on Monday nights we played at the Gondola. And if I hesitated, he would make me feel as if I had killed him, or as if I had done something really bad to him. So I gave it to him and told him that as soon as we finished playing that night, I wanted my money back. But that night when the show was over, he would come to me and say, "Ah, Allenko, you know that we are going to play on Thursday. So I'll give you one pound of the three now, and I'll give you the rest Thursday." That was how it worked. I could never get my money back in full. And before he paid me the other two pounds, he was coming to borrow more!

That's the kind of guy Fela was when it came to stuff like that. He had his own way of doing things; I'll put it like that. For example, I used to have very bad stomach problems. I had ulcers from the age of eight, and all my life it's been a problem. Once when I had my stomach problems very badly, Fela's doctor brother Koye wrote a note on a piece of paper and told me to give it to Fela. He told Fela to give me two weeks off. But when Fela saw it he asked Koye, "Why did you give him two weeks off? He has to play." Koye said, "Man, the guy's sick with a persistent ulcer. Your work is too rigorous. You have to let him rest a bit. Don't worry him." But still Fela was coming to try and wake me up in the middle of the night. I would tell him, go get John Bull to cover for me. Or Remi

Kabaka. But no one would cover for me, because they were scared of the music. They respected it, but they could not handle it. Fela tried both of those guys when I was sick, but it didn't work out. So that meant no gigs for the band.

That particular weekend, they managed with John Bull for the first night. But the second night there was a band coming from Ghana and we were supposed to play together. Fela couldn't face one of these great bands without his drummer. So I was sleeping in the middle of the night and there was a knock at my door. It was Fela, telling me, "You have to come to the club. You have to play." I asked him, "What about John Bull? Isn't he there?" Fela said, "He's there, but he cannot do it." "But your brother said I should be resting." "I know, but you have to come." He told me he was going back to the club and that I should come with a taxi and the ticket guy would pay the taxi driver when I arrived. I took my shower, dressed up, and got a taxi to Afro-Spot. Everybody was waiting for me there, and as soon as I arrived, I just saw everybody shouting and jubilating. But I was fucking sick, man! After that night I told him, "Please, don't call me tomorrow. I ain't coming." And I was out for the rest of those two weeks. I knew the band was gonna sweat a lot without me. But I couldn't help it because I needed my health.

I needed my money too, but I didn't put the music and the bread in the same category. Even though I knew this shit was wrong, I accepted it and managed because I had another job maintaining the printers at Associated Press. That was what was saving my neck and allowing me to pay my rent. Working with Fela, it was either one or the other—the music or the money. It was a question of "take it or leave it." And I knew which one I wanted to take at that point in my life—it was the music. Because the music was improving, and I felt like I was improving a lot myself.

But some of the guys couldn't take this situation. Once Ojo even pulled a knife on Fela because of money. What happened was that sometimes Ojo wasn't learning the parts quickly in rehearsal. On this particular day he played just one note incorrectly, and Fela tried to fine him. Ojo didn't want to take all that shit, you know? He was like, "You're playing with my money." So he reacted. He wasn't going to do anything to Fela, he just tried to frighten him. We cooled down Ojo and Fela didn't fire him. If he had fired him, then he would have to start all over again to train another bass player anyway. So he just had to accept that it was settled, and move on. But in his mind, Ojo had already decided that he was gonna leave one day, as soon as anything else opened up for him.

It was around 1968 that Ojo left to go into the Nigerian Army Band, along with Isiaka and some of the others. Actually, many musicians were joining the army band at that time, because it was a good gig. I was going to do it, too. But when I got to the barracks, I found out that the music director of the army had gone to school with Fela in London. His name was Major Olu Obokun. He knew all about the Koola Lobitos, and when he saw the list of all of us that enlisted, he went directly to Fela to say, "Man, you are dead!" Fela asked him what had happened and Major Obokun told him, "Don't you know how many of your musicians have enlisted in the army?" Because Major Obokun was Fela's mate from school, he came to talk to him about it first. That meant this guy really didn't want to destroy Fela's band. He wanted to make sure before he signed all of our enlistment papers.

Fela summoned everybody and asked us if it was true. And we told him yes: Ojo, Isi, almost everybody had enlisted. He asked me if I had enlisted too, and I told him yes. That day was the first time in my life I saw Fela cry, right in front of all of us. He really bawled like a baby, because he figured he was completely finished. But by me seeing him cry that day, I thought this thing was hitting him too hard. So I just stopped going to the barracks. And in the end, Major Obokun didn't sign everyone. He just signed Ojo and Isi, and we kept the Koola Lobitos going. We replaced Ojo with a bass player from the East named Felix Jones, and we replaced Isi with a percussionist named Henry Kofi. Kofi was Nigerian, but part of his family came from Togo or Benin, which is where the name Kofi came from. Inside the band, we called him "Perdido."

In a way, the type of music that Koola Lobitos was performing was too far ahead of the country. It wasn't straight highlife, so there were no tunes that anybody knew. They'd rather go for the straight highlife that they already knew. Or soul music, which had a very big impact. That was our biggest challenge. For example, people loved James Brown, and Brown was a big star in Africa. Then Geraldo Pino came in doing his thing, imitating James Brown. Pino had been in Ghana in '66 and '67 with his band the Heartbeats. And they were playing a real carbon copy of James Brown—singing, dancing, everything. But at least he was doing it in Ghana, so it wasn't a problem for us. But then he started to have problems in Ghana, I think because he was messing around with the wives of some of the top politicians there. So they deported him from Ghana, and he came to Lagos with his band.

And they completely took Lagos, man! This was another big challenge for us. We were already struggling to establish our feet in the middle of the highlife thing. Now we had to deal with the soul thing.

Fela tried some things like arranging Eddie Floyd's song "Knock on Wood" and some other soul numbers in our own highlife-jazz style. But really, we needed to escape Lagos, because Pino had it and there was nothing we could do. So it was around this time when we met a guy named Tunde Fademolu. He's the brother of the guy that runs Jofabro, the label that recorded the *Music of Fela* album with "Trouble Sleep," "Roforofo Fight," and those tunes. A lot of our fans were students, and many of them went on to study in places like the States. Fademolu was one of those students. He was living in Washington, DC, and he wanted to promote Nigerian music in the States, but he didn't want to take Pino to the States. Pino *owned* Lagos at that time, but it would have been a big joke in the US—after watching Pino do his James Brown thing once, the people would never come back again, because the master himself was there!

Fademolu liked Fela and he liked the Koola Lobitos's music, so he wanted to take us to the States for a tour. He came to the Afro-Spot to negotiate with Fela one day in the beginning of 1969. At that time, the band was eleven pieces plus one dancer, so we really had twelve performing every night. Fademolu only had a budget for ten people, so we had to lay off the clefs and maracas players. We needed the dancer to go with us to animate what we were playing for the audience, because they weren't going to be familiar with the music. And even before we laid off the percussionists, Fela used to look at my drumming as if I already had maracas and a shaker in my drumming, because of the way I played my hi-hats. My hi-hats are constantly going, so it's like they're representing the shaker. We missed the real one in the band, but not too much. So we were going to the States with a nine-piece band, plus our dancer Dele. We decided to leave Lagos to Pino and give the US thing a try. Fela felt that highlife-jazz needed to be exposed in the States anyway. We didn't really have any opportunities there aside from what Fademolu was promising us, but Fela wanted to go for it.

Plus, the civil war was really on in 1969 and that was affecting everybody's movements. Like the tour in '68 with Millie Small and Jackie Edwards. The gigs in the western part of the country were okay. But then we were supposed to go east, into the war zone, and it was more dangerous now than the time we went to Port Harcourt to play for Adekunle. At the airport in Lagos, the promoter Steve Rhodes got a call from General Ojukwu, who was the leader of Biafra. Ojukwu told Steve that although he himself would like us to come, he couldn't guarantee our safety. So Steve said, "Let's go back. We cannot go to the East because we are not guaranteed any safety."

The next scheduled gig was in the North. We had the Hykkers as the opening group to play before us, and they were all Igbos. So now we had to take these Igbo boys to the north, where they had been massacring Igbos! We didn't know what might happen. But we did it, and they were safe because we were like a shield for them. And I even remember that some people in the audience were trying to jump in and start something because of the Hykkers. They wanted to attack them right onstage! When we were in the van leaving after the show, we barely escaped.

The war was also killing off the nightlife in Lagos. There were black-outs in the night, no streetlights, and no lights in people's compounds. You could only have lights in your individual rooms. Imagine us going to play in the night and coming home in the darkness, in the midst of all this. Sometimes we encountered soldiers from the federal army, and we had to deal with all the atrocities they committed. They would just take women from the men that were driving home in the night. They would pull the man out of the car and take him away, do whatever they were going to do with the woman, and later they would release her. And this woman, who is she going to complain to? There was nobody you could complain to! But even with this shit, people were still going out in the night, at least at first. But after a while bombings started happening, ter-rorist attacks. Like someone would drive a car full of explosives into a petrol station, and when the mechanic lifted the hood up—boom! At the Yaba bus stop near my house in Lagos, a Mobil petrol station was blown up like this. Another time, they parked a big petrol tank truck right in front of a cinema, and when the audience came out, the truck exploded and killed a lot of people. So Lagos was becoming like a ghost town at night, and we all felt like "Let us get our asses out of this place!"

4 We left Lagos in early June of 1969. We had a stopover in Dakar, and Miriam Makeba flew over from Lagos with us. She was on her way to Guinea, but she always liked to visit Fela. That was because Fela was Hugh Masekela's friend, and Masekela was Miriam's friend. Miriam told us that it might be very tough in the States, but we were all looking forward to the tour anyway.

We landed in New York and changed planes for Washington, DC. When we arrived in DC, I thought about the fact that the money was never paid properly with Fela and that I didn't really know what we would face in the US. So after five days, I decided to look for a job. I knew that my former boss at Associated Press, Mr. Zeitlin, was now in the New York office, because they rotated them every three years. So I called AP and Mr. Zeitlin asked me, "Where are you?" I said, "I'm in Washington." He said, "Did you come with the band?" I told him yes. He told me that if I came to New York, there was a job waiting for me. The job was maintaining the printers, the same job that I had done at Associated Press in Lagos. It was a good job. But I told him it wasn't possible because we were in the US on group visas. He told me not to worry about that. He said, "If you can get yourself to New York, I'll give you a job and I'll get your papers, passport and everything."

I told myself, "This is big." Because many Nigerians at that time saw America as "God's own country" and dreamt of getting a good job there. It was a serious decision. If I had done that, it might have meant the end of the band. They would all have to go back home. There's no way they could do it without me. Even if they found another drummer, there would have been no way that Fela could pay the person in American wages. So I told Mr. Zeitlin that we were going on tour and that I'd get back to him when we were finished with the tour. But in my heart I knew that although that was a good job offer, and although I thought about leaving the band, I was meant to play music.

We had some buddies in DC who put us up for a while, different Nigerian people accommodating us. That was lucky for us because we found out very soon that Fademolu didn't know shit about promoting. It was as if we came to the States to only play for Nigerian parties! Why are we in the States if it is only Nigerians we are playing for? We could have stayed home and done that! This went on for two months with this guy. Going back and forth between DC and New York. He did get us a few good gigs. We played for one big party at the Roosevelt Hotel in Manhattan. That was good. But most of these gigs were in small basement clubs, and it was too slow for us. We weren't making any bread. Fela told Fademolu, "Look, I never came all the way from Africa to America to play for a handful of Nigerians. Is this a joke?" And that's where the problem started between them. Later, an African American guy named Michael started to help us get club gigs, because Fademolu couldn't handle big clubs. He didn't have the connections for the big clubs. I can't remember this Michael's last name, but he came with us when we left DC. We rented some Chevrolets and a U-Haul and drove out west caravan-style. First we stopped in Chicago and did a week there, playing mostly for Nigerians. Most of the students who were our fans back home were studying there. It felt good. Everywhere we went, the Nigerians there came out and gave us a good welcome and opened their homes to us. That's one thing that I liked. For example, they used to take us to strip clubs to see the dancers. Nowadays, there are a lot of strippers in Nigeria, but not at all back then. That was new for us.

Chicago was really cool, but I wanted to go back to Nigeria. First of all, I was sick. I still had an ulcer, and it was getting so painful one night before a gig in Chicago I was rolling on the floor. Who was going to pay for a doctor there in Chicago? There was a bed there, but I couldn't even handle the bed. It was too painful. Actually, I had been scheduled for an operation before we left Nigeria, but Fela's doctor brother Beko convinced me that I shouldn't have it. He told me that I should leave it alone and take medication. He said it was a dangerous operation and that I might lose too much blood.

That night I remembered that there was no grass smoking in Nigeria at the time we left. The military government was very heavy about that. And we hadn't been smoking in the States. The point is that I had gone a long time without smoking any grass. But when one of the Nigerian students saw how much I was suffering because of my stomach, he went out and came back with one joint. I took just three or four puffs, and it was like magic. That night, everything came back to normal and I was feeling good. The pain diminished completely and that was it. I slept like a baby. From that time on, whenever it came back, it wasn't as strong anymore.

So I didn't go back home. We continued the journey. After Chicago we took two and a half days of driving to reach San Francisco, and we stayed with some Nigerians in Palo Alto. I liked Frisco. There were a lot of foreigners there, not strictly American whites. It was a mixture of people. At this point we had been touring for two or three months, but we hadn't really met many African American people yet besides our manager Michael. But there was one African American girl who saw Dele dance in Frisco. She got so excited by the music that she jumped onstage and asked us to repeat the same song that Dele just did, because she wanted to dance to it too. We were playing "Ako." And so we repeated it for her and she tore the place up completely! By the time we arrived in Los Angeles, Dele had combined that girl's style with her own. And she became the best dancer around—the best. It was a great experience, and it was all because of that African American girl.

Dele was from midwest Nigeria, from a town called Obiaroko. That's in the Benin area, going toward the Igbo area. She was a natural dancer. She never went to any school of dancing, because there wasn't anything like that in Nigeria at that time. But Dele could dance to *anything*—she could dance to solos, and she could even preview where you were going in the music. You can imagine such a dancer in front of you—she inspires you all the time.

Fademolu was still involved, but it was our manager Michael who arranged for us to live with a judge named Morris Washington. He was a black guy who lived in Inglewood, and he saved our necks because he had connections and he knew an African American woman who owned a club called the Bill of Fare. Michael was able to pull some strings for us to get into this place. The woman really liked us and we were well treated. We were playing every night except Monday, and we were living with Morris Washington in his house until we could find our own place. Morris had a big house with a champagne fountain in the middle, and we slept two people in a room.

It was around this time that Fela met Sandra Smith. We went to play this open-air party at a big place on Wilshire. I think it was a benefit for the NAACP. That's where they met, and they hit it off immediately. Sandra was just coming off the Black Panther thing, you know, and Fela believed in Pan-Africanism. He was a family friend of Kwame Nkrumah and he liked Nkrumah's ideology. So he and Sandra gave each other ideas and that really started to bring the political side out in Fela. Besides that, it was like she was the only woman who could handle Fela, because Fela liked to have many women. Sandra was the only one able to handle this guy. And that's why they fell in love with each other and lived together. Even though he still went out to play around, she was his number one priority.

We were working six days a week, so we didn't really have time to go out and see other bands. If we did, it was just by chance. For example, we wanted to see James Brown, but Fela and James never met while we were in the States. In fact, we were supposed to play a gig at a place called the Factory that was owned by Sammy Davis Jr. It was a big place, like a complex, and we were supposed to play along with different bands. James Brown was supposed to be there, Sly and the Family Stone were supposed to be there, and the Temptations also. We were supposed to play one after the other. We were really looking forward to seeing Brown, but at the last minute they announced that he was not turning up. That was our only opportunity to see him and for him to see us. But one band I did get to see live that I really dug was Dizzy Gillespie's quartet with Kenny Clarke on the drums. We heard them one night in Orange County, and I remember Dizzy asking me about one of our ministers in Nigeria that night, a man named Njoku. I think they had studied together somewhere in the past. So Dizzy actually knew about Nigeria and Africa.

We played for a lot of those Beverly Hills parties, birthday parties and wedding receptions. I remember playing at a party for the famous African American footballer named Jim Brown. Another time at the Bill of Fare, Muhammad Ali came down. He had a good time with us. We discussed a lot. He had been to Nigeria before then, and he knew what Nigeria was like. He was very interested in talking to us. At least I can say met him face to face. That was during the period in which he was not fighting. They had taken his belt away because of the Vietnam thing. So he was just going to parties, having a good time.

Eventually we moved to a better place called the Citadel d'Haiti, owned by a guy named Bernie Hamilton. And we started to make a name for ourselves and to pull a crowd. Fela was enjoying himself. In fact, nobody back home had heard anything from Fela for a very long time. One day I got a letter from my parents asking me what was I doing in America now that Fela was in jail? Somehow a big rumor had gotten started in Nigeria that Fela had been sentenced to seven years in jail for committing rape. That wasn't true, but the truth was that in all those months we hadn't really accomplished shit. We were always driving around to Capitol Records and meeting with them, but nothing ever happened. The main problem was that we had bad visas. With the type of visas we had, they shouldn't be discussing business with us at all, because legally we couldn't work. All of this was Fademolu's fault. He hadn't even arranged the proper work visas for us!

After a few months, there were some Jewish businessmen who were friends of Morris Washington. They liked our music. They bought brand-new instruments for the whole band and took us to a factory where they showed us the costumes they wanted us to appear in. They wanted to sort out all of these immigration problems so they could get the business straight. Everything was set up. They had even arranged visas that said we could bring our wives from Nigeria. But Fademolu came again to spoil everything. He felt he was losing control over us, even though he never did a fucking thing for us! He said he had paid the money for us to come to the US. The Jewish guys were even asking him, "How much did you spend on these guys?" They wanted to pay him off. But he refused—he didn't want it. He said it was the principle behind the thing, and he reported us to the US immigration authorities. The Jewish guys had to drop the whole affair. They said, "We wanted to help you out of these problems, but your guy has come in and fucked up everything, so we can't do anything anymore."

Our big problems in the US started there. After Fademolu reported us, we were detained, and Immigration scheduled us for a deportation hearing. They could have taken us to prison that very day, but they let us go. The hearing was going to come after the beginning of 1970, and we even got a few temporary visa extensions, so we did what we could before the hearing. The main thing was that we wanted to record, and luckily we got a break from a Ghanaian guy named Duke Lumumba. Duke wanted to help us record the music that ended up on *The Los Angeles Sessions*.

That's when the problem came with Felix Jones, the bass player. Felix left because of the Biafran situation. The war was still going on and he was an Igbo from the East. He came with us for the tour, but in his head he wanted to stay in the States, and the only way he could do that was to declare himself to be a Biafran. He told the US authorities that he didn't want to go back with us, because if he did, we would kill him once we got to Nigeria! So even though we were all having visa problems, the American government took him aside and he was treated differently than the rest of us who were just hanging on. They told him, "You'll have no problems with these guys anymore." So he disappeared. How were we going to play Koola Lobitos music without the bass!?

Shortly after Felix split, we had a gig at a place called the Bayoux, and on that particular night Frank Sinatra and his people passed through. We were hoping that if we impressed Sinatra, we might get some kind of a break. But Fela was really suffering that night without a bass player. He had to try to play the bass *and* sing at the same time. Believe me, it was a tough night. We managed in the end, but after that night it was hard for him to play the trumpet for a while because his fingers were all fucked up from the bass. So the Sinatra thing was blown.

Meanwhile, the recording was coming up and Duke Lumumba was ready to pay for the session. He had even paid us a session fee in advance. We had to go and beg Felix and drag him back. We told him, "Just come and do this recording with us, and when we have to go back, if you want to stay, stay. But help us finish the recording." Because there was no way to bring in any bass player in the States that could play this music properly. Even if Fela wrote the music out for the bass player, it wouldn't be easy. So Felix came back and did the recording with us. We recorded on eight tracks in a small studio, and that was the first time Koola Lobitos recorded on multitrack. Then Felix disappeared again after the recording. When we were coming back from LA to Washington, he stayed behind, and he's still there today.

I loved the music the band was playing, but Fela's latest tunes w still too busy, in a way. He himself didn't think of it that way at that For him, it might have been that he was showing what he had l⁄ showing that he knew what he was doing. But from the poin⁄ of selling our music, it wasn't really working. In fact, we h⁄ named Mr. Wendell, a black guy who always came down to listened to the music. He was a musician from Beverly Hills. After one show, he asked, "Fela, do you want to make money?" Fela said, "Yes, I want to make money, of course." So Mr. Wendell said, "Well, your music is great but you're wasting music. Too many ideas in one tune." He said, "One of your songs is like three songs." Mr. Wendell advised him to keep it simple. Fela listened to him, but he never really applied that principle while we were in the US. He started experimenting with tunes like "My Lady's Frustration," but really he waited until we got back home. And it was almost like instant success after that.

As for me, I also changed my drumming in Los Angeles. When I got back to Nigeria, my playing was completely different because I got some techniques in LA from a guy named Frank Butler who used to play with Miles Davis and John Coltrane. Frank Butler was my good friend, man. He heard me play almost every night. When he told me he was a drummer and he had been playing with Coltrane before, I became very inquisitive, because Elvin Jones was one of my heroes and Frank had subbed for Elvin sometimes. And with Koola Lobitos, even though we played the highlife-jazz stuff, we also used to play some twelve-bar blues tunes just to show that we knew the rudiments of jazz. So one night Frank Butler was in the club and I told Fela, "I want to check out this drummer tonight. Let's let him play a twelve-bar blues." I stood there and listened to this guy play and—wow! It freaked me out completely. I told myself, "You've got a long way to go, man!"

After he finished playing, I called him aside, and I said, "Look, man, you are wonderful." He said, "No, *you* are wonderful. Too much!" I told him that I didn't see anything that I was doing that he couldn't already do. But Frank loved my playing, and he was looking at me like I was a magician for the way I was playing all of those Koola Lobitos songs, like the way I could change things from one section to the other, and the way I was syncopating with the horns. He thought I was wonderful, and me, seeing him play, I fell in love with his playing immediately. His hands were so fast and flashy. And he was even using all of his fingers individually on the snare. With the sticking and combination, everything was just cooking!

I asked him, "How did you develop those things?" "Oh," he said, "it's simple. You just have to do it every day. By the time you do it for one month, you'll be okay." I said, "What is *it*?" He told me, "When you wake up in the morning, take some pillows and play on them. Play until you can make your sticks bounce on the pillow when you're rolling." Then he told me that when I started to roll, that I should roll, land on the other pillow, and come back. Land and come back. Land and come back. Land and come back, without breaking the roll. And he told me that I should try to do everything with my wrists. That I shouldn't try to push it, but let it fall. It sounded simple, but I began to try it. It's not easy for a stick to bounce on a pillow. But every morning when I woke up, I did this pillow thing for one hour until I started to see my sticks bouncing on the pillow. And it was true — it started to change my playing. My wrists loosened up and became less stiff. That pillow game made me become very free, and more in control. One night Frank came into the club and he was standing right in front of the stage watching me play, and he ran up to me and said, "You got it, man! You fucking got it!" Because I really did get it. It was like a month later that I realized that yes, it was happening — my drumming was different.

But I learned about some other things from Frank, too. He used to come by my house at maybe six o'clock in the evening, like a dead man. He would say, "Tony, I'm sick." I didn't know what was wrong with him. I would try to get him some aspirin and he would say, "No, just give me ten dollars." I didn't know what he was after. I just knew that this guy was sick and he's telling me, "Ten dollars." "Ten dollars is gonna make you be alright?" "Yeah." I wasn't looking at the money at all. I was just pitying him. And then two hours later when I saw Frank, he was bouncing like a ball! He was a normal guy again, not the guy I saw two hours earlier. I didn't know what was happening. But Henry Kofi had a girlfriend from the Philippines named Annette who worked there in Bernie Hamilton's club. And Annette told me, "Don't you know anything, man? Frank is a junkie! He's a heroin addict. He's sick because he needs the stuff." I didn't really know anything about heroin and shooting up and what it does to you and all that, so that was when I found out. And the way I used to see Frank looking so sick and pitiful at times, I would never believe that I myself would be tested by this same shit later in my life! But I will never forget Frank because he taught me what I wouldn't have known. He never charged me for this knowledge, but I was able to take care of him a little bit. I respect this guy so much. I added what he taught me to my own style of drumming, and when I arrived back in Nigeria, I was untouchable — no doubt about it!

The other way I found out about heroin was one night when we were getting ready to go play. You see, the band had moved to a house that belonged to Bernie Hamilton. The place had an upstairs and a downstairs.

Some of our musicians lived upstairs, like Christopher and Tunde. Me, Isaac, and Henry, we were in a different building in the backyard, kind of like in a compound. But there was also a black American guy named Joe living downstairs in the main house.

The cab was waiting outside to take us to Hollywood to play, and when we came outside, we saw that the police had the whole compound surrounded. Actually, it was the FBI! They stopped us and started asking us many questions, but when they heard our accents, they decided that we were not the ones they were looking for. So then they cornered Joe's room and started to break in. They broke in there and found Joe hiding under the bed. It turned out that Joe and his whole gang had all kinds of shit going in there, man. First of all, they were pimps. But they were also transvestites and they were selling heroin. They would dress up in the night like women, pimp women, and sell heroin. We didn't know anything about this shit, so the cops let us go. But Annette later told me that Joe got five years for that. So that was the other way that I found out about heroin.

A few of the musicians in Koola Lobitos smoked grass like myself, Fred, and a few of the others. But Fela himself was still totally clean when we got to America. He was "Mr. Straight." The only thing that was in his life was maybe too many women. But smoking, drinking—no way. In fact, smoking was strictly forbidden in the band. Fela would really give you a big problem if he knew that you were smoking in his band. For example, one time back in Nigeria, we were getting ready to play the Afternoon Jump in Kaduna, and a joint dropped from Fred's pocket onto the stage. Fred picked it up quickly, but Fela saw it and said, "Hey, what is that?" And he started calling for the police, to have Fred arrested right there on the stage! At that time, one joint could get you ten years in prison in Nigeria! We all jumped in and stopped it. So he just fined Fred. But he was always telling us, "When you smoke, you don't play properly." He was watching everybody, because he knew we were smoking. Any wrong note, even just slightly—a five-shilling fine. Five shillings was a lot of money, man! I remember one day in Ghana the saxophonist, Christopher Uwaifor, went to smoke his joint in the toilet, and then came back onstage. Fela went to him and noticed the way his eyes looked, and he said, "Come, I want to smell your ear." He was not smelling his mouth, it was his ear—and from that he concluded that the guy smoked! That's how straight Fela was at the time. We laughed about that. But that was another five shillings gone for Uwaifor, in Ghana.

I was the only one that was really able to smoke. Because Fela was always watching us during set break, to see who was smoking. And I always had my bottle of beer and my joints, sitting and smoking and doing my thing. But he never said anything—he just waited for everybody on-stage. Waited for them to come back onstage and start messing up, so that their money would start flying away. One day he said, "Allenko, I watch you every time you smoke. But every time when you smoke, you play wonderfully. Your playing becomes super! How can you do that? You are the only one that delivers positively after smoking." I told him, "I don't know. I think the smoke stimulates me positively."

Then he told me that the reason he didn't want people to smoke is that when he got his diploma in London, he went to a jazz club with his friends JK and Wole Bucknor where one of the popular jazz bands was playing, and he asked to sit in. JK made him smoke grass before play-ing. And Fela went onstage and he said he remembered his fingers were running faster than his brain. His brain was not controlling the fingers, so he was just playing nonsense. The musicians stopped him and kicked him off the stage and told him never to come back again. Meanwhile, JK and Wole had disappeared because they were so embarrassed, and since they were holding his trumpet case, they took it with them! So Fela had to walk out of the club holding a trumpet without the case. That's the humiliation he got as a result of smoking that one time, and that's why he didn't want any of us to smoke at all. I told him, "Well, everyone has a different constitution. If your body doesn't like it, then your brain can't handle it. So don't touch it."

Anyway, Fela was living with Sandra, and that is where all the political and cultural awareness came from. But it was also through Sandra that Fela started smoking grass. The first time he really shocked me with it—he came to my house late in the night and asked me for two joints. Sandra was waiting for him outside, in the car. Out of the blue like that. Two joints, not one. And he was not even dabbling in this stuff before. I said no, but he insisted. I rolled two joints for him and he left. Then I started to notice that if I went to Sandra's place to visit him, he was smoking even if he was still in bed.

When Fela started smoking, he told me he loved it so much that he couldn't believe that he had been missing out on that all along. But if you knew the Fela of the first five years and this new Fela, it was a big contra-diction all of a sudden. The difference was too big. Grass does different things to different people, and the old Fela was gone overnight—his personality changed *completely*. And the first time he bought grass when we were back home in Nigeria, he bought a cement bag full! It's like now he had to be the king of grass, giving it out to everybody, and he wanted it to be legalized in Nigeria. And that's what gave him the most problems, because the government didn't want him to challenge them.

The race thing was very heavy in the States at this time, but personally, I didn't experience a lot of problems. The only incident I really remember vividly was when we were on the road driving from the East Coast to the West Coast, we passed through this place called Wyoming. We had been driving overnight, and in the early morning we just parked at the petrol station to fill up the tank and have breakfast. There was a café there, so we went in to eat breakfast, and fucking hell, man—everybody was just staring at us when we came in, like we were coming from the jungle, or maybe from outer space. We felt that this wasn't gonna be cool, but we went to the counter to order. The waiter wasn't even answering us, he was just ignoring us. And when he finally had to face us, he just said, "Do you know where you are?" We said, "Yes." He said, "You are not wanted here." So we left.

There was another time in Watts when a black taxi driver stopped me because he saw me walking on the sidewalk with a young white girl. He just pulled up his cab next to me and said, "Hey, brother—what the fuck are you doing?" I said, "What have I done?" He said, "You don't know what you're playing with, man. You better leave that girl alone. Go your way, and let her go her way." He said that if the police happened to pass at the time, they weren't gonna take it kindly. He said, "They will give you problems." So I left her to go, and I went back home. This incident happened after we had moved to the house in Watts that Morris Washington found for us.

For most of the trip, we lived in that run-down house in Watts, and we really suffered in that place. When we first arrived there, there was not even any gas, only electricity. There was no way that we could cook until one of the ladies in the neighborhood lent us a hot plate. Watts was rough. Where we were living was only blacks and Mexicans. And these were not the kind of successful black Americans like Morris Washington. I never saw a white American there except for the police, and they didn't live there. Friday night used to be dangerous, especially for the old guys that had just received their pensions. The thieves would grab them right in front of me. I used to see the way they handled them, ripping the old guys off right there in the street or in telephone booths! And every night there were gunshots. We didn't even know where they were coming from.

LA itself was hot when it came to race, but when we were in Watts, it wasn't really the whites that did anything, because the whites weren't really there. It was the blacks, our neighbors, that sometimes made problems for us. They would ask us shocking questions like, did we fly here to the States, or did we swim? They asked us, "Do you have planes in Africa?" Ridiculous questions! I would ask them, "What did you learn in the school? You never learned any fucking history or geography?!" That's when I discovered that not all Americans know geography and that many African Americans didn't know anything about Africa. At least, not at that time. They just know where they are, where they live. Many Americans in general don't really want to know about any other place. If you say, "I'm from Nigeria," they will ask you, "Is Nigeria in Ghana?" They don't even know the difference!

The kids from the neighborhood came into our house all the time. And I remember one morning they were just bending down, pretending to fall down on the floor, looking under the towel of Fred, the guitarist. And so Fred said, "What the fuck are you doing down there?" And one of the boys said he was just trying to check and see if Fred had a tail! So Fred told him, "If you want to know if I have a tail, go back home and check your father. If he has one, then I have one." Some of the guys in the band got aggressive and mad. I had to keep telling them, "It's not their fault. They were never taught anything about Africa." But these same small boys came back to turn our house upside down and steal our money. We had gone to play one day, and they broke in and messed up the house completely. Every box and every suitcase was thrown upside down. Cornflakes, rice, everything, they sprinkled it around everywhere in the room. They smashed all the eggs on the wall. They poured Clorox all over Isaac's room, on his clothes, on his bed. A few days later, they came back to tell us that it was they that had done it. They said it was because they saw a white girl come into the house in the afternoon. And actually this girl was Sandra's friend! She used to help us drive to the gigs.

There was another funny incident at the Bill of Fare. This African American woman put up a huge banner which said, "You are here now, but where were you four hundred years ago, when you were selling us into slavery?" She put the banner across the front door from one side to the other. And when we arrived she pointed at us and told us, "Yeah, the banner is for *you!*" We didn't say anything, we just went inside and spoke to the club owner. We asked her, "We've been playing here for weeks, and why are we getting this treatment tonight?" She came out with us, saw the woman and the banner, and she told us that we shouldn't worry about it. Just leave her alone, she said, because this woman's a nutcase. But after the gig we went back and asked the woman, "Where were *you?* Where were *you* four hundred years ago?" She told us, "Resisting." So we told her, "Look, you were not there. We were not there either. So why are you asking us this ridiculous question? We can't answer this. Sorry about that . . ." So she packed up her banner and took off.

We had a lot of fun in LA, but overall it was a lot of suffering. We were supposed to be living on allowance in the States, and Fela's allowance was only five dollars a day, paid out on a weekly basis. And it wasn't even possible to get that because for many months we were not even working! So maybe out of a week, we would get two or three days of payment. And when we started working, Fela was not paying us properly. He told us he was getting a certain amount from Bernie, but we found out he was actually getting more. It became a small argument between Fela and Fred, and Fred decided he wasn't going to play one night and he took off. Fela and me chased Fred along Sunset Boulevard for about six to eight blocks that night. We caught him, carried him back to the club, put him onstage, put his guitar in his hands, and he played. The way Fela wrote his music, if even one part was missing from the band, it was a big problem. Fred knew we couldn't do it without him, so he played that night. But we were all getting fed up with the money situation, and we went on strike for a while until we got this shit straightened out.

Meanwhile, I had been working in a record-pressing plant owned by a white guy from Texas. He and his wife had never even heard of Nigeria! One night I invited them to hear the band. They watched us play, and then I went to have a drink with them at their table while we were on break. They asked me, "What time do you finish here?" I told them two o'clock. They said, "You mean you do this every night and you get to work at seven thirty in the morning?" I told them yes. The wife just shook her head and said, "Tony, you can't continue like this. When do you sleep? You'll be dead soon." They told me that from then on, I shouldn't come in at seven thirty. He said, "When you get home, just try to sleep. And when you wake up, you come to work." I told him I appreciated that, but that I needed forty hours a week, and if I do as he's saying, there's no way I'm going to get my forty hours. But they insisted, so I took their advice and started to come later. That week, I only clocked in twenty-eight hours, and that wasn't enough money for me. So, after going to pick up my check, the boss asked me, "How many hours do you have there, Tony?" I told him I had twenty-eight hours. He said, "Make it forty. Just write forty there." So they took me in as one of them and tried to help me and treat me with respect. They were very nice people. If it weren't for people like that and the Nigerians who helped us like Yomi Willington and Olade Dos Santos, we would have starved in Los Angeles.

It got to the point where when I told Fela, "Look, what are we doing here? Let's go home, man. We haven't achieved what we came here for. What do we have to show for this trip until now?" I told Fela that this whole thing had become too much. After all, I had my family back home, my wife was pregnant, and we weren't making any money to send back. Plus, the civil war had finished by 1970. If the war had still been on, we could have stayed in America, because the US government wouldn't have sent us back to Nigeria with the war going on. They had already given us "voluntary deportation" and renewed our temporary visas several times. But now that the war was over, our status had changed and we had to leave.

Why not at least go visit home? Fela refused. Then I told him that I had gotten a job offer and that if this thing got too crazy, I could always take off for New York. I told him that the reason I hadn't already taken the job was because if I quit, the band would be finished. Either they would have to go back home or they would have to change their professions in the States. And he agreed with me. We were sad to leave LA, but between all the struggling, the end of the war, and the immigration situation, we knew it was time to go.

Fela flew from Los Angeles to Washington, DC, but I drove the band back and we had to rent a camper for the trip. Man, that was the most driving I've ever done in my life! But we only covered a few miles before the camper broke down. This was supposed to be a brand-new camper, but the rental company had never put oil in the transmission, so the thing was rolling dry without us knowing it. We were just a few miles outside of Flagstaff, Arizona, when the camper just stopped and refused to move. The next morning, heavy snow started falling and we were stuck in the middle of the road, with snow falling like water. We were stuck in that spot until about ten at night when one guy finally passed. He told us that he would go to Flagstaff to find a tow vehicle. After a few hours, a very strong tow truck came and towed the camper with all of us in it. Since it was Sunday, the driver told us he was just gonna drop us at the front of the Dodge garage, since it was a Dodge camper. That way, they would see us there on Monday, when they arrived. That meant we would have to spend the night in the camper, and there was no heater in this fucking thing! I never suffered like that in my life before. I'm talking about cold, man! When you stepped out of the bus, there was three feet of snow. We took all the paper we had and made a fire on the floor of the bus. It wasn't enough, because the papers burned up quickly, so we had no choice but to add some of our clothes to the fire.

When the garage guys arrived in the morning and opened the bus and saw that there were people inside, they freaked out! The first thing they did was send all of us into a warm room, with hot coffee and hot tea. They told us that we were lucky to be alive, and they said the only reason we survived was because there were so many of us inside the bus. It took them one whole day to fix the bus, but we were going to have to sleep in the bus again the second night. Fademolu was with us in the camper. We all told Fademolu that he had made us live this miserable life in the States and that we were not sleeping inside that bus again. We made him get us a motel for the night and pay for it himself.

When we finally got to Washington a few days later, we had a couple of weeks to kill before our flight from New York. Even though we were living with some nice Nigerians again, I worked for two weeks in DC, be-cause we didn't play any gigs until we went back to Nigeria. I was working at a Howard Johnson's restaurant, just to have some small change on me and to buy gifts for people back home. The day we got to Kennedy Airport in New York, I called the Associated Press office in New York, just as I had planned. The new guy's name there was Mr. Rosenblum, and he told me, "Please go back to Nigeria. Your job is still waiting for you. All the machines are broken in the Lagos office, so please go back and get them working again!" So it all worked out in the end — forty-eight hours after we arrived back in Lagos, I was back at AP!

I also remember that the same day, Tunde Fademolu came to see us off at the airport. He called me aside asked me, "Are you sure you want to go back with Fela?" I told him, "Yes. Why not? I am looking forward to going back. We were supposed to be here for two months but we ended up stay-ing for ten." And he said, "But why you are going back with this guy?" I told him that we came here with Fela and we have to go back with him. Then Fademolu started telling me that he doesn't trust Fela. He told me, "Tony, you are too nice to have to work with this guy. You'd better stay here in the US. If it's the passport and visa and green card and all of these things that's making you unsure, I can help you get all that." I looked at him and I said, "Thank you very much." But from where I was coming from, I didn't want to desert Fela. Because the band was in a very difficult time right now. Already our bass player, Felix, was staying behind. On top of that, for me to stay behind too, no. I couldn't do that. I liked the States, I had a good job waiting for me in New York, but I never took it because I wouldn't want to stay behind on account of Fela.

Fademolu tried to convince me. "It's not Fela's platform you came on, it's my own platform because I'm the one that paid for the tickets to the US." I told him that I didn't look at it like that and that if I wanted to be here in the States, I would rather pay my own money and come back on my own. Otherwise I'd look like a saboteur. I already had a reputation for dropping out of bands, like when I was in with Sunny Lionheart and Sivor Lawson before I joined Koola Lobitos. At least this way, no one could say anything about me. Furthermore, Nigeria is my home, not America. I could stay in America for fifty years, but I would still have to go back to Nigeria one day. If I had stayed like Fademolu was saying, what type of reception could I expect if someday I decided to go back to Nigeria?

With all the experiences I had in the States, I know I was in God's hands. I was there to follow my destiny and to prove to myself that I wasn't being a lazy motherfucker in life. I'm not someone who waits for something to come to me. I've got to look for it. Maybe that's why I was troubled with my ulcer, but I never gave a shit, man, I just continued like that. It wasn't a mistake for me to leave the States, but people were telling me that I was a fool when we got back to Nigeria. They said, "You had an opportunity to stay in 'God's own country' and you threw it away and came back. Don't you see that even the bass player never came back?" I told them, "Yeah, that's him, but not me. I have a family here." Time shows I made the right decision because things took off just after we came back, and we were already on tour in England by 1971. And what I gained with Africa 70 in those eight years after we got back, I wouldn't have learned in any university in the whole world. If I had stayed in New York, I would have just been another guy maintaining the machines at Associated Press.

Early in my career, I wanted to end up playing jazz. But I wouldn't reach nowhere, because this jazz we're talking about had been introduced to the world by the Americans. If I want to dabble in jazz, then I have to be competitive with the Americans. And no matter how good, being an African, we can never be as good as the ones in the States. It's not a matter of talent. It's because of the way of thinking about music. It's the same as if an American guy came to Nigeria. We have different ways of thinking about music. So to me, it's better I leave that one alone. I passed through it, and thank God I got my experience from it. Jazz was the thing that enlightened me so much. And Frank Butler came into my life just like somebody who could let me go back home with something extra. So I was eager to go home, to just show all the drummers there that I was back. There was gonna be a difference between the Tony that left and the Tony that came back. I wanted them to know that from now on, it's gonna be a different game. None of those other drummers could touch me now!

SWINGING LIKE HELL!

5 As soon as we returned to Nigeria, Fela changed the name of the band from Koola Lobitos to Nigeria 70 because we arrived back at the beginning of 1970 and everyone was feeling optimistic about the future of the country. The Biafran War was over and people were ready to celebrate! That was the time of President Yakubu Gowon, and things really cooled down. Everybody was enjoying the country, and even though there were lots of soldiers around after the war, the soldier boys mixed with everybody. That was when we started to grow. All throughout from 1970 to about 1977, Lagos was fucking jumping, man! That city was swinging like hell and so was the band!

Fela remembered Mr. Wendell's advice in Los Angeles about keeping it simple, and his composing started getting better immediately. That's when he started writing new music like the stuff on *Fela's London Scene* and other tunes like "Black Man's Cry," "Beautiful Dancer," and "Jeun K'oku." It was after "Jeun K'oku" that everything exploded for us. We went straight to the top and stayed there. All those tunes are simpler, without so many fireworks, and the music was really starting to move. It was much better, compared to Koola Lobitos. And that's why when James Brown came to Lagos with his band around the end of 1970, we blew their minds! They were staying at the Federal Palace Hotel, but they stopped by the Afro-Spot every night, because they dug the music, there were a lot of girls around, and they wanted to smoke, too. Brown himself never came down to the club, but Bootsy Collins was playing bass with him and I could see that he was a fucking genius bass player. To this day, Bootsy says that seeing our band was one of the greatest experiences of his life. I would meet up with Bootsy again years later, when I started working with Gary "Mudbone" Cooper in France.

That's also when Fela started coming out with his "blackism" message, which he had developed in the US after meeting people like Sandra. I supported him, because musicians in Nigeria in those days didn't have the foresight to challenge anything, such as atrocities being committed by the government. Nobody would *ever* sing to challenge the government in those days. They were only singing praise music. African music, on the local level, is mostly praise singing anyway. All the traditional musicians are always singing the praises of someone in a high position. And juju music was number one with the praise singing. The Muslim styles like sakara, apala, and *fuji* got heavily into it a little later. It was a bit less like that on the highlife side. Highlife was never heavily into praise singing.

In the early '70s, though, Fela wasn't really criticizing the government. If he sang anything critical at that time, he made it into a parable. Like "J'eun K'oku," which was a parable about greediness. But he was mostly singing about black power, black pride, and all that. About buying African products. Songs like "Buy Africa" and "Black Man's Cry." It was a kind of a cultural revolution, and he did a very good job at that, in the music. That made Fela kind of like a politician. If he had gone to study politics, he might have ended up somewhere in the country's House of Assembly, or maybe even higher than that. But he didn't want to be part of them, because he wouldn't have had a chance if he had been a strict politician. No politician in the country could have been so outspoken, not to Fela's extent. Nobody even tried. So the music was good for him, because it allowed him to get his messages through. Even some of those guys that would become future heads of state, like army guys or business guys — they knew Fela and they were passing through the club, listening to what he had to say. I'm talking about guys like Murtala Mohammed, who later became president, or M. D. Yusuf, who was head of the police in Lagos. These guys were our fans. They didn't have the same politics, but they loved the music, and even when Fela was singing about them, they would laugh. Like when Fela would sing a song such as "Shenshema," he was singing about those guys. But they still liked it, and later, when they became powerful, some of these guys never touched him. I even remember later in 1976, when things were hot between Fela and the government, Fela recorded "Zombie" for Phonogram and their A&R lady kind of freaked out. She didn't want the company to release this thing and have the military government come down on their heads. So she first sent it to Shehu Yar'Adua, who was chief of the army at that time, second in command to General Obasanjo. And Yar'Adua actually approved the release of the song! I think he looked at it like a caricature, or a humorous song, because in Europe or America at that time, people in the newspapers could caricature the government or insult them freely, with no consequences. So maybe deep down inside, Yar'Adua might have felt that even though Fela was singing against them, a song like that might be good for the country; maybe he thought it would help keep his own guys in line. It didn't stay like that forever. But it shows you how optimistic people were about the future of the country in the '70s.

So things were looking up. The public started to pick up the vibes properly. Our records were selling and there was only vinyl back then — no tape or CD or anything like that — so there was no piracy and that meant that we finally started making some real money.

We were very busy at the Afro-Spot, too. We played Tuesday, Friday, and Saturday nights, and we played the Sunday Jump in the afternoon. That meant more money was coming in at the gate. From way back, even before the States, Fela owed us a lot of money, and when we got back home he told us that he would start paying us the back money bit by bit, along with the new pay we would be earning. In fact, he told us he would pay us half of every old week, along with every week of our current pay. But Isaac calculated that it was impossible for Fela to pay all this back money. He said that at the rate Fela was paying, he would only get all the money he was owed when he was nearing his grave! There's no way anybody could get all the money they were owed. Isaac was not the kind of person to fuck around. When he said something, he meant it. So as soon as we arrived back from the States, Isaac resigned. And it turned out that Fela never paid what he promised, because sometimes it was even tough to get our normal pay after that!

For myself, I said, okay, let's forget the back pay and just go for the fresh one. And I started to get a little more of my own money because Fela made me the bandleader after we got back. But some of the others started to leave. Besides Isaac, Dele also left. Dele confronted Fela about money, and Fela asked her why she couldn't make some extra money by hustling, since she was a woman. Of course Dele didn't like that. When we went on tour in Ghana, she met Ebenezer Obey and then they fell in love. So she left. She is now one of the wives of Obey, and they have a daughter together.

Fred Lawal also left. We replaced him with a guy from Ghana named Peter—I cannot remember his family name. Tunde Williams left too, but he came back later. And since Felix Jones had left in the States, we replaced him with a bassist named Morris Ekpo. Meanwhile, we replaced Isaac with Igo Chico, a tenor player from the Midwest who played great solos on all of those early songs we cut after we got back.

Chico was a big name in the country, and everyone knew him in Nigeria. There were a lot of saxophonists in the country back then, but Chico's style was unique. He was a very good musician and his solos always had feeling. Chico was the best tenor player Fela ever had, but the problem was that he had a drinking habit and he was sick. Sometimes when he came to play, he couldn't play. And sometimes he would play and then lie down somewhere on the side of the stage. Fela didn't like that, and he was always telling Chico to get up, but the guy was in pain. Fela felt like he was in pain because of what he was doing to himself, so that's why he wasn't accepting any excuses. One day Chico resigned from the band and went to play at the University of Lagos with Akin Euba, who was a big composer there. And since he was at the university, he went into the teaching hospital there, free of charge. He got well in the hospital, and when he was going to be discharged, they told him, "No more drinking—don't touch that stuff again. If you drink again, please don't come back here!" Because it wasn't regular alcohol Chico was drinking, it was *ogogoro* (native gin), which is much stronger. But the day he arrived home from the hospital, the first thing he did was go for a bottle of ogogoro, and that was it. He died from liver problems very soon after that.

One thing that was difficult for Chico was that he was living completely off of his music for a living, and when he got sick he couldn't play, so it was hard to make ends meet. So for me, even though I was now bandleader, I always had something else going on, just in case. Associated Press Lagos gave me my job back, even though I had told them I was only going for two months and it turned out to be ten. When we arrived in Lagos, I went straight back to the job. I ordered the parts and got all the machines working again. The subscribers were all getting their news properly again, so they knew I was back. I started that job in 1963 and kept it all the way until 1973.

Soon after we got back, word started to get out about my drumming. Everybody was saying I was now like a magician. Fela's brother Beko couldn't believe it. He told me, "It's like *you* took everybody to the States, instead of Fela." He could hear the difference in my playing, and he told me it was like I had gone to the States to study. So that was my pride. But you see, it was really just the beginning for me. I had developed the drumming concept for Afrobeat from many things that I heard while I was growing up, and now I was starting to put it all together. It was a fusion of beats and patterns. There was highlife, there was local Yoruba music like apala and sakara, there was jazz, and there was Western popular music like funk and R&B. There was *atilogwu*, which is an Igbo dance from the East of Nigeria. There was also some of the traditional music from Ghana that you could hear in the fishing villages in Lagos in the early days, like *kpanlogo* and *agbadza*. So the techniques I learned from Frank Butler were like the final piece in the puzzle—that just made everything catch on fire. I had discovered certain things, and now that we were back, it was time to develop them. I could never have done that if I had stayed with AP in New York.

I tell you, I had gone clear of all the other drummers, completely. There was no drummer that could stand next to me! Shortly after we got back in 1970, we went on tour to Ghana. I've already told you about the great drummers in Ghana, and how much I respected them because Ghana was where all the great musicians were. Those guys were like my idols. They all knew how I was playing before we left, and they respected me, too. But by the time we got to Ghana in 1970, they were all telling me, "You're wicked, man!" A few years after that, we went on tour in Cameroon and it seemed like all the musicians were waiting there to meet us. We arrived late in the night, and they were all waiting! These were like copyright bands, and they wanted to see the guy who played the drums on "Lady" and "Shakara" and all of those songs. Because they could hear it, but they couldn't understand how to play it. There was one drummer named there Bele Njo who told me that I was his idol. He came to my room at three in the morning and wanted me to go to the club at that hour with him, because he said their whole band was waiting in the club to meet me! I told him that I had to get some rest, and to come back the next day. The next day he came back and I went with him to the club, along with Fela. All they wanted was for me to pass through and sit in with their band on "Shakara" and "Lady." So Fela sang the songs and I played drums. They played "Shakara" and "Lady" note for note and solo for solo! Everything. It was just the drums that were the problem. And when Bele came to see me playing it, he was gasping—it was like another school for him!

We played for a long time and they were asking me how I could play so long. You see, I don't feel pain or discomfort or anything like that when I'm playing. I can go on for as long as it takes. My body is used to it. And that's because when I'm playing the drums, I sit straight. I'm not leaning on any side. I'm right in the middle. That's how I get my balance properly. It's when you are leaning that you might be emphasizing too much on one thing. Drummers all have different ways of body movement. Some of them, their body is playing more than what the drums are doing! I see many drummers like this. They put so much in the body, but when you really check what is happening, it's just a simple motherfucking thing that he's playing there. Meanwhile, the body is playing the whole world! But maybe that's what he thinks will make him a drummer. You have so many things in front of you as a drummer, maybe he thinks that he has to let the audience know that. Maybe he thinks he has to them show them a lot of action. But I never look at it this way. People think I don't put effort in my playing, but there's a lot of effort in what I'm delivering. And if they can hear it, they know what is happening there. Forget about this fight you want to put on the drums. Don't fight the drums, just deliver coolly. I don't like using force to play the drums, because I know when I have to hit them hard. I know when I want something to be stronger. So I'm playing in between—it's like a kind of caressing. And at the same time, I could be brutal. I'm exercising both of those things in my playing. That's why you don't see much movement when I play. When I was learning to play highlife from Ojo I decided that I wanted to be a smooth drummer, not a noisemaker. Because I saw a lot of noisemakers in front of me in those days—it was sometimes like thunder on the drums! I didn't want to play like that. I saw that the drums have different tones. And you must make those tones relate—it's just like singing. That's the way I look at it. Aside from that, the flow of the Afrobeat has to enter the audience easily. If you don't catch them quickly with this feel, they might just be standing there and looking at you.

Mostly what I do when I'm playing is that the music is in my head up there, and I just use my hand to supply what is coming from my head. If it's a pattern that I'm laying down—okay, I could repeat the pattern every time, if that's the pattern I want to use for that song. But I cannot repeat myself when it comes to soloing. Because it's like my solo work is coming as things appear to me at that moment. So you can never see any of my solos being repeated like the one you heard yesterday. And my solo work was much better with all the stuff I learned from Frank Butler.

Me (left) with my friend Bashola, around 1957. CREDIT: TONY ALLEN

My parents with my brother Kunmi and my sister Jumoke, around 1960. CREDIT: TONY ALLEN

My wife Ibilola in 1970.

CREDIT: TONY ALLEN

My daughter Nike.
CREDIT: TONY ALLEN

My daughter Kehinde. CREDIT: TONY ALLEN

My daughters Abidemi (left) and Ibiyomi
(right). CREDIT: TONY ALLEN

Me (left) with Sivor Lawson's Cool Cats, 1960. Lawson third from left, with tenor sax.

Playing at Tip-Toe club with Koola Lobitos, Accra, Ghana, 1966. CREDIT: TONY ALLEN

Koola Lobitos in Lagos, 1967: (left to right) Ojo Okeji, Adisa, me, Fred Lawal, Isiaka, Christopher Uwaifor, Seyi. CREDIT: TONY ALLEN

With Nigeria 70 in Los Angeles, 1970. Top (left to right): Me, Lekan Animashaun, Henry Kofi, Fred Lawal. Bottom: Tunde Williams. CREDIT: TONY ALLEN

Me with the Koola Lobitos dancer Dele in Liberia, 1970. CREDIT: TONY ALLEN.

Me with my friend Sola backstage at Afro-Spot, 1970. CREDIT:
TONY ALLEN.

At Apollo Theater in Accra, 1973. Top (left to right): Tunde Williams, female friend, Igo Chico, three male friends. Bottom (left to right): Henry Kofi, female friend, me, Patrick (Africa 70 road manager). CREDIT: TONY ALLEN

Relaxing in front of Fela's house, 1975. CREDIT: TONY ALLEN

Me (middle left), Kologbo (front center), Henry Kofi (back right), and Laspalmer (middle right) with some of the "area boys" at Kalakuta, 1976. CREDIT: TONY ALLEN

Tee-Mac Iseli. CREDIT: TONY ALLEN

"Drum Convention" at National Theater in Lagos, 1979: (left to right) Remi Kabaka, Kofi Ghanaba, me, Bayo Martins. CREDIT: GERWINE BAYO-MARTINS

Me with Jumbo van Renen and his wife Marie during the recording of *N.E.P.A.*, 1984.

My band The Mighty Irokos, Paris 1986. Top: Jumbo, Olivier, Claude, Udoh, Sami. Bottom: me, Martin, Shirley, Ben. CREDIT: CHRISTIAN MAUVIEL

Me in Paris, 1987. CREDIT: TONY ALLEN

Martin Meissonnier (center) and Sunny Ade (left) at Olumo Studio in Lagos, 1984.

Me in 1993 with Martin's wife Amina and her group. CREDIT: TONY ALLEN

Me and Tunde Williams in San Francisco, 2000. CREDIT: TONY ALLEN

Me and my keyboardist Jean-Phi composing, 2000. CREDIT: TONY ALLEN

Tony, Damon Albarn in Lagos, 2004. CREDIT: TONY ALLEN

Being interviewed in Lagos by reporters from *Music* magazine, 2004. CREDIT: TONY ALLEN

Me playing at La Cigalle in Paris, 2009. CREDIT: TONY ALLEN

My sons Segun (left), Baptiste (middle), Arthur (right), and Remi (front). CREDIT: TONY ALLEN

My family in 2011: (left to right) Arthur, me, Baptiste, Sylvie, Remi. CREDIT: MICHAEL VEAL

Custom snare drum made for me by Guillaume Carballido. CREDIT: GUILLAUME CARBALLIDO

Custom drum set made for me by the Ghana Arts Center in Accra. CREDIT: GUILLAUME CARBALLIDO

With all those techniques I had brought back, it was just too much for these drummers! Plus, all those subtle things I was doing inside the groove matched up beautifully with what Kofi was doing on the congas. Kofi played the congas with his hands and with sticks as well, and he was a master at getting all the different tones out of the drums. He played on the head, he played on the side of the drum, and he played on the rim. We sounded great together.

We were very disciplined. If you're talking about discipline, it was very strong in that band. Even though nobody liked Fela's system of fining them for mistakes, the point was to get his music right. That's the way I looked at it. And I think the discipline was reflected in the music, because the music in that band was untouchable. Nobody in the country came near it. It was much too heavy for them! When "Shakara" and "Lady" came out, we went up to another level. But even that wasn't the limit, because Fela just kept on writing and writing. And it was like that all through the 1970s. I really considered Fela to be a genius when it came to composing.

"Confusion" was one track that really had people talking about my drumming. That was around 1974. When we played it live, people would stand next to my drum kit to try and see how I was keeping that pattern going. I was proud of "Open and Close," even though I wasn't happy with my solo. But the groove was very nice. That was around 1972. I liked "Unnecessary Begging," with that nice slow groove. "Colonial Mentality" was very good too, because of the triple-kick drum pattern. We were playing that around 1976. I really liked that one because Fela's composition was so nice that it made me flow. Those were some of the good ones.

Then there were the really fast ones, like "Roforofo Fight," "Slap Me Make I Get Money," and "Alu Jon Jonki Jon." "Alu Jon Jonki Jon" was over 120 beats per minute! You had to dance in half-time to that one, because it was so fast. Everybody used to watch me on that one, because the band was like a locomotive. "Question Jam Answer" was another great one. In fact, Fela had a close friend named Kuster back then who used to hang with him all the time. Kuster would spend twelve hours with Fela in the house sometimes. One day after the release of "Question Jam Answer," we were all sitting around joking, and Kuster said, "Fela, let's speak the truth—if Allenko were to blackmail you now, what would you do?" Because he didn't think he had ever seen a drummer who played like I played on that song! Fela just laughed and said, "Allenko is not the type. He would never blackmail me."

And those were just the records. For me personally, I preferred playing live to recording. In the first place, look at the recording time—it's not the normal time, it's in the afternoon. The studio atmosphere is not the same. Even though we've been playing a song onstage, it's very different when it's time to record it. In the studio all the small details count and you can get bored when you keep on repeating the same song. When you're playing live, you don't repeat anything twice. You play it once and you put your everything inside it to make it go properly. But when you're in the studio and you do the proper one, the producers say it's not right, and they ask you to repeat it again. Then it's deteriorating. Each take, it's deteriorating. So at the end of the day, when they say, "Yeah, it's good," that's bullshit to me! We have thrown away much better takes than that one, in my own opinion. Well, it's not my recording, so it's not my business. But when we played those songs live, it was a real kick in the ass, man! The record always limits you, but live is *dangerous*. The live of "Confusion"? Dangerous, man! The live of "Alagbon Close"? It was so heavy you can't even imagine it!

You know, one had to spend time with Fela properly to understand his way of composing. He would sit down, looking over here or over there, staring off into space, and all of a sudden you'd see him clucking his teeth together in rhythm. Then he would quickly pick up a pen and some paper and jot something down there. By the next day, he would have all the parts for the songs; rhythm section first, and then the horns. That means he was going to call a rehearsal for the following day, and he would tell me to get everyone together. The rehearsals themselves were like shows. We would rehearse in the Shrine and the public was allowed to attend, so many people would come from the area to watch us get the music together. Manu Dibango once told Fela how lucky he was to have a band like that, ready to go at all times. Because Manu himself was living in France at that time, and it's not easy to keep a band together in France. Everyone there wants to get paid, and if they get a better-paying gig, you can believe they will take it. So Fela was lucky to have us on call like that. Anytime he came up with a new idea, we were there to play it.

For a while, Fela wrote out the horn accents for me, just like he did in Koola Lobitos. But then he stopped doing that and started to ask me, "Allenko, what are you going to play on this one?" I would try out different patterns, and all a sudden he'd stop me and say, "Keep that one!" So I had a lot of freedom now, but I never used my freedom any more than to make sure that things were tight, man. I decided to just keep the groove instead of accenting so much. I heard the way he was writing, and it didn't need a lot of overplaying. For example, when he was playing a solo I kept it steady, but at the same time, I was interacting with him, like a jazz drummer. It was really like telepathy between the two of us. Sometimes when we were onstage, he would turn around and look back and give me a thumbs-up, to say like "Man, you're great!" And sometimes he would just shake his head while we were playing, because he too could not understand how we could communicate like that. It was like we were seeing inside the head of each other. But the point is, that musical connection came out of our closeness. If any drummer wants that kind of connection with the bandleader, he must know the person inside out — musically, his way of life, things like that.

I was a crucial part of the band. If I was sick with my ulcer, that meant no gig that night. Even if it was a full house, Fela wouldn't even come to the club. He would just send a message to the gate man to return the money back to everybody and cancel the show. I never felt good about that, because some people in the audience had come from far away, planning to return back home in the morning. Plus the little money the other musicians would make that night, they weren't gonna get it, because Fela will tell them, "We never played," and he would refuse to pay them. That's why I always had my sodium bicarbonate next to me onstage. That was my ulcer medication and sometimes I would start drinking it right there onstage, while we were playing. It was Fela's doctor brother Koye who advised me to do that.

The Afro-Spot was packed every night. We toured Ghana in 1970, we toured all of Nigeria in 1971, and we went to the North, the West, and the East. That's the tour when Ginger Baker filmed us in playing Calabar. The people loved it all around Nigeria, and they began to see that this was different from what all the other bands were playing. Rex Lawson and all those guys, they were still playing highlife, but ours was something completely different. It was like another education for the people. But it wasn't always easy. Some people already had a problem with what Fela was singing, and then he began to talk between the songs, what we used to call "yabis." That wound them up even more! Sometimes people would disagree with him and call out from the audience. For example, Fela was always talking against the Koran and the Bible, and since he was known as the son of a reverend, many people just found the things he was saying unacceptable.

That made him be even more aggressive in what he was saying, and that meant that sometimes when we were leaving the gig, we had to fight our way out of there!

We were becoming so hot that we toured England in 1971. It was Ginger Baker who organized that tour for us. I don't really know how Ginger and Fela got to know each other, but I think it was through EMI. Fela had never told me anything about Ginger before 1971. Ginger was really getting into African music, and he loved Fela's music and his way of life. He was also getting ready to set up a new studio in Lagos, so he became very close with us. When we got to London we were living in Bayswater, which is near the center of town, and we played at places like the Speakeasy in London. We also toured some other cities like Reading, and we went to Wales. We were playing mainly for British people, plus some Nigerians who knew us from back home. The reception was great everywhere we went and they were all good concerts. Ginger was guesting with the band throughout that tour. Usually he and I would play together for one song each night. Sometimes Mitch Mitchell guested with us too. Mitch was Jimi Hendrix's drummer. On that live album that we did, Ginger's playing with me on the song "Egbe Mi O." The rest of the album, I'm playing alone. I liked Ginger and we became good friends, but personally, I wasn't crazy about the double drum arrangement because it just sounded like a jam, and we played with precise patterns in Africa 70. I could see that Ginger and Mitch were both great rock drummers, but on the Afrobeat it sounded kind of cluttered. So I just laid back and let them do the driving on that song. I was mainly playing the hi-hat part.

On that tour I met a Nigerian guy in London named Dusty, through another Nigerian musician named Johnny Haastrup, who was a member of a group called Monomono. Dusty and I became good friends, and he hung out a lot with me and Fela. He was always at our side while we were in London. After he discovered the kind of music we were playing, he said that Fela was playing militant music, and when we were leaving, he gave Fela a book called *Black Man of the Nile*, by Dr. Yosef Ben-Jochanan. That book really influenced Fela and you can hear it in many of his songs.

During that tour we were able to record the *London Scene* album, which we did at Abbey Road studio. Then after the band left, Fela invited Sandra to London and they did Ginger's *Stratavarious* album together. The tour was such a success that we planned to go back to England in 1972. But that was canceled because of a problem between Fela and the authorities in England. What happened was that one guy was flying from Lagos to

London and they caught him at Heathrow with a big African drum that was filled with grass. When they asked him where he was coming from, he told them, "Fela." And when they asked him who he was visiting in the UK, he told them "JK and Ginger Baker." JK was Fela's old friend who was now living in England. So we had to abandon the '72 tour.

It was not too long after our England tour that Ginger drove the equipment for the studio from London to Lagos, all the way across the Sahara desert, in a big army truck. The complete studio was in there, so all he needed was the land and a building. That's when he went into partnership with one of those big businessmen—I can't remember the guy's name, but I remember that he was the uncle of Remi Kabaka. They managed to get fifty or sixty square meters of land in Ikeja and they built a very good studio, which was called ARC. We already had Decca in Akoka and EMI in Apapa, but ARC was the first sixteen-track in the country. The others were all eight-tracks. When the band first got back to Nigeria, we did most of our recording at EMI, on eight-track. But once Ginger set up ARC, we started recording there a lot. ARC started a lot of competition among the studios in Lagos, because when Ginger set up his sixteen-track, everyone else had to go for sixteen tracks. Then EMI upgraded to twenty-four. Ginger was in and out of Lagos all the time in those days. When he finally left, it was around 1973 or 1974, and that's when his studio was bought out by Phonogram.

After a certain point, there were some problems with the ownership of the Kakadu, which was where we had the Afro-Spot. That place was run by a guy named Landa, and we had been leasing the spot since before we went to the States. While we were away our band manager, a guy named Felix Osijo, handled it for us and we resumed playing there when we came back. But now Mr. Landa wanted to take the place back. So we had to look for another place, and we ended up moving to the Surulere Night Club in '72. That was where Fela started the Afrika Shrine. The proprietor there was a guy named Mr. Balogun. We moved there in 1972. That's where Paul McCartney came to see us while he was recording at EMI. But because of a big argument about money between Fela and Mr. Balogun, we had to leave there after about a year too, and that's when we moved the Afrika Shrine to the Empire Hotel, which was right across from Fela's house on Agege Motor Road in an area called Idi-Oro. All during the 1960s, the Empire Hotel was a place that was rocking, so it was a known place.

Idi-Oro existed in the '60s, but for a person like me coming from

Ebute-Metta, going to Idi-Oro was like traveling out of town! You would never say that you were going from Ebute-Metta to Idi-Oro unless there was someone specific that you were going to visit. The roads were not wide there back then. The main road running through the area was Agege Motor Road, which leads to the airport. The other main road running through there now is Ikorodu Road, and even that road wasn't existing in 1964, when Muhammad Ali came to Lagos. But later, development made it become part of Lagos. We moved there around 1973. The proprietor of the Empire Hotel was a guy named Mr. Kanu. He knew Fela's family and I think Fela had known his sons since they had all been teenagers. The Empire would fit about eight hundred, with a full house.

The organization was getting bigger now. It seemed as if Fela wanted to develop things just by making them bigger. Up until "Jeun K'oku," we had kept the same formation, which was a ten-piece band plus one dancer. Then the band started to grow, because Fela started to recruit more dancers and singers. We soon had about forty people around us on payroll. Then Fela decided that, since he was recruiting so many people, he wanted to bring the whole thing under his control inside his house. That's when he changed his way of living. After that, the house on Agege Motor Road became like Fela's headquarters, not just his home. All of Fela's friends that he studied with in school were passing through at any time and staying as long as they wanted. I'm talking about high-level guys like Wole Bucknor, who led the Nigerian Navy Band, and Olu Akarogun, who was a journalist. Fela's brother Beko even had a clinic in the house. But with all this stuff going on it was quickly becoming rowdy, and he could not afford to have his family in the house anymore. It would have been like an invasion on them. He knew that he had to get them out of the mess that was about to start, so he found Remi and the kids an apartment in Aguda, and they moved out of his place on Agege Motor Road. Remi didn't leave Fela. In fact, the kids were still coming to the house every day after school to play with their father and Remi had to drag the kids back to Aguda! That's really how it was.

Since we were now playing right across the street in the Empire Hotel, the whole area was becoming kind of like "Fela's area." That's when things began to get crazy. Nineteen seventy-three was really the beginning of the craziness. I could see Fela's attitude changing, and his way of dealing with people. Back when we started the band, you remember Fela had promised me that we would share everything as a partnership. But once the machine started to roll, it's like he forgot about that. It's true that he made me bandleader when we got back from the States, but it was still difficult to even get my basic pay—even after we were the most popular band in the country. And when Fela had that money dispute with Mr. Balogun back in 1972, the police had to be called because Fela jumped behind the counter of the bar, went crazy, and broke up everything! That wasn't the Fela I knew, because Fela wasn't a fighter. He had his own fighters who stayed with him in his house. Fela didn't have to do any fighting himself. But he was changing now. Some people have put blame on his mother, but I wouldn't blame her for anything. Fela's mother was just a nice lady that was supporting him, and she could not stop him anyway because she was old by that time, and Fela didn't want anybody telling him what to do. She wasn't what she used to be before, as the famous Mrs. Ransome-Kuti.

Fela began to be surrounded by a lot of parasites, people who were hanging around but weren't contributing anything to the organization. But even though he was surrounded by these people, what he didn't like was "yes men." I mean, he liked to have them around him, because he was a guy that could not be alone. He wanted to have people around him at all times. But secretly he saw them as his enemies. Because as soon as it turned out that someone was with him every day, his attitude inside was "Who are you?" If you can come and sit down, wait for him to wake up and you're going to be with him for twenty-four hours, that means you have nothing else doing. So now he can treat you the way he likes, and you cannot even open your mouth. That started a lot of the craziness.

Another thing that made everything crazy was all the girls that were coming around. They came on their own because when Fela was looking for a dancer, plenty of girls came. Our first four dancers after Dele left were Kemi, Adia, Paulina, and Eva. Adia we called "Yansch Controller." Kemi was called "Shakibo." But many others came, and some of them didn't want to go back because the house was big and there were so many things going on. The music was exciting for them. But with all of those girls around, there was bound to be a lot of craziness, and sometimes it got to be too much. For example, Ginger Baker once gave an interview where he said he subbed for me when I was sick. But that's not really how it happened. What really happened was that on this particular day, it was my mother's fiftieth birthday and my family had a big party for her. I wasn't even supposed to come to play that night, but I knew that by not coming to play, the band wouldn't play. I didn't want to disturb the business because of my mother's birthday. People would say that I was disrupting business for luxury. Plus, it was salary night and I needed to get paid. So I went to my mother's party and then I went to the gig after. I don't know what was going on in town that night, but for some reason the club was not filling up quickly. But it was just the beginning of the night, so there wasn't anything special about that. The people were just coming in slowly. So I arrived and started up the band.

After we had played for a while, Fela came in and he saw that the place was not full. That was about eleven o'clock in the night. And so he spoke to some of these stupid people he used to have around him. Fela always put the wrong people in the right place. He always put thieves there to guard his money. He would never let any normal person take care of his money. He always let thieves do it. That was because of what he called his "politics." He would always choose the raff off the street to handle his money, and most of them were robbing him. One of these motherfuckers was in charge of collecting all the money of the night and telling the figure to Fela. And whichever figure he tells to Fela is what Fela believes. It wasn't even written anywhere. So a lot of the money that came in at the gate, that was money that we would never see. And on a slow night like that, they're already taking care of themselves, you know? So when Fela came, he asked that guy "What time did Tony start playing with the band?" He thought the place was not full because we had started playing late. And that idiot there told him that we had just started at that moment. That way, he could pocket all the money from earlier in the night. Actually, we had been playing for about 45 minutes to one hour!

Fela came over to my drums and told me that when we finished that song, I should see him backstage. So when we finished I went backstage, and he asked me "Why are you starting now, at this time? Why are you starting late like this?" And then he started saying a lot of crazy things, man. I told him "Hey Fela, it's not like that. It's the politics of these guys up front." And I told him "You never even asked me about nothing, you just started on me with this shit! Why didn't you come to me coolly and ask me yourself? I don't like the way you are talking to me!"

He told me that if I didn't like the way he talked to me, I could resign. I said, "What? I could *resign*? Then I'm doing it now—I resign!" And I just walked away from him. Then he ran into the club and told the gate guys that they should return the money back to everybody, so that they could go home. No show that night. Everybody was asking, what is the matter here? They had been enjoying the night coolly before Fela came, and all of a sudden they have to go back home!

But Ginger was in town at that time. And it just so happened that as I was getting ready to leave the club, Ginger was coming in. When Fela saw Ginger, he said, "Ginger, man, come on and play with me, man!" And he yelled at the gate man "Stop, stop, stop—don't give them the money back!" Ginger was asking, "What happened to Tony?" Because I was standing right there. I told him "Look Ginger, I cannot say anything right now. If he wants you to play, the drums are right there. Go ahead." So he took over that night, which was a Saturday night. I just stayed backstage and sat down, smoking and doing my thing. Ginger knew all the songs anyway, because he'd been hanging with us all along. But to actually get up and play them was a different thing. Well, Fela just happened to be playing rock music that night. It wasn't Fela's music anymore, it became something else. Fela was trying to play his music, but he suffered a lot to have Ginger behind him, playing it in a different style.

But that wasn't even the end of it, man. Right in front of Fela's house, I had set up a small boy there, to sell some small things like omelets, yams, and tea. Because when we came back in the middle of the night, everybody wanted to snack on something. It was just to make some small change. He knew that that was my own business there. So, when Fela came back home, you know what he did? He told his bodyguards that they should go and kick over all of this boy's eggs, yams, pots, that they should just break up everything! And they did that.

Meanwhile, the next day was supposed to be Sunday Jump. And before the starting time, his so-called friends that "advise" him came to my house. They saw what happened the night before, and they told me that the music was not happening. And they asked me, was I going to remain at home like this? I told them that I wasn't going back there. These guys begged me and begged me. So finally I told them that I could come to the Jump. I had nothing to do at home at that moment anyway. I could just come to the Jump and watch like any other person. But I wasn't playing any fucking drums. And they told me that, no, they don't want me to go there like anybody. They want me to go there and play! Because they were my fans and they loved what I was doing.

I got there and the musicians were waiting to start. So, who was going to start them? Ginger couldn't start up the band. Animashaun could not do it at that time. So for their own sake, I went and tuned the band. Then I played the warmup tunes with them. But as soon as Fela and Ginger entered, I walked off and left the drums for Ginger and went backstage to smoke my joint and drink my beer. Fela did not have the guts to call me to come and play. So, they managed again that night, but the people were getting crazy in the club! Fela himself heard all the people shouting out my name, asking what was going on? So when they finished that night, he announced to the audience that from that day, there would be no more music and that the next show would be announced. And only God knew how many months that was going to take, for him to regroup!

Well, the truth was that all this bullshit happened because of all those girls that were around. It was just a question of me screwing one girl that was his favorite. But nothing stopped him from screwing that girl also, because she lived in his house. So, who was the master—was he not? If the girl followed me, it was because she wanted to. I never dragged anybody by force! She was not my wife, and I never put any emblem on her, so why was he making a problem with me? And on that very night that the shit went down, that girl was standing right behind me when he was facing me and talking to me like that backstage. So he just gave it to me properly in front of that girl, to let that girl know that he was the boss. Which everybody already knew, anyway.

So I went back home and relaxed. Then, Fela slowly started to send his delegates to me. The first one he sent was Wole Kuboye, who was his lawyer and his friend. We used to call him "Feelings Lawyer." And Wole came to me with allegations that I have fucked some of Fela's girls. I have fucked this one. I have fucked that one. I have fucked the other one. It was all true. But you have to understand something. These girls were not his wives at that time. There were girls coming and going all the time, and they were there for anybody to pick. In fact, Wole himself was picking one any time he wanted. It was only that particular one that was Fela's favorite that caused the problem.

I told Wole that, since these allegations have been made, that we have to go clear this up. I told him, let's go to Fela now. But as soon as we entered Fela's house, Fela ran up to me and said "Allenko, let's forget it. Let's forget about this completely." And he said "I'm very sorry for what happened with your shop there. How much did all that stuff cost?" He told me that I should just give him the bill and he would pay it. And I asked him, "But what about the matter that brought me here?" He told me that we should forget about it, that we should not even mention it.

And then he asked me "So, when are we playing again? Are you still playing?" I said "Alright, finito—it's finished."

It was very seldom that Fela apologized for anything. But he did it that time because he could not afford lose me at that time. Especially over some stupid bullshit like that. I think he must have checked the level he had reached with me, and realized that it would have crippled him for a while and when he woke up, he wasn't gonna get his machine rolling the same way anymore because there is no drummer in that country or from any part of the world that will replace me when it comes to playing Afrobeat. So after I accepted his apology, he ran out to call his press attache, to put it in the newspapers quickly that we were back on. That's what really happened when Ginger subbed for me. It had nothing to do with me being sick.

Between the two of us, there was always a lot of ego tripping, man. For example, any time Fela came and saw me with a new girl sitting in front of the stage, I knew it was gonna be a problem. Because in his mind, I'm sure he was thinking "Ah, this one must be with Tony." My job as bandleader was to make sure the band was in tune. And then we would play our warm-up set. We would start maybe one and a half or two hours before Fela came, playing my own instrumentals—no singing, just groove and solos. And I would keep the crowd on their feet dancing the whole time! Some people would tell me that when I was playing was when they were enjoying the music the most. It wasn't competition with Fela's music, it was just that when Fela came, many talkings were going to go on. He had his politics business and sometimes it took the whole night for this. One song would last like maybe twenty-five or thirty minutes and with all the talking between songs, he might only play four or five songs in a night. So some of the people commented. It's not that they didn't like Fela's show, it's just that there wasn't too much dancing going on anymore. It became what they used to call "mouth dancing," they used to be yelling out that Fela was dancing with his mouth!

But when he came onstage the first thing he had to do, if I had a girl there, was to show everyone that he was the boss. He would turn around to me and say "Allenko, did you tune up the band?" I would say "Yes." And then he's gonna start his shit: "Ah, the band is not in tune! You didn't tune them well." I mean he would say this publicly, on the mike! And the band was right in tune, anyway. So I laughed and told him "Okay, if they are not well tuned, you are the boss—tune them yourself! I play my drums, and my drums are in tune." You see? I gave him back the answer like that, publicly. Then he had to walk over to tune the guy's guitar for him or whatever, and the guitar was already in tune! All this shit just to show off in front of the girl.

So when we finally started the tune, I would just play it straight and clean. Fela would be playing his solo, and I wouldn't be giving him any extras to make it exciting. That means things were slipping, and that was a problem for him. He would start to look back at me, to see what was happening. And me, I wasn't going to look at him! I just turned my head to the side! I felt like "You are the leader, so go ahead and drive the ship . . . !"

Then he had to try and find a way to bring me back to life after insulting me. So after a song, he would start to ask me questions. "Okay . . . Allenko . . . hmm . . . what do we play now?" I would say, "Well, who's driving the ship?" He wanted me to say we'll play this tune or that one, and I wouldn't say it! And sometimes when we finished a tune, he'd come back to me and ask "How did it go?" And it was his own music he was asking about! The point is that it was some psychological shit he was tripping on and you couldn't fall into his trap, man!

This small stuff was nothing compared to what happened when we went on tour in Cameroun in 1974. That's when I really began to see how much this guy's attitude had changed. It seemed like everybody in that country was screaming for "Shakara" and "Lady," because those were our big songs at the time and they were very big hits there. So our first gig was in the big stadium in Douala. The stadium was completely full with about 60,000 people and first of all Fela was very late, as usual. He would never come onstage until everybody was screaming for him. But I was there already with the guys, warming up the crowd up with the band's set. Finally he came, and we started to play all the songs that we were doing at that time. The gig was going fine, but after a while people started shouting for "Shakara." In fact, the whole stadium started shouting for "Shakara." So I said to Fela, let's play "Shakara" now! But he went to the mic and told the entire stadium that he wasn't going to play "Shakara" and that if they wanted to hear it they should go home and play the record. That was always Fela's policy, you know—he would not play any song live that we had already put on record. He would always tell the audience that if they wanted to hear those older songs, they should go and buy the records. And then he turned to us and said, "Let's play another song."

The audience actually thought he was joking and that he would come back to it. But we played for a long time and eventually we had to finish the gig. We never played the song. And after we finished, it took us about three hours to get out of the stadium with an army escort, because the audience wanted to tear the whole stadium down, they wanted to destroy the place! It became a big problem between Fela and the promoter because he had brought us all the way to Cameroon and Fela refused to play our most popular song. But we managed to escape that situation.

The next gig was in Yaounde, which is their capital. When we arrived there, the promoter put us in some kind of shitty hotel, maybe a one-star or a no-star hotel. It was just a place to sleep and wake up, and we started to complain about that. But the president of Cameroon at that time was a man named Ahidjo, and Ahidjo was a big fan of Fela's music. Ahidjo heard that Fela was in Yaounde and that we were going to play in the stadium. He asked his people, "Where are they staying?" And they told him that we were in that no-star hotel. So he told his people that they should go check all of us out of that shitty hotel and take us to the five-star hotel in Yaounde, which was the Hilton. The Hilton was built up on the mountain, and it was like a paradise up there. There were three days until the gig and Ahidjo told us that we should eat anything and drink anything we wanted, as much as we wanted. Open tab. We were having a ball, man! The day of the concert, you should have seen the stadium. It was totally full up, like for a football match. There were about seventy thousand people there! And the presidential stand was up there, too. And Fela did the same thing he had done in Douala—no "Shakara," no "Lady." He told them that he didn't play anything that he had already recorded, because he was trying to move forward and that if he kept playing his old songs, he would not move forward. And afterwards, it was another fucking riot!

I could understand his principle, but I thought that we shouldn't have applied that in this type of situation. At least he could have bent just a bit. He could have told them, "I don't usually do this, but I'm doing it for you people because you gave us such a good reception." Especially when the president gave us this red carpet treatment, you know? But he refused, and we never played those two songs on the whole tour! So that was the last time we ever played in Cameroon. They never brought us back there because of all the bullshit!

After the Cameroon tour, some of the musicians really began to get fed up. Going through all of this shit, and we weren't even being paid properly. All of this stuff was building up and the result was that there was a strike after we all came back from Cameroon. We were supposed to be playing at the Gondola in Lagos, and the musicians decided to send a petition to Fela. Animashaun was the one that drew up the petition. There were nine of us then, not including Fela. The other eight all signed the petition, and then they brought it to me. I myself didn't want to agitate. What could one tell Fela anyway? You couldn't tell him anything. He was a person that had his own way of life, he knew what he wanted, and he was going to do things his own way. I didn't want the same things as him, but if you want to work with a person like that, you have to be ready to compromise. I knew everything that I myself was doing for the organization, and every time I would see all of the bread just flying past me, and none of it coming my way. And I had also stopped working the job at Associated Press at the end of '73. It was getting kind of tiring, and after ten years of working two jobs, I was not really getting richer, either. So I told myself, okay, let me just face the music, and that's when all this shit went down in the band. So I could have been the first person to agitate. But I was the bandleader at that time, so it kind of put me in the middle. I had to be very diplomatic. Anyway, the majority carries the vote.

At that time, Fela was earning ten shillings per album sold, as a royalty. So the band asked for one penny per album. To give you an idea—if you have nine pennies, it is not even adding up to one shilling yet. So the band was petitioning for less than 5 percent of what Fela was already earning. I thought that this was minute. They never asked for anything exorbitant or unreasonable. You have to remember also that the band was not paid for recording sessions. It was part of our expected duties, and the recording fee was part of our salary. That's the way it was back then. So I signed the petition and it was taken to Fela.

When it came time for the Gondola show, there was no gig and I stayed in my house sleeping. But Fela came to my house in the middle of the night with his whole troupe—all the singers and dancers and everyone else—and parked the bus at the petrol station near my house. It was about two in the morning. I got out of bed, and Fela asked me, "Allenko, what's happening?" I told him, "Did you see the petition?" He said, "Yeah." So I said, "That's what's happening!" He said he wanted to see me in Kalakuta, in his house. My wife asked me where I was going at that hour, and I said, "To Fela's." So I got myself together and drove there. When I arrived, Fela's mother, his lawyer Kanmi Osobu, his friend JK, his friend Benson Idonije, and he himself were all there. Mrs. Ransome-Kuti was a woman that I used to dialogue with a lot, because she knew my family from Abeokuta. She asked me why I should be inside of this matter of the petition, since me and Fela were very old friends. I told her, "The majority carries the vote. And I'm not sure they're asking for too much." Then Fela said we had to close this matter, that he was going to talk to all the musicians the next afternoon.

The next day, everybody was there. Fela said that his reply to the petition was that he was not going to give anybody one cent from his royalties — no way! He told us that the only way to make money is to write your own songs and that if any one of us wanted to make our own money then we should do the same thing as him and write our own songs. And he told us that as long as we were in the band, he would be part of the project and he would support it. He would participate for free, he would take it to the record company, and he would not ask for any pay or any royalty. He made his point very clear, and he put the ball back into our own corner.

So that's where many of my own songs came from at that time. Like "Hustler" — even though that song was an instrumental, it was my way of saying that Fela had put me in the state of hustling for my own survival. As long as he's not going to give anybody any royalties, I had to do my own records to be able to get my own money. *Progress* was the next album after *Jealousy*. In between, we did a few more of Fela's albums. What I was saying on *Progress* was that, instead of fighting with Fela for money, I was trying to progress and create on my own. If I kept waiting around for money from Fela, I would still be in the Egypt 80 today! And where I am today, I could even have a legal case because my name is documented on all those Africa 70 albums with Fela. But I think I would be wasting my time instead of progressing and trying to create something for myself. You see? Progress is what a hard worker is looking for. I had to look for it for myself. The lyrics tell you that. Later on, I did *No Accommodation for Lagos*, which was referring to the housing shortage at that time. Well, at least Fela gave me the chance to have those on the market. Anytime I told him that I wanted to rehearse with the band, he would tell them, "Allenko wants to rehearse tomorrow and everyone is required to be there." So at least he was supporting me that far.

It was around this time that things really began to change between us. I was still part of the organization, but at the same time I was far. I had to operate this way because the truth is that Fela messed many people's heads up. I remember one Saturday night that we were doing what we used to call the "Comprehensive Show" with all of the dancers and everything. And I don't know how he managed to come up with this that particular night, but he stopped the music and told the audience that he was gonna preach to them. He asked them what they believed in, and most of the people there answered that they believed in God. So he asked them, which god? And he told them that if they thought there was any god, he himself was God. And he told them that if they thought there was any other God, that they should look up to their ceiling when they woke up in the morning and pray for God to give them their daily bread. And if they saw that bread drop down in front of them and they could eat it, then he would believe in their God. But he told them that as far as he was concerned, he was the only one that they could see in the morning and ask, "Fela, I'm hungry. Please give me some money to buy my bread." And since he was giving them money for the bread, he was their god now! A few people believed this shit, some didn't believe, and most of them just found it ridiculous. But they couldn't challenge him there, you know? I just kept my cool.

There was another time when the band was on tour up north in Kano, and he had his boys—those ones that believed in his gospel—he had them take all the Bibles of the hotel and use the pages to roll big jumbo joints. Because they were those old Bibles where the paper is very thin, like Rizla. I didn't like that. When they gave me one of those joints, I made sure to take that Bible paper off and use my own paper. When all of these things were happening, I was just talking to my own God inside of myself and saying, "Please, you know I never did any kind of shit like this . . . So please spare me any time you're going to drop the axe!"

Sometime around 1976, Fela made everybody in the Africa 70 organization change their names. Any European name had to be changed to some kind of typical Nigerian name, even including their family name. He himself took the "Ransome" name out of his name and put "Anikulapo" there. Everybody in the organization changed their names— musicians, workers, dancers, singers. But me, I refused. I told Fela, "My father's living and I'm not going to change my surname and disrespect him. Sorry. I'm *Allen*. And that's it, period." But since my father's middle name was "Alabi," Fela started putting that name down for me on the album credits. He took my middle name "Oladipo" and combined it with my father's middle name. That's why you see me listed on some of those albums as "Oladipo Alabi." That wasn't right, because my father never used Alabi as a family name. I would never be recognized by the real Alabis if I went around them. "Allen" was originally a slavery name, that's true. But I told Fela that that was hundreds of years ago and that today I wasn't the slave of anybody, so it didn't disturb me. That song "Colonial

Mentality" was written about this name-changing business. If you listen closely, you'll notice that Fela was mentioning the names of the people around him. But when he got to "Mr. Allen," he sang "Mr. Alien." He dodged it cleverly.

If there was any kind of dispute between us, usually he wouldn't confront me. But if we had something going on in the studio, that's when the bullshit would start. He might take his revenge in the mix. For example, if we were listening to something and I said, "There's not enough drums there," he would tell me, "Well Allenko, it depends on what you want to hear at a certain time." And then he would reach over and turn me way down in the mix. After all the work we've done! That's the reason you can't hear my drums too clearly on some of the records. For example, if you listen to that song "I Go Shout Plenty," you'll see what I mean. But if you can hear my drums very clearly, that means the politics were good in the band at that time!

The whole Africa 70 trip is something that I saw grow up in front of me, because I was there before the beginning of all that. From the time he started smoking, Fela changed completely from the guy that I used to know between 1964 and 1970. Believe me, man—many crazy things were transpiring around him. It was chaos, and the more you looked, the less you would see. I decided that it was better for me to be at a distance so that I could see clearly. The distance I'm talking about is not like the distance between people in different houses. I'm talking about what's in the heart of the person. Because even though I was the leader of the band, I wasn't going to accept everything that Fela was doing. The turning point was around this same time when I went to confront him in his house, in what they called the "court." That was where everybody in the Africa 70 organization aired out their grievances. Everybody had to be there. And I told Fela in front of the whole organization that day: "The one thing I will do with you for ever and ever is the music. I am with you. But the other things around it, I am not inside of them. These other things are not things I can handle." Fela then turned around and asked everyone, "Did you all hear what Allenko said—that he is not inside our philosophy?" Everyone said yes. And that was that. I had to do this because with all the shit that was going on, he might think that as long as I was with him in the music, I was with him in everything. Unless I clarified it, which I did. At least that cleared up my own side.

EVERYTHING SCATTER

6 Among the general public, Fela had some fans in the middle class. But most of his fans were either from the high class or the low class. The high class was like the intellectuals and the educated people. They appreciated his message. And the low class was like the people in the street. His songs inspired them to be able to stand on their feet. Don't let yourself be bullied around. Fight back. Look — these messages in the music were really sung for everybody. He wasn't singing for himself. He was singing for the public so everybody could learn from that. Because the things that those politicians would not even talk about, he was singing about them and exposing them to the public. The country needed someone like Fela at that time, because we were under military rule. With the soldiers, it was like "If you don't do it our way, you are against us." You understand? One-sided. No conversation. No dialogue. Meanwhile, the rich were getting richer and the poor were getting poorer.

That's why I give President Yakubu Gowon a little bit of credit. Even though he himself was a soldier, when the oil money started to come he gave out refunds for government workers from the surplus. The Udoji refund was the first, and the second one was the Morgan refund. Gowon built bridges, so that the people could reach each other. He built the National Stadium with the money from the oil. At least he made something happen there. But after Gowon, the corruption started to get to the highest level. I mean, Murtala Mohammed came in after

Gowon, but he was short-lived. He wanted to straighten out the heads of everybody, but they didn't want that type of person because it was too hard for them. He was making the former colonizers sweat because even though he was a northerner, he was following the politics of the South. For the most part, the ones in the South wanted the country to progress and stand on its own, and the ones in the North were in the pockets of the former colonizers. That's why they eliminated Mohammed right away. Obasanjo came in after Mohammed, but he was a stooge for the northerners. So you see, everything in the country was going haywire.

That was the system, and it was difficult for anybody to come up and criticize the government because nobody wanted to be on their bad side. The journalists were there, but how many people read the paper to get those messages? And even if the news was on the radio, how many people were educated enough to understand it? So there was little the journalists could do to criticize the government, on radio or the TV. And if they tried, the director of the program would be locked away somewhere. The music was an easier way for everybody to get messages, because even if they couldn't buy the record, somebody might put Fela's music on in a record shop and play it very loudly in the street, and everybody passing would stop and listen to the record.

As far as I was concerned, Fela's program was my program. I liked the fact that he was able to face these things squarely. It was just the craziness around the program that became a problem. The police were getting irritated because he was singing against them. And then he began to sing against the military. When Fela started talking about going into politics, the truth is that he could have become head of state if he had played the right role. To do something like that, you have to go about it in a way that will make the people be on your side and fight for you. But most of the people up there in the government didn't like his lifestyle. And even if they tried to ignore his lifestyle, it was impossible because their kids were coming to Fela's house, and some of them were staying! I'm talking about the children of magistrates, judges, politicians, and other people like that. These people didn't like the fact that their kids were coming to the house of Fela, the crazy musician who smoked grass and all that stuff. When we were on tour of Cameroon in 1974, the cops chased us all the way there and back because of some underage girls that were singing and dancing with the band. They took the girls away, but the funny thing is that as soon as they got them back to Nigeria, the girls escaped and came back to Fela's house! Many of these kids couldn't hear a single word against Fela. If you made the mistake of trying to lecture them about Fela, you would be in a big soup!

What pushed everything over the edge was when Fela began to challenge the government on the grass issue. The Indian Hemp (marijuana) law was one of the craziest laws that was ever passed in our country. It even ruined many of the higher-ups. For example, some big-time doctors and lawyers went to jail for ten years, for stupid bullshit like having one joint. I even remember meeting some policemen back when we were in the States. When they found out we were from Nigeria, they laughed and said, "You guys are from Nigeria? You people must have a good sense of humor over there! Isn't it in your country that for one joint, it's ten years in prison?" So they had even heard about this in the US! We just laughed along with them, but they were looking at it like it was complete madness because in California at that time, people were smoking everywhere. When President Yakubu Gowon came in, he never changed that law. But the majority of the people would not agitate on the grass issue, because nobody wanted to be agitating on behalf of drugs under the military government. That's something Fela took on himself. And that's when the big problems started.

It was sometime in 1974 when the police decided to jump on us for the first time. I happened to be at Fela's house that night. I was standing with Fela's mechanic, whose name was Olu, when a bunch of policemen arrived. They came in regular vehicles, not police cars. And they were all dressed in normal clothes—it was a plainclothes operation. There were female officers to take the girls away, and male officers to take the guys. The police went inside first and gathered everybody—about thirty people—and then they came back outside. I had two joints on me and I knew they were coming after these types of things. So I was able to destroy the joints outside of the compound. And then they came back out and they were about to take everybody away. But first they were asking the people outside, "Who lives here? Who's not living here?" The ones that said that they didn't live there, the police let them go. I myself didn't live there. I never lived in Fela's house, I always lived in my own home with my family. But when they brought Fela out, he told me that they found five sticks of grass in his house, and that made me feel something for him there. Like, it was gonna be a big shit for him now because of that ten-year possession law. So when they asked me if I lived there, at first I just didn't answer them. They realized that I didn't live there, but then I said, "I live here. But could you just let me go lock my car?" They said, "Yes, go do it."

So I locked my car and they took everybody to one police station. And that station refused us, because they didn't want to deal with Fela's people. So they took us to the next police station, which was called Iponri, in Surulere. They started to put us into the cell, but the desk sergeant there also said no, he doesn't want to be responsible for Fela's people. Then they transferred us to Central Police headquarters on Lagos Island, and we were refused there. They took us to Awolowo police station in Ikoyi, and we were refused there. They were refusing to take Fela's people everywhere, because no one wanted to have anything to do with Fela's people, and also because there were too many people. That's why finally they had to drive us to Alagbon Close, which is another jail in Ikoyi.

At Alagbon, there was just one big cell, but it couldn't contain all of us. So they had to use the offices there to create temporary cells for everyone, except Fela. Fela, they put him in the real cell, the one with all the hardened criminals. That cell was called Kalakuta. The police thought they might break Fela by putting him there, but actually they were all his fans inside there! There was a "president" in Kalakuta, like the top criminal in there. But when Fela arrived, that president stepped down for Fela to be the president of the place.

I myself spent three days in Alagbon without going to any trial, and I was bailed out the third day. Fela was bailed out a week later, and the first thing he did after coming out was to name his own compound Kalakuta Republic and tell everyone that the laws of Nigeria didn't apply inside there. And from that moment, things started going haywire. The government couldn't stand this "republic within a republic" thing. Especially because they themselves had critics all over the world because of all the craziness that Nigeria was going through at that time, with the war just ending and the oil boom and all the corruption. And people started to wonder, "What kind of government is that in Nigeria, when a musician like Fela can just toy with them like that?" Fela was always attacking them and ridiculing them publicly, and they were starting to write about him in foreign newspapers, like the *New York Times*. So the government kept trying to break him down. The raids started following each other, one after the other. For grass, for abduction, for all kinds of things. And it never stopped.

But what a lot of people don't know is that if some crazy things were coming, the soldiers would always warn him by coming to tell me first. Because the soldiers were in the Abalti barracks, which was close by on Folarin Street. And they knew I was the coolheaded one in the middle of all this craziness. The soldiers would sometimes tell me when they were going to come and stop us from playing in the night. And many times I tried to pacify them, to say no, you can't do that, because we musicians don't have any problems with you guys. We just play music, and if you come to stop us, you disturb us from our living. And so they would always tell me that I should go tell Fela to cool down from yabbing (insulting) them. Because you know, he was yabbing them so badly by this time. They would always tell me to tell him that he should cool down, otherwise they will come and do their worst. But whenever I went to tell him, he would always say, "Ah, Allenko, you have come with your theory." So what could I do? Every time I gave him the warning, he said it was only my "theory." And when the shit came down, it came heavily. Each time, it got heavier and heavier. But I wouldn't be there because I already knew when those people would jump. That's why many times I just played and went home.

Between 1974 and 1977 it was a hot, hot time. It was like we were caught up in a war zone, man. Fela even electrified the fence around the compound to try to keep the police out. I could have easily left the band then, but I stayed and I never complained because of how much I loved the music, and also because we were finally having some fun and making some money after all the years of struggling. Also, I used to tell people, "Why should I leave like a coward? The message this guy is preaching is right. It's just his approach that is the problem." But the truth is that it was getting too hot and I knew I would reach my limit one day. I didn't know when that day was coming, but I knew it was gonna come. You know, I don't take irrational decisions, just like that. I wanted to make sure that if someone asked me why I left, I had a good reason. I wanted to make sure that before I did it, I had enough proof. And as it turned out, that proof was coming soon.

All of this was right around the time of FESTAC (Festival of Black and African Arts and Culture), which was held for one month in Nigeria in early 1977. FESTAC was a good idea. At least for once in Nigeria, they gave some attention to cultural things. But the problem was that there was so much maladministration around the festival that nothing came out of it in the end. All of those artists should be recognized today, wherever they are in the world. But at the end of the day, there was so much corruption that you could never really see it as a credit to the artists, to the country, or to Africa.

That was the main reason that Fela refused to perform at the FESTAC. The government actually wanted him to represent Nigeria properly, and he went to a board meeting in Bagwada, near Kano, where they were planning the whole thing. But he dropped out halfway through the meeting because he didn't get along with anybody there. He also told them that the only way he would play was if the government would buy that book that Dusty had given him called *The Black Man of the Nile* and distribute it freely to everybody that came to the festival. The government didn't want to do that, so Fela came back to Lagos and told all of us that we were not going to play.

But the festival wasn't complete without him, and our Shrine became like the FESTAC spot for all the foreign artists. When they finished their performances at the National Theater, they all trooped over to our Shrine. Some of the musicians even sat in with us, like Randy Weston and Babatunde Olatunji. Randy loved Fela's music. And Olatunji actually set his drums up right next to my set. Hugh Masekela also sat in with us. Masekela was Fela's personal friend but he was in town for the festival and he used to come play. Another trumpeter that came through was Lester Bowie, from the Art Ensemble of Chicago. Lester loved Fela's music and ended up staying for a few months and playing with us. So you can see how hot we were at that time. In fact, Stevie Wonder also came with his brother one night. Stevie didn't play, but they sat him right in front of the stage. Fela wanted him to try some kind of African beverage, so they brought palm wine for him to drink! And Stevie stayed there until the end of the show. He was digging the music and having fun!

The Shrine was completely full every night of the festival, outside and inside. So many of the foreign artists were trying to pass through there that it was impossible to move. The government didn't like that, and they didn't like all of the attention Fela was getting. And Fela himself was yabbing them hard. Insulting them and ridiculing them publicly, in front of all the foreigners that were in Lagos. And this was being broadcast all over the world. So how long was it gonna take for them to jump again?

They waited until everybody had left town, and this time when they jumped, it was a real disaster. This was in February of 1977, about one week after everyone from the festival had left. At that time, we were finishing Fela's *Black President* movie, and even the very title of the thing was irritating the government. He had already proclaimed his place the Kalakuta Republic, and now it was like he was challenging them at every corner. So he was like a big pain in their necks. We had been completing the soundtrack at the Ghana Film Studios, in Accra. And it was really bad luck for Fela because the film was actually finished. The only thing left to do was to take the soundtrack to have it mixed, which they were planning to do the very next day. Another project that was planned around that time was for me, Fela, and Manu Dibango to record an album in Ghana with Ghanaian musicians. But then this thing happened and all of our plans went haywire.

What caused the whole problem this time was one guy named Segun who was one of Fela's drivers—actually, he was Fela's mother's driver. Segun disobeyed the traffic police and then drove the car to Fela's house. This kind of stuff happened all the time. Fela's boys would cause all kinds of trouble around Lagos, and a lot of it Fela didn't even know about, because he was in his house while his boys were out causing trouble. They would be breaking the law, abusing people, fighting with the police, and many other things. But whenever the police came to investigate the matter, Fela would always defend the boys, no matter what they had done. He would never hand them over to the police. Like I told you before, this was because of his "politics." So on this particular day when the police came to Kalakuta to try and arrest Segun, Fela and his people put loudspeakers outside and started playing "Zombie" to taunt them. So they went away, and Fela thought he had won. But then they came back, and about one thousand soldiers from the Nigerian Army came with them!

I was actually supposed to be there that day, because usually I was there in the house every afternoon. I would wake up, drive down there, and maybe stay from two o'clock until maybe twelve or one the next day. I would just be hanging and using the house as my base, taking care of different business, moving from there and coming back. The only day I didn't come was when we were playing in the night. Because I was tired and we were supposed to play that night, I told Fela that I wouldn't be there Friday afternoon, but that I would see them onstage in the night. But that was the gig that never happened.

The soldiers came there about two or two thirty in the afternoon. But even though I didn't live far from Fela's house, I didn't hear any of the chaos because I was at home sleeping. When it got to be about ten o'clock in the night, I woke up to get myself ready to play, and I noticed that my wife was late coming home, because she was usually back by that time. It was only later I found out that the soldiers had stopped all the transportation into the area. But a friend of mine came to knock on my door around that time because he saw that my car was still there. When I came to the door he saw me and exclaimed, "Thank god you are here!" I asked what was the matter and he asked me, didn't I hear what happened at Fela's house? He told me that there had been a complete massacre there by the soldiers and that Fela and all the girls had been taken to Abalti Barracks. But there were always crazy rumors and stories flying around Lagos. So I said, "Let's take a trip."

My house was very close to Kalakuta, like walking distance. I could walk there by Western Avenue, or I could walk by the railway. We walked down Western Avenue, passing behind Abalti Barracks. But when we got close to Fela's house, there was a roadblock and we were sent back by the soldiers. So we came back and went again. This time, we went through the railway line. But there was a roadblock on that side too. The soldiers had the area completely closed down. So finally we went back and got my car and drove over to Lagos Island, because it was the middle of the night. We went to a beer parlor and sat down and drank for a while. At three in the morning, I said, "Let's try again." This time I drove my car through the Mosholasi way, across the railway line. We finally drove in front of Fela's house and I couldn't believe what I saw — the whole house had been completely burnt down! The same house I was in a couple of days before! And the soldiers were guarding it. This went on for a week. Whenever you wanted to pass through that area, you had to pass the soldiers with your hands in the air. After one week, they dismantled the roadblocks.

By the end of the week they had revived Fela and moved him from Abalti barracks to the hospital, but when I finally got to see him, he was like a dead man. He was not talking, moving — nothing. They had broken him completely into pieces. He was almost totally destroyed. All the girls, they had raped them and violated them every way they could think of. The soldiers had mutilated the bodyguards with bayonets and their intestines were falling out. The doctors had to put the intestines back in and wrap their stomachs in plastic to keep the intestines in. That attack seriously wounded Fela. Apart from the physical battering that he received, they completely fucked him up mentally. Because of what disappeared that day, there's no way he could ever get back — physically *or* mentally.

I was at the tribunal afterwards, hearing all the testimony. Everything that the army alleged was untrue. For example, they claimed that Fela's bodyguards had burned an army motorcycle. That never happened. It was bullshit, just a way of finding something to put on him. Because if they could prove that his boys burned an army motorcycle, that would justify total war. And when he tried to sue the government, they dismissed his suit and said the house had been burnt by an "unknown soldier." So he was left with nothing in the end.

He even lost his conveyance for a piece of property in Ikeja that he had bought from my family back in 1970 or 1971. That land had originally belonged to my grandfather. And I remember that Fela called me one day and he told me, "Allenko, you know that I don't own the land your father sold to me in Ikeja anymore, because the conveyance of the land burned up in the fire." He was keeping it in his home, and when it was destroyed in the fire, there was nothing he could show to anybody to prove that he owned that land.

This is when the people around me decided to give me a real kick in the ass. They asked me, "Tony, are you crazy? Fela is going to sell this fucking land and it's going to be worth a million naira now!" They proposed that I should sell this land, get the money, and give Fela back his original amount, because the land was worth much more now than when he originally bought it. I didn't want to do that, so I went to my father. My father pitied Fela for what he had lost, and he agreed that we should do another conveyance for him. He didn't take advantage of the situation, because my father was not that type of person. He even paid the lawyer himself. My father never asked Fela to pay. He just went and did it, gave the conveyance to me three days later, and told me, "Now Fela has his land back." When I went to give it to Fela he just told me, "Thank you." That's all.

In that period after the fire, it was like one insanity after another. People were starting to leave the organization. To be a disciple of Fela and to preach his gospel, was becoming too crazy then. Like Lemi, a painter and graphics guy who did many of our album covers. I don't know precisely how he and Fela fell out, but I'm quite sure it was because this matter was getting too tough for him. So he just stopped and got another job. And then some other people left because Fela was becoming paranoid. He started to accuse some people close to him of being agents from the CIA, and he would order his boys to whip these people.

When everything was finished with the tribunal, the next place that Fela and his people lived after his house was burnt was the Crossroads Hotel. That hotel was owned by a lawyer named Mr. Ogun who used to hire bands to play there. We couldn't gig anywhere else in Lagos, because the army wouldn't let us. Anywhere we tried to gig, they stopped us. It was only at the Crossroads that we created a stage to do our Sunday Jump. And that was because Mr. Ogun was also an army boss, so the place was kind of under his protection. But the Jump wasn't bringing in much money. Although the place was always full, Fela had to pay a lot of money to the hotel because the entire troupe was living there.

We couldn't do anything in Nigeria, with the army stopping us every time we tried to play. So we went to Accra to try to record a new soundtrack for the film, because the original one was destroyed in the fire. That means we were trying to redo the music, dialogue, and everything. After a while we gave up, because it was too difficult. But fortunately for us, we had got a steady gig at a club called the Apollo Theatre, where we were playing three times a week and on the weekends. The band was still intact and still tight. So we were making money again — just a little bit because we were living in the hotel for six months and we had to pay hotel bills, too. But it was still craziness. I remember that Fela actually slapped a guy onstage while we were in Accra. That was Y.D. Williams, who was the elder brother of Animashaun. Y.D. was playing tenor sax with us at that time, while Animashaun was playing baritone. Fela gave Y.D. a real dirty slap in front of the whole audience at the Apollo Theater, because he thought Y.D. had insulted him onstage. And after he slapped him, he tried to call his thugs to come and discipline him. I got up from my drums and stopped playing in the middle of the song, and I told those guys, "If you touch that guy, you will all be dead! It's gonna be war for you guys!" What kind of discipline is that? Animashaun himself is already older than Fela, and Y.D. was Animashaun's elder brother! How could you slap somebody older than you like that? And then he was about to be disciplined again by some of Fela's riffraff! Anyway, they reversed back and never touched him. And Y.D. refused to play anymore. He just left the stage.

After the show I went to meet Fela, and I told him, "This surprises me a lot! You can even slap an elderly guy like Animashaun's brother?" I said, "Since I've seen you do that to this guy, I think I myself I could be expecting such a thing the next time!" Fela said, "Ah, no, no, no — never, it can never be!" He was trying to tell me that Y.D. had insulted him. I said, "But how can I trust you now when you have done it to an elderly guy like this?" That was just about the end for me.

After six months we were deported from Ghana, because the problems started again. One night we were busted in the hotel when they found a big bag of grass, and another time Fela got into a dispute with a Syrian man in front of his shop. And the government in Ghana started to look at Fela like "Oh, this guy has a problem in his own country and he wants to come and start another one here."

Fela went free of the weed business, but the government just waited for us to go back to Nigeria. Fela had announced to everybody that he was going back to Nigeria to marry his twenty-seven wives, and that was covered in all the newspapers in Ghana. So they just let us leave Ghana, but after the wedding we were supposed to be coming back. And luckily for me, I never left Lagos by plane with the band, because I was supposed to be driving. They left by plane in the afternoon and I told them that I would drive over to Ghana in the night and arrive in Accra the next afternoon. So I was still preparing myself in the evening when I ran into those same guys that had left in the afternoon by plane! And I asked them, "What are you doing here? You are supposed to be in Ghana!" And they said yes, they had arrived in Ghana but they were sent back with the next plane. The government told them that the musicians could come in, but not Fela. Well, if Fela was not going to come, what were the other musicians going to be doing there? I was lucky not to have taken off yet, otherwise I would have gone to Accra just to find out that those guys were not there.

So then they all moved back to JK's house in Ikeja, and it was from there that they moved to the Decca offices, because of a dispute. The problem was that Decca had asked Fela for eight albums a year, which is incredible! How did they want to sell eight albums in one year? So to fulfill the contract, we just went into the studio and did eight albums in three days—two long songs on each album. Lester Bowie was guesting with us at that time, and he played on a few of those tracks. Fela was just composing those particular songs on the spot. But that caused another problem, because when the year was finished, he wanted to record for another year but out of the original eight albums, only one or two had been released! The others were just sitting there in the can. Some of them are still unreleased today. Decca was refusing to release Fela's music, probably because they were afraid of the government. But Fela wanted his money, so he sued them for breach of contract. It became a war between him and the record company, and it was because of that that he took all of his people and moved them into Decca. They took over the whole Decca complex for about one or two months. Negotiations were going on, but Fela told them that no, he just wanted his money.

But the good thing that happened during all of that craziness with Decca is that that was where the contracts were signed for the Berlin Jazz Festival, which was scheduled for September 1978. So that's when Fela relaxed a little bit and they all moved back to JK's place. By the time the Berlin gig was arranged, Fela owed us so much money — about four months of back salary — and we all felt happy because this big festival gig would finally allow him to pay everybody for the work we had been doing. Because really, things had gone completely haywire ever since the army burned Fela's house down. But he promised everyone that at least the gig would allow him to pay us our back pay. And this was a huge paycheck — about 250,000 US dollars. This was the most he had ever made for a live gig. And it was the most the festival had ever paid a performer. They really wanted him!

For me, I was nearing the end of my rope — not only because of all the money Fela owed me, but because there was just too much insanity inside Fela's organization. People used to come to me all the time and ask, "What the fuck are you doing — why are you staying with Fela? Are you crazy or something? You're too coolheaded for these types of problems. What is it there that's so special for you? Was it Fela's mother that nursed you?" Many of these people were even Fela's friends — members of the elite that he had gone to school with — who used to tell me the same thing. They themselves knew that nothing was coming to me and they used to tell me that I should be shining too, that I should be getting some money and recognition. Because at that point, I'd been putting up with different shit for more than ten years, and even though we were now successful, it wasn't really getting any better. It was only getting crazier. And Fela had already put me in a very difficult position, by making me bandleader when he wasn't treating the band well. That put me in the middle. But maybe he did that deliberately, because his friends used to tell me that when they confronted him about not treating me well, he would tell them, "Ah well, Allenko is a weak leader. He would never agitate." But even after the house was burnt, I still didn't leave right away. Because that was a very crazy time for them and I never left them in the middle of shit before. And the house thing was the worst shit. The worst. So I couldn't leave. I wanted Fela to at least be back on track before I took my decision. And that's what I did when we went to Berlin. Even though I didn't tell many people before we left Lagos, I had told myself that what happened in Berlin was going to be the decider of whether or not I would stay in the band. And as it turned out, what happened there was complete bullshit.

First of all, we went to Berlin with seventy-one people. That means airfare and lodging for seventy-one people, and meanwhile only twenty-eight were actually working! The others? Besides Fela's family, which was only about six people, they were all his imbeciles—the parasites and riffraff that he decided to have as part of his entourage. We should have gone three or four days before the gig so that we could see the city, done the gig, and then left. That way, Fela could have paid us all our back pay and still been sitting on a treasure for himself. But what happened was that all the riffraff that was living in his house in Lagos went on that tour, to do nothing in Berlin, and the whole troupe stayed for two weeks! Fela and his family were staying at the Palace Hotel and the rest were in the Hotel Kampinski. The festival organizers were paying for everything—they knew exactly how the money was being spent, and they couldn't believe it. They weren't thinking that he would come with seventy-one people! So that $250,000 became nothing at the end of the day.

Then it was time to do the gig. We played in the Philharmonic Hall there. The organizers asked me and Ginger Baker and Henry Kofi to open the show with just percussion, and we got a standing ovation—they wouldn't let us leave the stage! And then everyone was waiting for the legend to appear. The gig was good, but Fela tried to lecture the audience about his politics and there were people in that audience that were much heavier in that kind of thinking than he was. They didn't like the way he played the sax and the keyboards, and after a while they started to boo and whistle. The festival paid him that huge fee because he was a legend, but I watched him fuck it up by his manner of approach. After Berlin, we were supposed to tour West Germany and play some other cities like Hamburg and Cologne. But the tour never happened because the newspapers had already printed all the negative shit about the show. Those promoters that wanted to bring him to those other places canceled the gigs. Even Fela himself, when he read the papers the next day, realized that there was no way that he should proceed further. So we had to go back to Nigeria—just like that! The manager called me at the hotel and told me that at eight o'clock, the bus would come to take the band to Fela's hotel and then directly to the airport. This was the day after the gig. And it wasn't supposed to end like that.

But the straw that broke the camel's back was when the musicians came to me as bandleader and asked for their bread so they could go shopping. After all, the guys wanted to change their look, because we were in Europe. They also wanted to buy presents for their people back home because it was getting close to Christmas. But when I called Fela about this, he asked me why hadn't the guys saved their daily allowance? How could he ask us something like that when the allowance he was giving us was twenty deutschmarks per day?—that's twenty deutschmarks to cover breakfast, lunch, and dinner! It was madness, and now he was telling us that he expected us to have money saved out of that twenty! These guys were going back with kids at home, and they couldn't buy a single handkerchief! This was Fela's biggest paycheck ever, and everyone was going home empty-handed. I don't know where the rest of the money went, but at that time Fela was supposed to be running for the presidential elections in Nigeria and so he had to use the money for his campaign. At least, that's what he told me.

When Fela told me that I called the guys and I told them that, first of all, I was no longer inside this Africa 70 thing—as of *today*. And then I told them that Fela said they should have saved their allowances if they wanted to go shopping. So then they asked me, but what about their salaries? And I told them that Fela said he doesn't have one penny to give to anybody now. Forget about the back pay. Forget even about being paid for the gig itself! We never got paid a single cent for the gig. As soon as I gave them this news, they all entered their rooms, took their bags, and walked out of the hotel. I didn't know where they were going, but I wasn't going to stop them. Even some of them didn't know where they themselves were going. But about eight of them just took off, like that. Some of them are still living there in Berlin today.

Before we left Lagos, I had already told Fela that I would be going to London after the end of the tour. Henry Kofi and I were doing some work with Ginger there, and Virgin wanted to license my album *Progress* for distribution. And he told me it wasn't a problem. So when the bus arrived, I went to Fela and told him that I would meet them in Lagos, and asked him for my own money. Because while I was talking to him about the band's money, I never mentioned my own money. And he called to his assistant Steve Udah and told him, "Steve, give Allenko, eh, fifty deutschmarks." Fifty fucking deutschmarks—it's ridiculous, man! At that time, fifty deutschmarks was like eighteen Nigerian naira. I didn't want to argue with him in the bus. And then he left Berlin without even giving me my ticket back to Lagos! I had to make the festival people call him and tell him to send me my ticket. Remember—this was the same year that my father drew up a new conveyance for this guy! This was the final straw for me.

At the time, I still planned to go to London, and that meant I had to deal with the German immigration people. Luckily for me, I had an old Ghanaian girlfriend named Felicia who was living in Berlin at that time.

And she told me, "Tony, you cannot go to the immigration people without money in your pocket." So she took me to the bank the next morning and withdrew one thousand deutschmarks for me. But the woman at immigration was giving me so many problems. She acted like she didn't speak English, so I told her, "You people, you come to my country, you get employment, you live there coolly and nobody tells them to move your ass out of the country. So why are you giving me this problem? Do you think I want to live in this country? I'm not even dreaming of it! Even if you asked me to live here, I'm not going to live here. All I want from you is a reentry visa from you, so I can go to London and then go back to Nigeria." Then she spoke English with me and gave me what I needed. But once I had my ticket to Lagos in hand, I decided to stay there in Berlin for about a month and a half. I never went to the UK.

The festival organizers really helped me while I was in Berlin. They liked me a lot, and one of the organizers named Bruno even told me that if I wanted to live there in West Germany, he would arrange everything for me. I thanked him, but I didn't accept their offer because their way of life in Germany is not for me. I didn't feel the atmosphere, and after a month and a half I went back to Nigeria.

When I finally arrived back in Lagos I went to Fela's place. We sat down and smoked, then he asked me, "So you are back. How was Berlin?" I didn't want to say anything much. I just said looked at him and said, "My money." "Ah," he said, "Your money. Come tomorrow." The next day when I came back, he said I should give him two weeks. After two weeks, I went back and he called his cousin Fola, the paymaster who handled the money. And he told Fola, "Whatever amount Allenko is owed, give him half of it." He said this right in front of me! I said, "Why half? Look, you don't remember that this is long-time-ago bread? It's not bread of now! You owe it to me. I have worked for that!" He told me he was going to give me the rest, but it was that we just came back from Europe and the money was gone because of his political campaign. So I should just give him two weeks more. So they gave me the half, but when I went back two weeks later, the rest of my money still wasn't there. I went back again two weeks after that, and the money still wasn't coming. So I stopped asking.

Meanwhile, every time I went to Fela's house I saw him rehearsing, trying to get another band together. Some of the previous guys were still there, because in the end some of them simply weren't able to leave Fela.

And some of the others stayed because they were not sure of whether or not I was saying the truth when I told them I was leaving. They were rehearsing with four drummers, and I knew three of them — Ganiyu, Ringo, and one guy called Sunday. The fourth guy I didn't know. You know, Fela always had ways to trick people into doing things. Maybe he thought that by seeing all those other drummers, I would get uptight and want my gig back. But I didn't give a shit, because I had already taken my decision. So I never paid any attention to the band business.

But as it turned out, nothing was happening with the four drummers and Fela saw that I wasn't coming to play. A little while after that, I was hanging with some of my friends in the old Kalakuta area in Idi-Oro, and some of Fela's musicians came from practice and told me that he had disbanded because the music wasn't happening. He told them that anybody that wants to play should reapply. That's what all the Nigerian bandleaders do if there's a dispute. They disband and then force everyone to reapply. Then everyone has to beg for their job back, usually at a lower salary. So when those boys came to tell me that Fela had disbanded, I jumped up and said, "Yeah, that is it!" I never actually told him that I had left, but now he was starting to realize it. One month, two months, three months, and then he was forced to disband. And that was good for me because when he didn't see my application, then he'd know that I had left for good. In the end, Fela got a new band together after many months, but it was never gonna be anything like what we had with Africa 70. So I was very happy that day and I was drinking all over the place. I made sure I celebrated. Now I was properly free!

At this point, some people came to me and asked me to come back to Fela's band. They told me, "Don't worry about Fela, we will pay you ourselves." But I just told them, "Thank you, but it's not your problem." You see, they were my fans that liked my playing and everything, but I was not working for those guys, man. Three months later, some of Fela's wives went to complain to him that since I'd left, the music was getting weak and they didn't feel like dancing anymore. And Fela told them that no, I hadn't gone, I had just decided to rest for a while. They told him, "You must be crazy — he's gone for good!"

And so Fela sent for me and I went. And he asked me, "Is it true that you've left the band?" I told him yes. He asked me, "What is the reason?" And I told him, "Three reasons. One: one of your wives — as long as she's your wife in this organization, — I can never be there, because we don't get along. She's a troublemaker for me. I cannot tell you to send your wife away. So I have to find my own solution. Two: I see that Animashaun is now the leader of the band. So what do you want me to do — come back and make Animashaun step down again? No, I ain't gonna do that because I'm a Lagosian and I don't want to wrestle a fight where I don't see my opponent." You see, on the plane to Berlin I had told Animashaun about my plans to leave if Fela didn't pay us. I confided in him as a friend. And he told me that it was going to be his last gig too unless Fela paid us. But on the plane going back to Lagos, he revealed everything to Fela. Animashaun did this because he himself wanted to be bandleader, and he saw that this was his opportunity. Fela himself told me this that day when we were talking.

Then I reminded Fela about everything that happened with my album *No Accommodation*. We recorded that track at the same session as "She and She" ("Shuffering and Shmiling"). "It took us three days to finish 'She and She,' but it took us six months to finish 'No Accommodation,' because you insisted on redoing your tenor sax solo, even though the first solo was excellent. It took you two months to do that! Every day, you kept telling me to book the studio, and I waited in the studio every day for two months, morning 'til night, and you never showed up! Finally, you came to the studio to replay the solo. This one was not as good as the first one, but it was still okay. But you told me that that solo was still not good and that you had to replay it. That took another two months! And what could I do? It wasn't finished until you said it was finished because you had the contract with Decca and you were producing the album. You came in to do the third solo two months later, and it was the worst solo I've ever heard. But I accepted it. Then when it came time to mix you told me to book the studio for the next day, and it took another two months for you to come in and mix! So in the end, I waited every fucking day for six months!"

But, you see, there was another side to the story about "No Accommodation." Fela had produced my first album in '75, which was called *Jealousy*. He had produced the second one, which was called *Progress*, in '76. Then it came time for the third one, which was in the making around '78. And one night Fela came down to the club while the band was already playing. In fact, we were playing "No Accommodation." He listened to it and said, "Wow! Who wrote this?" And they told him, "It's Allenko." And Fela told me, "Allenko, you are there — now you are really there!" He said to me, "The way you write, it's going to take a jazz bass player to play your lines!" That was his way of complimenting me. Because we had two different ways of composing. Fela was composing like a trained musician. For myself, I never went to music school, but I was gifted my own way. You see, I write like a drummer, and if you check the way I'm writing sometimes, you don't see any instruments clashing. Composing Afrobeat, everything is supposed to be interwoven. That's the way I look at it. It's boring if it's like a monologue. It should be like a conversation. And whoever is writing the music has to make sure we all have something to say in the conversation. The instruments must be talking to each other. That means the instruments are all going to be playing different things. That's how the great traditional guys did it, like Haruna Ishola. You see, I've learned my lessons from listening to traditional music, man. And it took until *No Accommodation* for me to really get my composing right. But when it came time to actually record it, I don't think Fela wanted me to succeed.

But I wanted to end on a positive note. I told him, "Let us just stay as brothers and friends. It's better like this, and I'm still at your service. If you need me on your recordings, I'm still available." Then he asked me, "How do you live now? What are you doing for money?" I simply told him, "There is a God." And he said, "Oh, yeah, I understand your God." And then I walked out of his room.

I still saw him every day anyway, at least for a while. We would talk and discuss different things. One day he told me that the *Daily Times* was promoting a tour of Nigeria with him and Roy Ayers, and he wanted me to come on tour and assist the sound engineer because I knew his sound. I agreed to do it since I wasn't on his payroll anymore; the *Daily Times* and the tour organizers were paying me, you know? So I went with them on that tour for one month, and we ended up in the studio with Roy Ayers. That's where Fela wrote "Africa, Center of the World." It was like an instant composition in the studio, and he asked please would I play this one for him? So that's why I played on that song. That was the last one. And then I went my own way.

When I left Fela, it was because God told me to do it. Fela used to often say that any musician who left his band would never get anywhere. It was almost like he was putting a curse on them. And some of the guys that left did end up coming back. But in my own case, God just entered my mind and said, "Now is the time. You don't know what you're going to do, but if you don't do it this time, you'll never be able to do it. So just go." I wasn't going to try to make Fela aware of all the things he did to me over the years. That was beneath me. All the things I did for him over the years, I was treating him like a brother. So if what he did in Berlin was the only way he could think to pay me back for all of my loyalty, then thank you very much. I never even tried to contest it. And I never looked for revenge. Revenge is not in my dictionary. I don't believe in it at all because the people that do bad always get it back. It might not be from the same person they did the bad to, but it must always come back from somewhere.

Fela could have had a realization. He could have felt like "I've lost almost everything. Let me not lose this guy, too." But I wasn't really expecting that from him. In 1978, he had too many problems to face. Too many distractions. One, his mother had died after the attack on Kalakuta. Two, he didn't have his house anymore. Three, he blew all of his Berlin bread on the presidential election, and in the end they did not even let him register. Four, he needed to play to make some of his money back again, and the band was going haywire.

And so Berlin was my last show with Fela. In the end, all the Nigerian bandleaders have the same style when it comes to money. Fela was doing the same thing that all the other bandleaders had done before. His music was new, but not his way of handling the money. The lifestyle of a musician is like gambling—it is a risk. I gave up a steady gig with Adeolu and the Western Toppers back in 1965 and jumped into a big shit with Fela. I had a good, steady life with the Toppers, but I left for where life was going to be crazy, and there was going to be a lot of bullshit! And it took me fifteen years to get that bullshit off my neck. But it was worth it for me musically. I was interested in playing with Fela more than the others because I was thinking about the future more than the present. I never felt that I lost anything by staying for fifteen years. Sometimes it seemed like a waste of time, but today I can say I'm reaping the benefits. That's the way I look at it.

If it's money we are talking about, even then, I'm not sure I should be lamenting anything. Even when I left, it was more about principle than money. The money was lacking, but you cannot have everything at the same time. And if it had only been about money, I would have left way back at the beginning when I saw where the money was going and how it was being spent. When the army burned his property down, things were lost and there was no way anyone could retrieve them. It was impossible. But, you know, life continues. You must keep living. But after that he was getting so involved with the issue of the government and it became really scary for everyone around him. That's when I left. That was our destiny. It had been written that we would do something very powerful together and at a certain point we would part.

I stayed as long as I did because I was musically happy, and looking back on it, I feel great about what I did with that band. Back then when I was doing it, I just thought of it as my handiwork. It was my job and I simply had to deliver. So I just kept on going. It's only when I look back on it now and listen that I start to ask, "Really, is that me that played all this stuff?" I can hear that I've really done something significant in the past!

PROGRESS

7 It was now 1979 and after fifteen years I had finally left Fela, but I didn't have anything happening on my own side. So I decided to do some freelancing and see what was gonna come next. After a while I thought, as long as there's music involved, let me check out what's happening in the church, just to get something going. I'm talking about what they call the "Celestial Church" in Nigeria. Some of the guys in that church were my friends, and they asked me, "If you're not doing anything, why not come play church music, and maybe things will be fine?" Well, why not? If we're talking about God, maybe the nearest place to see God is wherever he's located. At least, that's what I thought. And I can adapt quickly to anything. So I started going to this church near my house on Tejuosho Road and playing in the band with them.

As a matter of fact, I was born Catholic, so this Celestial Church thing was not really my style. Their style is what we call a "free church." It doesn't have all the rules of the Catholic Church. But it's good music in that church, man! In that band we had trumpet, sax, drums, bass, guitar, and keyboards, plus a lot of chorus singers. The music was for dancing. It's not couples dancing. You will dance where you are, and when they stop the music you can pray for some time, and then the music starts up again. It's kind of like gospel music. But as time went on, I found out that there were a lot of things happening in that church that I didn't really fancy. There was a lot of hypocrisy of people trying to preach one thing and doing something else behind. For example they always say, "Don't drink, don't smoke, don't do this, don't do that," and they themselves were doing all those things after church was finished. Well, I didn't say what they were doing was wrong, because I'm not going to tell anybody what they're doing is wrong. But I don't want anybody in front of me trying to tell me this is how it should be, or this is what you should do, while they themselves are going to do something else. As long as they try to put both of those sides together — what they were calling "the bad" and "the good" — then they are part of the bad side, too. Still, I believed in God and I knew that God has done a lot for me. So I decided that from then on, I myself should be talking directly to God for what I need rather than having somebody trying to communicate for me. That's why I left the church, and from then on I decided to have my own way of communicating with God.

Another interesting thing I did around this time was organized by my friend Bayo Martins, who was my friend from the Koola Lobitos days. In 1979, Bayo organized a "Drum Assembly" with himself, me, Remi Kabaka, and Kofi Ghanaba, at the National Theater in Lagos. That show was put together by Bayo along with the National Theater and the Reverend Sisters, which was an organization of Catholic nuns. Bayo was always on the intellectual side of things — besides being a drummer, he was also a writer and a journalist. Remi was my old friend. Kofi Ghanaba was coming from Ghana. That was actually my first time meeting him. He was like the father of African drum set playing, and we all knew him from when he was playing with E. T. Mensah, back when he was known as Guy Warren. I really respected him because when he went to Europe and the US back in the '40s, he was not playing congas or percussion, he was promoting himself as a drum set player, and he played with some very heavy jazz musicians like Charlie Parker. Even just seeing his own drum set up showed me that this guy was a real original. He had invented his own style of trap drums using traditional Ghanaian drums instead of tom-toms, but with kick drum and cymbals. I saw that as like the opening of what we are all supposed to be doing with the traps in Africa.

It was a beautiful show. The first part was a choir and the army band from Abalti Barracks, directed by Olu Obokun, playing the "Hallelujah Chorus," with Kofi accompanying them on his drums. Seeing him play those drums with the "Hallelujah Chorus" was great, man! After that, it was just the four of us playing for the rest of the night. All of us played trap drums except Kofi, who was playing his own set. One of us would solo while the other three just kept the groove. That was really a fantastic show! So you see, I was even playing some religious music now. Fela would be totally against something like that, but I didn't give a shit because I just wanted to be myself and I didn't want to be under the umbrella of anyone dictating to me what I should be. It took me a long time to be able to reach that conclusion in life.

After that, I stayed at home a lot, and also continued freelancing. Sometimes I would work with a juju band led by a guy named Oludayo who had a group called Oludayo and His Rhythms, but I cannot remember his last name. I did some recording with them in the studio, and I also worked a little with one of Sunny Ade's guitarists, a guy named Bob Oladeniyi. Later on I started to play with a guy named Tee-Mac Iseli at a club called the Lords which was near Ikorodu Road. Tee-Mac is a flautist and he had an Afro-rock band called Tee-Mac and the Afro Collection back in the '70s. He also did some other things in the music business. Tee-Mac is a very successful businessman and a guy that always treated musicians with respect. His band was the best-paying gig in Lagos. We were playing gigs at the Lords, and we also recorded television programs there. We actually recorded thirteen weeks' worth of television programs that were broadcast on the Nigerian Television Authority (NTA). So I hung with Tee-Mac until that year ended. That was around the end of 1979.

In that period when I was freelancing, I also did some gigs with a guy named Steve Rhodes. Steve was a writer and arranger and he had his own band. He was also putting on some shows on the NTA, so he was recording on location in the main hall at the University of Lagos. One day he told me that there was a part of the show where he wanted to use two drummers together, along with a guy named Jimi Solanke who was singing a type of traditional music that we call *ewi*, which is kind of a Yoruba "native blues" type of thing. The other drummer was Remi Kabaka. But what happened was that Steve only gave us notice like two weeks before the thing was supposed to be televised, and in the meantime, Remi had gone away to London. On the day of the show, I arrived there with my drums, and Steve had another drum set there already, waiting for Remi. I kept on asking Steve Rhodes, "Uncle Steve, where is Remi?" It got later and later and Remi still wasn't there. So finally I asked, "Since Remi is not here, can I play double bass drums?" That means two bass drums, two pedals, and all the drums. Actually, Steve himself was asking me if I would be able to do that.

Well, I had never played double bass drums before, even though I had seen Ginger and Mitch Mitchell do it. So I said, let's give it a try! I put my snare in the middle, and switched back and forth with my left leg onto the hi-hat. I tried it and balanced it for the television engineers, and the show came on. I really enjoyed playing like that, but one thing I didn't like about it was that I was missing my hi-hat at times because of all the switching between pedals. But it was a nice show, with Jimi singing his ewi music. Just singing and drumming and no other instruments, and it was really something, it was actually fantastic! But since then I haven't played any double bass drum stuff. It's not really my thing.

It was during this freelancing time in 1979 that I got my album *No Discrimination* together. The album came out on a label called Shanu-Olu records. Mr. Shanu-Olu was the proprietor, and he had a chain of different businesses in Lagos—like a bakery, and he also made cement bricks for building. He had also built his own recording studio, which was a huge complex out in Ijebu-Ode, which is about one hundred kilometers from Lagos. Mr. Shanu-Olu heard that I had left Fela and he knew that I had already put out three strong albums. So my vocalist Candido Obajimi and me went to meet him and he gave the money for the recording. So this man kind of rescued me. It was because of him that I had my own record out and I could continue into the '80s with my own band, and my own original music to play.

That *No Discrimination* album is Afrobeat, but it's got a very different and a very unique sound. If I wanted to continue doing this Afrobeat thing, I was going to have to make it completely different from what I was doing with Fela, because there's no way I would be able to do Fela better than Fela. Now that I was free, I was trying to put in things that were not usually there in Afrobeat. I was trying to use more modern instruments like synthesizers, for example. If you program them and find a good sound, it's good for the music. Fela refused to use them in his music, but me, I wanted them. Actually, I suggested them when we were producing my own albums with Africa 70, but Fela said no. I also included some guitar solos on that album. That's why the *No Discrimination* album sounds like that, and it's a great album. Not everybody in Nigeria liked it, though, because they were used to Fela's typical Afrobeat sound. Unfortunately, Mr. Shanu-Olu's studio was only running for about two years, and then it went down the drain because of mismanagement. After that his headquarters burned down, with all of our printed records in there. It was like his life's work went up in smoke, man—just like that! Mr. Shanu-Olu died shortly after that.

It was sometime after that, probably in early '80, when Animashaun's brother Y. D. Williams called me. You remember that Y.D. had left Fela's band after Fela slapped him onstage in Ghana. But Y.D. had a friend in Lagos named Mr. Lawal that he had schooled together with—I think it was in Manchester, in the UK. Mr. Lawal was a marketing manager of one of those Indian factories in Lagos where they print cloth, like for clothing. He was a nice guy that had some money. And because Y.D. had left Fela's band, he needed money. Mr. Lawal felt that the best way to help Y.D. was to help him get a band together. It takes bread to get a band together, man. Someone has to buy the instruments and everything, and that's why every band needs a sponsor or a patron. The band also needs someone who knows how to compose. Y.D. was a player, but he was not really into composing and all those things. So he asked me, why don't I come meet his friend and give him the list of what we need as instruments, and start a band? Y.D. also wanted me to write the music for the band. It was time for me to try to do my own thing anyway. So I went to meet Mr. Lawal, who was just living walking distance from my house, and we arranged everything. Soon after that I met him in his office, we went out together to the bank, and he gave me the money to buy all of the instruments and amplifiers and PA system for the band. I already had my own drums.

And that was it. It was really my band, and I named them the Mighty Irokos. The iroko tree is a huge tree in Nigeria—it's so big that you could build a house inside of it if you wanted! It's kind of a spiritual tree that is so mighty, it looks like it could live forever. That's where I got that name from. I wrote all the compositions, and my friend Candido was the vocalist. I also got Tunde Williams to join, from Fela's band. I rehearsed them in a club just near my house called Club Chicago that was owned by the highlife musician Roy Chicago. I asked them to let me rehearse there to get the repertoire together, and then we would play on weekends.

Meanwhile, another contract had come in from Calabar for a gig at a place called the Maryland Hotel. The proprietors were Mr. and Mrs. Oku, and they wanted discuss a one-year contract in Calabar. They wanted a guy named Willy Bestman to sing, because I guess they had heard him in Calabar before. Actually, Willy Bestman was a very good singer. So we decided to go on to Calabar and leave Lagos alone for a while. We were supposed to go for one year, but I stopped it at six months, because things were not too good with Mr. Oku and his wife. They started to play tricks with the money, and I didn't want to pass through that bullshit again. We needed money to eat, and they were only thinking about their commission.

We also started to have problems when we went on tour to the North, because Tunde Williams and Y.D. got into an argument in Kaduna and it ended up that Y.D. was refusing to play the concert that night. I told him, "Look, we have only two horns. If you let Tunde go up there alone, it's not funny, because we are playing in a nice club." I was mad with him and I didn't care whether the instruments were coming from his connection or not. I just told him, "You cannot continue to blackmail me like this. If you don't come to play tonight, it's going to be the end of you in this band!" But he never came for the gig. He stayed in the hotel and didn't play. So the band had already started falling apart.

We also all got locked up in Jos. Jos is a city with so much corruption, but we weren't involved in anything. It was just that we were playing a club and they also had call girls living in there. That was none of our business, but when the police came to raid the place, they arrested us too as musicians. All these ups and downs with the band, man—I was thinking that I couldn't do one whole year with these people! And it wasn't really happening on the musical side anyway. So after six months I got tired of all the hassles and told everybody that we had to go back to Calabar. Y.D. took off straight to Lagos, on his own. But when I told Mr. and Mrs. Oku that I was going back to Lagos, Mrs. Oku took all the instruments and had them locked up in the police station and said that only Mr. Lawal would be able to retrieve them. Well, I had my drums with me anyway. So I went back to Lagos and dropped the musicians off, and then went to meet Mr. Lawal. I told him that his instruments were impounded in the police station in Calabar and that I wanted to give them back to him. He gave me a note and Y.D. and I took it to the police in Calabar. We arrived back in Lagos with the instruments, and I drove to his house and dropped everything off there. I told him, "Here you are, you can give them to anybody now, to go and make money with. But me, I wash my hands of this whole deal!" And I took my drums and I went back home. So that was the end of the first Mighty Irokos. That was around the end of 1980.

Back in the '60s when I was with Koola Lobitos, there was a young boy named Seyi that I had brought into the band to play shaker. Fela had asked me, "How are we going to pay him?" I told him, "The boy is living in my house with me and eating my own food. So he can play for you but just find something to give him. At least, at the end of the month, you can just give him something." Then when Seyi got a little older he left the band, and I took him to where I was working at Associated Press because he had just got a place to live and he had to pay his rent. They gave him a job taking over for me when I was not around.

Well, by 1980 Seyi was a big boy. And he had all these brand-new musical instruments—Pearl drums, bass guitar, keyboard, amplifiers, and all these things. I don't know how he managed to get them, and I didn't ask any questions. But he wanted to get a band together. So I asked him to let me use the instruments so that we could make some money together. Meanwhile I had some Camerounian boys around that I had met while we were in Calabar—they followed me back to Lagos. Since they didn't have anywhere to live, Seyi lodged them in one of his houses. We started to work, but as soon as these boys received their first salary at the end of the month, they disappeared and we never saw them again! Well, I had to employ others just to keep going. But then Seyi himself started to get a very big head. At least, that's what it seemed like to me, because he freaked out one day and insulted me at the club. I said, "Oh yeah? If you can talk to me like this, now it means you're coming to me like a boss! Boss of who? You will never tell me anything about being a boss of anyone! Because I don't want to say 'I made you,' but I think I made you. Whatever you are today, I made you, and so what is it that you have done to make you feel so arrogant?" I just told him, "Take your fucking instruments—take them away! I ain't touching those instruments anymore!"

After that I went to see Tunji Braithwaite. Braithwaite was Fela's lawyer, and they were supposed to be collaborating for Fela's political party. But they fell out. So I just went to his office one day. He was always curious about what I was doing, and when he asked me what I had happening, I had to tell him the truth, which was "Nothing." I told him, "Every time someone gives me a set of instruments, there's too much bullshit around it." He asked me, "Is that your problem? How much does it cost to purchase a set of instruments?" I told him I should be able to do it with maybe three thousand naira or something like that. He told me that he was going to the States that night, but that I should come to his office the following Monday and the secretary would give me the check. I thought he was joking! But I tried my luck anyway. I went Monday and the secretary was waiting for me. And she gave me the check—immediately! I couldn't believe my eyes! So I went straight to the American Bank, cashed the check, and put the money in a plastic bag because it was a lot of money. Straight away I left from there and went to Seyi's house. I asked him, "All your instruments, how much do they cost?" He said it was about twenty-five hundred naira or something like that. I told him I that I could give him two thousand in cash, right there. He agreed, and I put all the instruments in my car and drove them to my house. I still had one thousand naira left, and I finally had my own instruments! So I was ready to start up the Mighty Irokos again, and I got back some of the guys who originally went with me to Calabar, like Tunde Williams and a few other guys who had left Fela's band, like Leke Benson, who was a guitarist; Jallo (Kalanky Jallo Clement), who was a bass player from Liberia; a saxophonist named Patiki (or something like that); and another guitarist named Idowu. Then I had Benjamin Ijagun on percussion. Ijagun actually started out as a guitarist from the army band under my old friend Ojo Okeji, but before that he was one of the artists from Osogbo doing the "spirit" paintings, like Twins Seven-Seven, who is famous for that. Ijagun is in the States now, and Idowu also left later on to study in the States. Then I got a guy named Raimi Olalowo to play trombone, who used to play with Osibisa in London. Once I got the instruments, it was easy to pull the guys back together. So when all those guys came to join me, the band was rolling, and we started playing at a club called the Pussycat, which was on Wakeman Street (they later renamed it Borno Street), in Yaba. This was in the first part of 1981.

The only problem we had was with the singing. Candido had sung on my other albums, but he left as soon as we returned from Calabar, because he said he wanted to move into sound engineering. So I had to start trying different guys, like Lekan Oke, who was a good singer. You see, I would deal with any singer who was on my own wavelength. But I didn't want to deal with any singer that thinks he's the leader of the band just because he's out there in front singing. I've dealt with many singers like that, and that kind of shit drives me crazy! So that's why the band was kind of on and off. The funny thing is that around that same time, Fela had his spies to come around me and check out what I was up to. He was always sending his spies, and these people went back to him to tell him that "Allenko is okay, he just has a problem finding a proper lead singer." And Fela told them, "That is his only problem? Then Allenko himself is going to sing one day. He's definitely going to sing." And that's exactly what happened, because right after that I started singing myself. That was a tough job, man — to sing along with playing my drums. I was trying but it disturbed my regularity on the drums, you know? But I started to do that, very slowly. I didn't want to force myself too quickly.

It wasn't easy gigging in Lagos in those years, man. If I have to tell you the truth, the music thing in Lagos was finished since around 1978 because nobody was safe in the night anymore. Back in the highlife days when we were getting started and Lagos was really swinging, I remember starting to take my shower at twelve midnight, just to get ready to go out! And when I went out, it was like daytime for me—I could go anywhere, without disturbance. Even by 1977 it was still cool, more or less. There were some robbers out there, like some boys that would snatch your jewelry at night when you were coming from a party. But they were just normal petty robbers. They might gang up to catch two or three people, and take their things and let them go. They never harmed anyone. But when Shehu Shagari came in with that rigged election in 1979, that's when the real problems started. Although it was supposed to be a civilian government now, the soldiers never really left, and there were guns all over the place! There were already guns inside the army barracks, but now there were a lot of guns outside too. On top of that, there were many guns left over from the civil war. All the guns that came into the country for the war started to circulate. After the war, nobody could give any account of how many guns were issued. If they issued a gun to a certain soldier, and that soldier is dead, then where's the gun? They killed so many on both sides, and the guns that were taken from the dead soldiers ended up on the black market later. So there were no more normal thieves chasing you, man. It was no more petty crime like before. Armed crime started happening, and by 1978 it was becoming rampant. Because of all this, people started lynching criminals. The lynching started from around 1978.

All this is why by the '80s, nobody wanted to go out. Living in Lagos was almost like living in a prison. People weren't free in their own fucking country. To go out to enjoy yourself at night was like looking for trouble. The only two people pulling a crowd in Lagos at that time were Fela and Sunny Ade, and they made it because they had their own clubs. Sunny's club was called Ariya, on Ikorodu Road, and of course Fela had his new Afrika Shrine out in Ikeja. What that really meant was that if you went out to Sunny's club, you didn't want to go back home in the middle of the night because there was too much armed robbery on the road. You would probably stay in the club until like six o'clock in the morning, when everyone started going to work. Then you could go back home because the sun was up and everybody was on the street again. It was the same thing with Fela's Shrine. If you went to the Shrine, you had better stay 'til dawn! Some people would even decide to go directly to work from there. And that's why whoever was playing had to be very strong to draw a crowd. Because whoever puts his feet in that Shrine knows he's not going to leave until daybreak.

It was very hard for Fela around this time, too. He had been through a lot of shit, and people were starting to say he had gone mad since he got into his spiritualist stuff. It was really a witchcraft type of thing. He and his people went completely into the black magic way of life. Probably some of his wives got him into it, along with some other people. Everybody was counseling him against this stuff, including me. We had all passed through this stuff because it's part of our culture. But he himself never grew up with that in his own background, because his background was Christian. I even remember an argument that Fela had back in the Koola Lobitos days with our percussionist Isiaka. Isi was talking about how these *babalawos* (Yoruba traditional herbalists) could affect you—how they could create illness or insanity, or even eliminate you altogether without being anywhere near you. And Fela jumped up and told Isi that he was talking nonsense and superstition. He told us that people used to refer to his own mother, Mrs. Ransome-Kuti, as a witch because of all the powerful things she accomplished. But Fela said that was all nonsense—that she wasn't a witch, she was just a very clever and strong woman. Isi didn't like this, and he told Fela that he had the mentality of a child and that he didn't have a deep understanding of African life. They went back and forth, but the point is that you can see how Fela felt about these things at that time. He was not the type of guy that believed in all these things.

But after all the stuff he had been through, he was getting into black magic now and he wouldn't listen to anybody. I used to go talk to him as a friend at his house sometimes, and it was a big surprise for me to see them pounding different kinds of substances together, like herbs and tiger skin, for the things they were doing. He was believing that this stuff could protect him from the soldiers and that he could use it to communicate with the spirit of his mother. Some of his friends even hinted to me that Fela was doing some little things behind the scenes to get me to come back into the band. I wasn't worried about that, but he was so much into this shit that he was hardly leaving his house anymore except when he was playing. But his music was still excellent, man. I would go to the Shrine, and the new music he was composing was so heavy, man, I would get completely lost in it sometimes. Just because I left, it doesn't mean his music died, man—no! The only thing missing was the engine, and that was making his music suffer. And we both knew it. He would look out and see me sitting there, and I knew what was going through his mind. And he knew what was going through my mind. Sometimes I would find myself wishing that I was up there playing those fucking drums, man! All kinds of ideas were passing through my head about which patterns I would play inside that music. But when I thought about how much bull- shit I would have to go through all over again, I chased those thoughts out of my head.

People were also really listening to Fela's music in Europe, and it was around that same time — 1982 — when Martin Meppiel and his brother Stefan started coming to Nigeria. They were from France, and they were working with an Afro- beat group called Ghetto Blaster that they wanted to take to France to produce. They managed to get about three guys from Fela's band — Ringo, who was a drummer, Udoh, who played congas, and a guitarist named Kiala. And then they got Willie Nfor, a bassist from Cameroon. The only thing they were missing was a good singer. The Meppiels were coming to me because they wanted me to play in Ghetto Blaster. I played with them for a little while, because they were using my instruments in Nige- ria since my band was not happening too much at the time. I was also in their video. But Ringo was there, so why did I want to play as two drum- mers? It was kind of like they didn't know exactly what they wanted to do, so I just told them, "Go ahead and leave Ringo there, because I'm not going to Europe. So, just get this thing done and take them." That was it, and the Meppiel brothers took them on to France.

It was also around this time that I met Martin Meissonnier. Martin is another French producer who was really into African music and he wanted to do something with Nigerian music. He really helped me a lot in my career. Actually, he wanted to do something with Fela at first. They started on some things, but then they fell out because Martin brought Fela to Europe two times, and the second time was his downfall. He went bankrupt the second time he brought Fela to Europe. But he kept going. After that he worked on a project with Fela's old friend Sandra, from Los Angeles. Sandra had her own project going as a singer, and Martin was going to produce her. They went to Fela and asked him to write eight songs for her, and he told them that they would have to stay in Nigeria for eight months and that he would write one song a month. They felt that was unreasonable and they didn't want to do that, so when Martin came to Nigeria, he and Sandra came to watch my band at the Pussycat.

Martin told me afterwards that he didn't like my band. He thought that it was me alone that was happening in the band. But we had made contact and he said he would find me when he came back to Lagos, because he wanted me to work on Sandra's project. Tee-Mac was involved too. So even though I was having a lot of problems keeping my band going, it was really at the Pussycat that things started happening for me.

When Martin came back to work on Sandra's project, it was sometime in 1982. Chris Blackwell and Island Records put up the money for the project. We started rehearsing in Lagos, and then we went to do the recordings in Lome, Togo. After we finished our work on the backing tracks in Togo, they took the tapes away to London to put Sandra's vocals on and to mix. But Sandra later told me that it was very strange, what happened in London—every night when she went to the studio to record her vocals, she lost her voice—it just disappeared and she couldn't sing anything! Chris had already dealt with these kinds of strange things in Jamaica, and he felt suspicious that something was going on somewhere, and he decided to forget about the project. But they did eventually use one track that I wrote, called "Traffic Jam," as part of that documentary about Fela called *Music Is the Weapon*. They used it without the lyrics, under the film credits. I don't know what happened after that because the rest of that music was never released. That was the business of Martin and Island, and probably the music is still there in their cupboard.

We're now around the beginning of 1983, and I was still playing with the Mighty Irokos at the Pussycat. Martin came back to Lagos, and this time he was working with Sunny Ade and having a lot of success in Europe and America. I knew Sunny from back in the old days when Koola Lobitos used to play with them at island clubs for the elites. At that time, he was very rootsy. Not like the Sunny of today with all the electronic stuff. Martin wanted me to play on a track on Sunny's album that he was producing. So one night when I finished at the Pussycat, I went over to Sunny's Ariya club and I was supposed to be featured that night on the song that Sunny wanted to record the next day in Lome, at the same studio where we worked on Sandra's project. There was also a French girl there named Catherine that was working with Martin as the sound engineer. So I went there and played the song with Sunny's band, since my house was not too far from there. But as I was driving home past the Yaba bus stop, I got into an accident and I lost control of my car. That was very strange. I wasn't drunk and I was driving coolly. Leke was in the front with me, and Ijagun was in the back. Those boys got some serious bruises, man. And for me, the windshield shattered and went directly into my eyes. It was heavy pain for me, but I didn't want to go to the hospital. I just tried to treat myself with some eyedrops.

The next day was Sunday, and Martin and I were supposed to fly to Lome. I told him what had happened, and I tried to explain to him the strange way this accident happened. There was like some kind of trickery involved, as if someone didn't want me there at the club that night. It was like someone among Sunny's people just didn't want me to participate in that project. I didn't want to mention anyone's name specifically, but I knew.

When Martin saw my eyes, he said that maybe it was best if we didn't travel that day, that we should go on the following Tuesday. That gave me time to relax at home properly and treat my eyes. Tuesday came and Sunny's guys had already gone to Lome by bus. Martin and I arrived later by plane. Just as the taxi drove up to the studio, Sunny's guys were coming out the door, and the person in front was the drummer, Moses Akanbi. Akanbi was playing drums for a long time before he got with Sunny's band. He was coming from Eddie Okonta's band to Orlando Julius's band and from Orlando Julius to Sunny. Akanbi was good for the type of things we were playing back home. But there's only one pattern that he was able to take off me. And he was playing it in reverse.

When Akanbi saw me there, he was shocked! He said, "Ah, so you are here!" I was standing there with a patch on my eye and I said, "Yeah, Sunny said I should play one track." "Ah," he said, "that would be very good." We set up the studio that day and then everybody left for the hotel.

We came back the next day for the recording. Sunny was in the control room with the engineer and Martin. And suddenly something inside my head told me, "You haven't learned your lesson yet? You want more?" So I called Martin outside and I told him, "I'm sorry for this inconvenience and for the money you have paid for the flight, and I know you'll be shocked by what I want to tell you. But I just decided that I won't play that track. I'm not going to play it." He asked me, "Why?" I told him, "You are a white man and you don't live here. You are going back to your France and I'll be left here with the consequences. If you don't understand what I'm trying to say, I'm sorry. But I'm not playing this track. That's all." I really didn't care whether Martin understood or not, because I'm a Nigerian and I knew what I was talking about. So he said in that case, I should go tell Sunny.

So I went back into the control room, and I tapped Sunny and told him, "I want to tell you something." He said, "What is it?" I said, "Just at the last minute, I decided I don't want to play this track with you today." I thought he was going to get mad. But he looked at me and told me that I had taken a very nice decision. It was as if he had felt my vibes and he knew just where I was going. All of his guys were inside the studio, and Sunny was looking at them through the glass. He pointed at them and said, "Do you see all of them there? They are all devils. It's only God, my mother, and Jesus Christ that are protecting me." You know, it was just Yorubas talking to each other; we didn't have to say too much. It was very quick. He understood completely. So I walked away from that coolly and I never touched those fucking drums that day, man. I just went back to Lagos.

Timewise it was still 1983. Besides my own band I was still doing some work with other people too, like some juju bands and some other people. I also had some old fans, like people who had been following Fela's music since the Koola Lobitos days. They were students back them and now they were grown up and working, and some of them were making a lot of money and living the fast life. I didn't want to know how they made their money, and I didn't really care. Seyi was one of those guys. Another one was a guy named Kobena Stephan, and he approached me around this time. Kobena wasn't a musician, but he grew up around Koola Lobitos and Africa 70. After a while he went abroad to study, and then he came back with a white woman and a son. Kobena used to see me when he would come to the Pussycat to play cards, and one day he told me that he was thinking about doing something with his money. So I went to see him with Candido. At that time, Candido had come back and he told me that we should start again. I said alright to that, since I had never really groomed myself properly for singing. That took a load off of me. So we went to meet Kobena, and he told us that he was planning to open a club in a place that used to be the Amusement Park Hotel in Apapa, near the Apapa wharf. He was going to renovate it and reopen it as a big club called Grandpa's Moustache, and he asked me if I wanted to bring the resident band. This was going to be a step forward, to have someone coming behind me with support and not leave me alone just hanging in the air.

Because of this new gig, I wanted to add more instruments to my band. I wanted to add percussion, a very good conga player, a keyboardist, and a good PA system this time around. I also wanted to add horns, just to make the sound full. I told Kobena this, and we agreed that it was best to go abroad to buy some instruments. I got my visa, and he gave me five thousand dollars to travel and buy whatever I could with that money. So I flew to the UK, and I was supposed to be going on to Paris to buy those instruments. But I passed through some small problems at the customs because I only told them I was carrying two hundred dollars. The customs and immigration people searched my stuff and detained me for one hour because of all the cash I was carrying from Kobena. The immigration officer said, "You only declared two hundred dollars but you had five thousand dollars on you. Why did you do that? Why didn't you tell me that from the beginning?" I told him that the law in my country is that you cannot just transport foreign currency. For me to smuggle five thousand dollars out of the country, I said, it's a lot of money and it's a big risk. Then he asked me what my mission really was, and I told him that he could look at my visa and see that I was continuing to Paris to buy musical instruments. Then he asked me, "What do you want to buy?" I had a list of things and when he saw the Prophet 5 synthesizer on the list, he said, "Wow, Prophet 5? My advice to is not to go to Paris. The instruments are more expensive there. Stay in London and check the shops around. I think you will do better that way with your list." He just advised me like that and then went ahead and gave me the visa.

I went around London and bought the instruments. But then the problem was that I had to get the instruments back to Nigeria and I couldn't reach Kobena. Did he think I was going to carry them back on my head? Because I knew that at the airport they would say it was excess luggage, and even if I sent it air cargo, I would have to pay a lot for it and the bread was already finished. Fela was in London at this time, and I asked him for some money to help with the instruments, but he told me everything had been spent on his tour and money was tight.

Actually, I used to pass by Fela's hotel every couple of days with my old friend Dusty. Fela told me, "Wow—if I knew that you were coming I would have called you because we just finished recording and we had a problem with James Meneh." I guess he was having a problem with his drummers so he called James to help him. I offered to help him out, but it was too late because he had already sent the band back to Lagos. You remember that James Meneh was one of the guys that really inspired me to play the drums in the first place. Fela had used him on some recordings that they were doing in London, but it wasn't working out. James had been living in Europe for many years by that time. Fela knew James as one of the best drummers in Nigeria back in the old days when he was in London studying, and he thought that since James had been playing in Europe for so many years, he should be even better now!

I couldn't understand what kind of problem Fela would have with a drummer like James. But there was one boy that used to play guitar with Fela called Laspalmer Ojeah. He got stuck in Italy when the band left him behind, so he came to London. Laspalmer was trying to start an Afrobeat band there in London with James Meneh as the drummer. And it became a big argument between James and Laspalmer because Laspalmer wanted James to play his hi-hat separately on the offbeat, like in my style of playing, and James told him that that was impossible to play. Laspalmer told James, "Tony plays this easily!" and James kept saying, "It's not possible!"

I walked into the studio just as this argument was going on. James told me this hi-hat thing was impossible to play. I told him, "No, let me show you." So he got up, and I sat down and played it for him, just like that. It was simple, what I call the "first pattern" of Afrobeat. Then I said, "James, come on—try it, man." But he couldn't do it. This guy was one of my idols before, and I found out that he himself cannot even touch what I've done! So I knew then that I had done a good job for myself by trying to work out something unique over all those years. Even though I was struggling, it made me feel a little better. It showed me how much I had progressed since the old highlife days.

While I was in London, Martin Meissonnier phoned me. He was living there with his wife and daughter while they were working on the Sunny Ade thing. That's one reason why I went to London, because I thought Martin could help me with the instruments. He called me one day and said, "Hey, Tony, we're in the studio with Sunny! Do you want to come down and have a play?" I said, "What? Martin, you must be kidding, man! Did you forget what happened last time?" He said, "No, don't worry, it's not what you think—none of the guys are around this time. It's just Sunny alone. Just take a taxi to Island Studio and we will take care of it." So I went to the studio. It was just Sunny and me, and I started to lay drums tracks down, and Sunny sang "Oremi," which came out on his album. We spent three days in the studio and we did a few other instrumental tracks. It was Martin producing. He just made some work for me, to help me out. At the end of the session, I went to see him in Sunny's hotel and he gave me one thousand pounds. One thousand pounds was a lot of money for me—those instruments would definitely go home now! I got the money and went directly to the air freight company to send everything to Nigeria. I arrived back in Lagos, and I made Kobena go and clear it. I told him how much the money I had spent for freight, just so he didn't think that his five thousand did everything. And he told me that at the end of the day, those instruments belonged to me anyway. So that was a good start. Now all I had to do was to get the band together.

Kobena had finished renovating this Grandpa's Moustache club, and my band opened that place. I had some guys from before like Ijagun on congas, Raimi, Candido, and some others. But I also got some new guys, like Showboy on baritone sax. Showboy's real name is Rilwan Fagbemi. He used to be like a contortionist, back when he was a teenager. He used to perform onstage at the old Shrine, before the music started. When he got a little older he went into the Nigerian Navy Band, where he played under Wole Bucknor. Later he went on to play with Fela for many years, but my band was his first gig. In fact when he joined up with me, he was still working for the navy. Showboy also learned how to repair saxes in the navy. He's a master of that—he can break a saxophone completely to pieces and put it together again. But to actually play music practically, it was my band that he started from.

So the band was on and we were sounding good. But it became a problem to get the musicians' salary at the end of the month as Kobena had promised, because he was starting to go crazy with drugs. He was taking coke and heroin together, and he started to go haywire. He was doing it a lot, it's like his whole day was taken up with this shit and he got fucked up in the head. What happened was that some Hausas from the North snatched his wife, and when the woman left, she also took the son. Maybe it was connected to his gambling, because he used to play a lot of cards, and there was a section in the Pussycat for serious card playing. It was a real professional thing and he was very good in that, he loved to do that. So maybe he was heartbroken about his wife and he went to drugs, but I could tell he was starting to ego-trip because he bought his mother a Mercedes-Benz and he was driving around in a custom-built Nissan— actually, he owned two of them. Soon he started telling me that he and Fela have the same way of life, because he was born on the fourteenth of October and Fela was born on the fifteenth—so they were similar. After a while, he wasn't concentrating on running the club anymore, and he wasn't doing any publicity for our gigs. Then he started to get into this bodyguard business, with all of these bodyguards around him, and it was hard to even contact him. He wasn't focusing properly anymore and I saw that this was becoming a waste of time. You see the kind of bullshit one has to go through to have their own band, man? I didn't want to leave one person that was ego-tripping and jump right into another one. I had been struggling for five years on my own, and I was thinking that I could either stay in this shit or find a solution.

Every since I left Fela, people had been advising me to go to Europe or America. People were always asking me, "What are you doing wasting your time here? Now that you have left Fela, why can't you just go to Europe or America to have a better life?" Everybody felt that with my ability, I was supposed to be abroad. But I always asked them, "Why should I go there? I was born here. My family's here. All I know is here. I learned everything I knew here, so why can't I make use of it here? You're telling me to go abroad. First of all, I don't know nobody there. When I arrive there, I'm going to have to fight just to live. Where's a job gonna come from? I wouldn't be allowed to work. Do you know all this? So thank you for your advice, but I'm not really up to it."

But eventually I had to start thinking that way. It was hard to be a musician in Lagos at that time because of all the crime, and it was getting even harder under General Mohammed Buhari and Tunde Idiagbon, who took power in a military coup at the end of 1983. The soldiers put checkpoints all over the city. To go anywhere you had to pass through so many checkpoints, so nobody was going out anymore. The whole country was retrogressing. And all this shit with Kobena made me tell myself, "Now is the time for me. I've got to consider this." My opportunity came after all of the Sandra and Sunny Ade business was done, when Martin Meissonnier arranged for me to get some publishing money for my past recordings through Closeau Music, which was also the publishing company for some of Fela's works in France. Martin was one of the partners in Closeau. He told me to come to Paris to sign the agreement, and then I went back to Nigeria to wait for the money to come through. I was praying to God every day, and one day I received a letter from Martin saying that the publishing money was ready and I had to come to Paris to get it. Just when I told myself it was time to make a move, this publishing thing came though for me. This was in 1984. So I went back and told my guys that I had to jump now. I had to put the cart before the horse and jump. I was leaving certainty for uncertainty again. I left all the instruments for them and I told them, "You guys take it from here. I'm gonna make my move now."

WHEN ONE ROAD CLOSE...

8 On the way back from Paris I passed through London, and that's where I was contacted by Pascal Imbert and Francis Kerketian, two French guys who were managing Fela at that time. Pascal was another French producer who used to work with Martin Meissonnier, but they fell out at the same time that Martin fell out with Fela. So Martin went on to work with Sunny Ade, while Pascal teamed up with Francis. Francis wanted to see me, because they were really pushing Fela in Europe around this time and now they were looking to take him to the US for a big tour, too. Francis told me that it would be nice if they could hire me to play drums for the tour, because he and Pascal didn't really like the drummers that Fela was using. I thought about it and told them that I would do it if they themselves hired me. I didn't want to be dealing with Fela with anything concerning money—no way! And Francis told me that it wasn't going to go through Fela, that they would pay me directly. So since they came to me that way—professionally—I took the job. Francis called Pascal and confirmed everything and told him to go to Lagos and tell Fela. Then they started to get excited about the tour. Martin Meissonnier was already pushing Sunny, and it looked like this was finally going to be Fela's big break in Europe.

As for me, I was in London and I didn't have any intention of going back to Nigeria. I wanted to stay put for a while. But Pascal was in Lagos and he called me to say that Fela had agreed to the deal, but on the condition that I come to Nigeria to rehearse with the band. Look at me here in London, and Fela wants me to re-hearse with him in Ikeja! I told Pascal no — no way was I going to let this guy get me stranded in Lagos. I gave them the condition that if I came to Lagos, whether the deal happened or not, Francis and Pascal had to pay my flight back to London. They agreed to my condition, so I flew back to Lagos and started to go to Fela's house every day, asking when the re-hearsal was. Fela kept telling me, "Yeah, we're gonna do it." Time was going and they were supposed to be leaving for Europe. Actually, they were now saying it might be a world tour because all the visas had been arranged. I myself had my visas for the whole tour. And you know what? Fela never rehearsed at all — there was not a single fucking rehearsal! I don't know why he wasn't rehearsing for his own world tour. I told Pascal, "You see?" But he told me just to go on with the band to Europe. It was no problem for me anyway, because while I was in Lagos I used to go to the Shrine, and I knew all of those songs like the back of my hand, man. That music was great! What Fela was doing by that time was like a big band Afrobeat style. I had been thinking about those songs and I knew I was going to play some shit on them that they never heard before, man!

When we got to the airport in Lagos, we had a problem with my first visa, which was to Italy. Fela's daughters Yeni and Sola had the same prob-lem. So the three of us all traveled together the next day, and because of that, I missed the first show, which was in Milan. They told me no problem, that I should join the band at the next show, which was at the Glastonbury Festival, in England. And it was a very big show because there were hundreds of thousands of people there and they were going to film the show. So we arrived in Glastonbury, and Pascal and Francis and everybody were happy that I was going to play. The festival lodged us in one of those Porta-Cabins behind the stage. Actually, our Porta-Cabin was right next to Weather Report's, because they were playing before us. It was like Weather Report was on the left side and Fela was on the right side. And when we arrived, the Weather Report people were standing there waiting for us, and they asked me, "Are you Tony Allen, Fela's drum-mer?" I told them yes. So they invited me into their bus to meet Wayne Shorter and the others. For some reason, Joe Zawinul couldn't make that gig. And Wayne told me that it was really a pity that Joe couldn't be there, because he really loved my playing. Then they asked me if I was playing with Fela that night. I told them, "Yes," and Wayne said, "Oh wow — we're gonna see the magic tonight!" And since they were going to play before Fela, they went on to the stage.

But someone in Fela's camp saw all the commotion that the Weather Report people made over me and went back to report this to him. Weather Report was already onstage and it was about thirty minutes until it was time for Fela to go onstage. And that's when some of his boys came to me and said, "Allenko, Fela wants to see you." I went back to Fela's dressing room and he said, "Allenko, you know what I just thought now? I just want to ask, if you play all these shows with me, will you be going back to Nigeria at the end?" I told him no, that I had never agreed to such a deal. He said, "Ah—you see now? That's why it's not good for you to play today, because you won't go back to Nigeria with me!" Then he told me that I could go on tour with them anyway, just to hang out and enjoy myself. But no playing. I looked at this guy and thought, what—is he trying to give me a holiday? I said, "It's okay Fela, no problem. No problem. I'll think about that and decide later." And I left the room, and went straight to Francis and told him, "Since I came all the way here, you're going to pay me whether I play or not." He asked me, "Why is that?" I said, "Because Fela said I'm not playing!" Francis started to get crazy—he just couldn't understand. He went to confront Fela and they had a big row over that backstage.

By this point, Weather Report had finished playing and it was Fela's turn. The band went up to the stage and I was just standing behind. And they started their fanfare for Fela to come onstage. The Weather Report people ran up to me and said, "What's going on, man?" They were expecting to see me on the drums at that time. I just told them, "I ain't playing. It's a long story." They said, "Are you sure you ain't playing tonight?" I said, "Yeah, I'm sure." All of the Weather Report people just walked down and entered their bus and drove off. They never even watched Fela play. They didn't give a shit. The band was still playing the fanfare and Fela hadn't even come on the stage yet.

Well, you know, the reason all of this shit went down this way was simply jealousy. Fela didn't want these famous people checking me out. When he suggested that I could come and hang on the tour, he might have decided to let me come up and play in one of those cities when not too many important people were going to be around. This is typical for Africans, you know. Our mentality is this way and everybody knows it. In the case of Fela, he would rather sabotage his own music than to let me get some recognition! And you can watch the video of that Glastonbury concert for yourself and see that Fela was struggling to keep the drummers on track.

So that was it. The next day we were supposed to be going to Holland. We drove to the airport in two buses. The band was in one bus, and Fela and his wives and family were in the other bus. When we got to the airport, he came out of the bus with all his women and he asked me, "Are you coming?" I told him yes. But I hadn't checked my luggage. I walked away and went straight to Francis and told him, "I ain't going anywhere. I am not leaving England, so give me my money now!" He told me that he didn't have all the money on him, and he gave me five hundred pounds. As soon as he gave it to me, I took my bag and went to get a taxi back to London.

I settled back into London to try and get my own career together. We started to work on my next album, *N.E.P.A. (Never Expect Power Always)*. When we were in London with Africa 70 back in 1971, we were living around Bayswater, which was near the center of London. But when I went back in 1984 I found myself living in Harlseden, which was in the Northwest. It was more of an immigrant sector—a lot of Indians, Jamaicans, and Nigerians. That's what I found myself in. As a matter of fact, I found out that there were some similarities there with the Nigerian environment—you know, the *ariyas* (parties) and all of these things. Those Nigerians had the same style of life as back home. But me, I wasn't even into such things back home—this type of partying, it wasn't my thing. So it made me shift my movement, to move more on the music business side, which was mostly white people. After a while Fela came back, because they had a gig to do in London. So I went to collect the rest of my money from Francis. And then Fela himself called and asked me, "Oh, are you still here? When are you coming to Lagos?" I told him that I didn't know. He said, "But what will you be doing here? There's nothing much to do musically, in London. It would be better to come back to Lagos." I said, "Fela, I don't know. I'm just trying some things. Let me work it out. Why are you asking me all these questions?" You see, what had happened was that they had gone to Paris and the drummer disappeared there! That drummer was a boy from Cameroon that they used to call Moustique, because he was very slim. I can't remember his real name. He was a very good drummer. He couldn't play like me, but he still had enough feeling to make the band move. So he jumped from the band in Paris and he stayed put here. But he's dead now. He was a heavy drinker and he was beaten to death by the police in Paris.

So the band went back to Lagos without a drummer, and now Fela wanted me to come to Lagos and do the US tour with him. But he wasn't speaking straight to me, and I told him directly, "I ain't moving my ass nowhere. I'm here now, I'm here." He understood me, and said, "Alright." And then he went back to Lagos to prepare for that tour. He was going to use Ijagun on drums for the tour. You remember that Ijagun had been playing congas with me in Lagos. So when it came to playing drum set, he was a complete beginner at that time, man!

Actually, Fela had been having a lot of problems with drummers since I left the band. I mean, he had many drummers, but he made them just play the patterns he told them and not to fill in anything too fancy. That was all he wanted to hear and he would warn them all the time. Some of my fans would come to tell me what was happening in the Shrine. They would tell me, "Last night, Fela stopped the show and asked the drummer, 'Are you trying to play like Tony? Don't even try it because you don't know what the fuck Tony's doing! Just play what I tell you to play and keep it going steady!'" It was a challenge just to keep the groove going— that is already discipline number one, and not all of them could keep it going. Fela couldn't get the sound he had with me, so he started to employ more percussion to make up for that, and he distributed the pattern among all of them. He was really trying to get something that I myself would have just played as one person. My friends were telling me that sometimes Fela got so frustrated in the Shrine that he would stop the music and ask, "Are there any drummers in the audience?"

So in 1984 the promoters hired me to make the show brighter, but Fela refused by making that stupid condition that I had to go back to Lagos with him. If he hadn't done that, I probably would have done both tours with him. And now he was going to use a beginner to play drums for his big US tour. That tour was supposed to be his big break, but it didn't matter to him. The guy was stubborn, man. He would never agree to anything that didn't come from his own mind.

But in the end, Fela never got to the States. At the end of 1983 we had a military coup headed by Mohammed Buhari, and Buhari threw Fela in jail when he tried to travel to the US at the end of 1984. So that tour never happened. You see? Once again I was guided by God, man! Because if I had gone back with him to Lagos, the tour would never have happened and I would have been stuck there, and I would have lost my British chance! I never would have finished *N.E.P.A.*! So I proceeded in finishing my album completely while he went to Nigeria and all these terrible things happened to him. I never prayed for anything like that to happen to him, man, because he had already received enough beatings in his life, and they threw him in prison for almost two years. And Nigerian prisons are rough, man. But it was just karma.

Fela going to jail at that time made things slow down for me. I didn't want to start pushing anything too strongly because it would look like I was exploiting his misfortune. So I just did *N.E.P.A.* for a label called Earthworks and settled down in London for a while. That album came out at the beginning of 1985, and it was the first album I did outside of Nigeria. Earthworks was run by a South African guy named Jumbo van Renen. I put the album together with a guy named Victor Addis who played bass and guitar, plus he was a sound engineer. So Victor played along with some of my guys like Candido, and we had the horn section from the reggae group Aswad.

At that time the Jamaican dub thing was big in London and we started to think about how we could use dub in the Afrobeat, to make "Afrobeat dub." I myself wanted to trip on that electronic sound a little bit, but not too much. Later I went into it more heavily. But for now I just wanted to make a fusion. Well, you can hear that the album is dubby, but the core is tight! The kick drum is solid. And to include dub mixes was a good decision because I didn't have too many new compositions at that time. I just had "N.E.P.A." and "When One Road Close, Another One Opens," and those two were written in London. So Jumbo felt like we should make it into an EP, just something to get my name out there in the market.

Things were cool in London. I had a girlfriend named Maya that I used to live with for a while. She was a hippie and she was a lover of this mushroom business, you know? Me, I didn't know nothing about mushrooms until one day she asked me, "You want to try it?" And I said, "Yeah, let me try it." Actually, I was playing a gig that night with Julian Bahula, the Zulu percussionist from South Africa. And I swear on my life—I will never take this trip again! It's longer than any trip of anything—like eight hours! And you start to see many things, man, many colors. The colors are too many. And you're the only one seeing these fucking colors! This eight hours, I was just waiting for it to end, praying to God, asking him, "Please let this mood die fast!" Praying during every song, asking, "God, please let me be able to finish this song!" And it's never finishing, because we still got to play more! I don't know how people can play under the influence of this stuff. I made it to the end of the gig, because I was praying to be able to make it. And when I flew off that stage, my girlfriend was dancing. She was enjoying herself on the trip. I was suffering. And I warned her: "Please—from now on, eat your mushrooms yourself!"

I didn't go back to Nigeria until sometime in 1985 and at that time, Fela was still in prison. His son Femi was leading the band, along with Animashaun. So I used to pass by the Shrine, and anytime I put my feet in the Shrine, Femi made me come up and play all those fast songs like "Pansa Pansa" that we used to play. I wasn't playing for the whole night, but I might play two or three tunes, and then their own drummer would come back up. It felt great because they were playing the music that I was playing before, and the people were jubilating to see me there. They were playing the old tunes, the Africa 70 stuff. I was up to it, but the point is that I wasn't trying to think about what I had done in the past. When I came from Europe, I realized that I must be broad-minded this time around, and not just stuck on one trip.

During 1985, I was traveling back and forth between Paris, London, and Lagos, and I was trying to make sure that I didn't overstay my visa in London. Meanwhile Martin was living in London with his wife and kid while working on the Sunny Ade thing, but then the deal between Sunny and Island was finished. Martin tried to change Sunny's music. He wanted to make it too electronic. They spent so much money on those recordings, but Sunny had to stop, because he never sold too many records in Nigeria with that style. The ones before it like *Synchro System* were still okay. It's just the one called *Aura* that never really took off, because it was way out for the Nigerian people. They weren't ready for modernizing juju like that, because it lost the rootsiness and it became something else.

So one day Martin decided to move back to Paris. I asked him if he was going just to visit but he told me that no, they were going back to stay. This was a surprise for me. I had already finished *N.E.P.A.* and it was getting good reviews, but I was still looking for a way to be stable in London, and Martin was my main contact there. So he asked me if I planned to stick around London and I asked him, "Stick around for what? You said you were gonna produce me and we haven't done anything yet! I produced *N.E.P.A.* on my own!" Then Martin asked me if I was coming to Paris. I told him I didn't have any way of going. I had some friends there like the guys from Ghetto Blaster—Udoh, Kiala, Ringo, and all of those guys that used to be with Fela. But I didn't have work there and I didn't have a visa to stay. Martin told me that if I wanted to come to Paris, he would work something out for me. And when he arrived in Paris, he got me a very good letter of invitation from Barclay, which was a big record company there. I needed that letter for my French visa. So it was done, and it was really Martin that enabled me to come to Paris. He was the one, no doubt about that. He really did many things to help me.

I moved to France around the end of 1985. I never in my life thought I would end up living in France. Back in the Africa 70 days, we used to play in French-speaking countries in Africa, like Benin and Togo. I played there, but I never wanted to live there, because I always thought, "This French-speaking place is not the life for me." Anytime we arrived at the border of Benin or Togo, the policeman there was speaking either in his native tongue or in French. We would joke with them, like "Ça va? Ça va bien." But that was as far as it went with the French. In fact, I refused the subject in the school. It was just a subject that was in the syllabus that didn't concern me. What was I going to do with French? I would never have dreamt of it at that time. But I found out Paris was not like England or America or Germany. It was a place that I arrived in and felt good in right away. At first I thought that even though the place looked good, I couldn't situate myself here because I could not speak the language. But as time went on, things changed step by step. I liked the culture, because what brought me here was the music scene and I saw that the African musicians had a stronghold here. Even Fela had already passed through Paris and he made it like his base of operations outside of Nigeria. He liked Paris better than everywhere and called it his "second home." All of the people handling his affairs were also from France, and the people there loved his music. The wife of President Mitterand, whose name was Danielle, even came to meet Fela. So I guess it was destiny. Nobody really knows where their destiny could lead them. But if I had known back when I was younger, I would have tried to learn my French back in Africa!

When I got to France, Martin kept his promise and immediately arranged a contract for me with Barclay, because the director of Barclay at that time was a good friend of his named Philippe Constantine. Philippe was a guy that was good for all of the black musicians living in France. Anytime you hear of a black artist who made it in France in the '80s, it was because of him. So Philippe signed me on for a five-year exclusive contract with Martin as my producer. I had used a little bit of the electronics on *N.E.P.A.*, and it was a good fusion between the Afrobeat and the electronics. *N.E.P.A.* was doing fine in London. Even the critics were saying that this was one kind of Afrobeat that Fela himself never played. It was completely new to them, and it got a lot of good press. So I wanted to follow up with the same approach on my next single, which was called *Too Many Prisoners*, and develop it better. I worked on it and it was really happening, like real Afrobeat, and I was happy with it. But Martin was producing, and after we mixed it, he told me that the production was bad. He wanted it to sound more electronic. So he went back to Barclay for a higher budget so that they could make a "slave," which means that the music we originally played was gonna be used to trigger some electronics, even drum machines. We copied everything to another twenty-four tracks and ended up with forty-eight tracks which were completely zero! I couldn't even recognize myself in the music anymore!

It wasn't my own idea to make myself sound like a drum machine. That period was the height of this thing when they were trying to put all these electronics into African music. I saw that this was something that was gonna be competing with the drummers, and that's what we were dealing with in the '80s. But I knew at that time that it wasn't gonna beat me because I'm a human being and this thing was a machine. The machine is limited. I felt it was too perfect, and too stiff. That is what those producers wanted at that time, they wanted Afrobeat drums to sound like that. It wasn't to save money alone, it was also the vogue at that time. But it cannot work. Because there is flexibility in playing Afrobeat. It can never be the same intensity all the time. I know that I'm creating patterns myself, and varying them. So to me, all that was just like an experiment. I was passing through different experiences and I knew that I would get to a point where I had to do my own thing myself, my way. Martin tried to do the same thing with me that he did with Sunny Ade. It was a big fucking mistake with Sunny, and it was a mistake with me too! So that's what happened to *Too Many Prisoners*. It came out in limited copies in 1986, and it never went nowhere. Plus there was no response to the record because even though Martin produced the record, he never stayed with Barclay to give them directions of how to promote it, so it received no promotion. He went on to work with some other artists and kind of left me hanging in the air with Barclay. But because of that contract that Martin got for me, I was able to get my *carte de séjour*, which is like a resident work permit in France.

Now that I was settling in France, I put a fifteen-piece band together because I still wanted to be on the road. Imagine — my own fifteen-piece band, man — that's bigger than what I had back home in Nigeria! I had three singers with me. One was named Sami Ama. He was from Rivers State, in the Delta region of Nigeria. He had his own band later, called the Bushmen. Then I had a Malian girl called Asitan Dembele. She was actually French-Malian, because her parents were from Mali, but she was born here in France. The third singer was a Senegalese girl called Julia Sah. She was the coolheaded one in the band. I was still calling the band the Mighty Irokos, like I did in Nigeria. It was a little more difficult because I wasn't working with Martin as much now, and I was more on my own. I was spending my own money for rehearsal, for instance. Even when there were no gigs, we rehearsed because I wanted to keep the band tight for when the gigs did come. But I had to pay for that. I had to pay for the rehearsal place, pay the musicians for their transport, and in the end they had to believe that something would come out of it. Later I found a manager to help me, a Camerounian guy called Joe Pando who lived here in Paris with his French wife. Joe was getting us gigs and keeping us working, plus he fixed me up with festivals.

Then one day, some of my musicians happened to run into Martin on the road, and they told him they were on their way to rehearse with me. The musicians told Martin that the band was sounding good, so Martin went to meet a guy named Jean-Louis who was the proprietor of a club called La Chapel de Lumba. That club was in Paris, near Bastille on rue de la Roquette. Jean-Louis wanted a band for his club, and Martin told him that he should go and check out my band. So Jean-Louis came to our rehearsal, introduced himself, and said he was sent by Martin Meissonnier. We just played two songs before he jumped up and said, "Fantastic!" He didn't want to hear any more, and he told me to come see him in the office the next day to discuss business. I went in and Jean-Louis told me that he wanted to give me weekends for one month—Friday, Saturday, and Sunday. So that was the first gig we had, at La Chapel de Lumba. And my musicians started to believe that the band was really gonna happen. Our first job was a steady thing for one whole month, and that's a good beginning! We were pulling nice crowds. Every night when I played there, it was full up, man!

After that gig, Joe Pando got me a big tour in Italy. And we kicked their asses, every night! But to be a bandleader trying to keep fifteen musicians in line was difficult because the more successful we became, the more the musicians started to get big heads. They started making demands on tour, like demanding more money when they already knew how much they were supposed to be paid for the tour. We had already agreed on that before we left Paris. But once we arrived at the gig, they started to agitate for more money. Especially when they saw the reception of the people, then they thought they could force more money from me. For instance, one would suddenly come to me before the show and say that she was not going to sing the song that she had been singing all along. We've been playing this song and everybody knows what they are doing, but all of a sudden somebody's going to start to say, "I'm not going to sing this song tonight!" This happened several times in Italy.

So I just told them, "Okay — I don't want no problem. If you don't want to sing, don't sing. But if you don't sing, you are going back to Paris directly from here. You are not going back to the hotel to be incurring bills while you are here not working. That's my deal with you — as soon as we finish this program, you are going back to Paris." And *bam* — I close my door and just wait for that song not to be sung! I conclude that I'm not gonna get this song today, so I will have to play something else. But in the end the motherfucker will sing the song! In fact, once we're onstage she will probably be looking back at me asking, "How come we aren't playing my song?" Even some of the Nigerian guys in the band that were supposed to be my friends, they made more trouble for me than anyone, especially when they were drinking. Another problem was that the musicians could not take Pando as my manager, so I was stuck between him and the musicians. Fucking hell, man. It's like sometimes I could become brutal and jump on somebody physically, because of their attitudes! Because of all these problems, I decided to disband when we came back from that tour of Italy. We played one more gig at La Villette in Paris, and after that I disbanded. That was around February or March 1988, right before I left for Lagos for the funeral of my father. That was it for the Irokos.

I was struggling, but one person who helped me a lot when I arrived in Paris was a Senegalese lady named Awa Ba. Awa used to be a girlfriend of Fela back in Nigeria, in the '70s. That's Awa with me on the cover of my album *Jealousy*. This is a woman that I had a lot of respect for right from Nigeria, because she was one of Fela's women that wasn't playing his Kalakuta game. Whenever she came from Senegal, Fela actually put her in a hotel with her girlfriend. She would come and visit Fela, but she never lived in Kalakuta. She was outside of all that Kalakuta craziness, completely. Awa left Fela after all the madness started and he decided to marry those twenty-seven women. But they remained friends and Fela eventually helped her open a Senegalese restaurant in Paris called Le Senou. Every time Fela came to play in Paris, she would cook Nigerian food for him.

As for me, I never saw Awa after she left Nigeria. I didn't know where she went; I thought maybe she went back to Senegal. So it was really a shock to run into her in Paris, because I didn't know she was here at all! But one day I was just taking a stroll along the street and who did I see standing in front of a restaurant there — was I dreaming? Was it Awa? She said, "Tony! Wetin you do here?" I told her my situation and that I had just arrived in France. It turned out that Awa actually owned that restaurant and it was only a block away from where I was staying at that time. So, *boom* — she took me inside for some food and drink and she told all the workers that even if she wasn't there, if I passed by they should give me whatever I want, free of charge. Awa knew I was struggling, so that was a lifesaver for me, man! Even though she was younger than me, she was like a mother figure to me, almost like a guardian angel when I first got to Paris. And she is still a very good friend to me today.

During 1985, I also met Sylvie Nicollet. I met her when I went to visit another friend of mine, an artist named Babatunde Okanlawan. Babatunde did some of my record jackets like *N.E.P.A.*, and he also did one for Fela. Babatunde had a friend named Esther, and Sylvie was a friend of Esther. I liked her direct, in other words, immediately! And so I invited her for dinner a few times, and that's how we got started. After this I went back to London for a few weeks, and then I came back to Paris around December 1985. Sylvie and I started to live together in early 1986. We were living in the 5th arrondissement on rue Guy Lussac.

I did the recordings with Barclay during 1986, and every time I went to record, Sylvie was there with me for the session. And during this year, she was pregnant. Our first son, Arthur — who's also called Toyin — was born in February of 1987. But this happened just as I was getting to the end of my carte de séjour. The problem was that my contract with Barclay was for five years, but the carte de séjour was only good for one year. At that time, I was still using my Nigerian passport. And as far as the immigration authorities were concerned, they didn't give a shit about the five-year contract! To them, I only had one year to stay in France.

Eventually it ran out. I had to leave the country to play, and every time I came back to France, they would only renew me for two or three months. This was really getting me mad because I wasn't even making any fucking money in France — I always had to travel outside the country to make money. And still, I needed their permission form to be able to go out and come back. To make any money abroad, I had to travel quickly, while the card was valid. And if I knew that I was going to spend a long time away, I had to obtain a new card before I left. That meant I had to go and spend a lot of time fighting with these immigration people, in their *mairie* (town hall).

It was the same shit every time. They told me to bring my bank statements for three months, but there was no money in the account, because I wasn't making any money inside the country, and what I made when I traveled, that's what we were using to live on. The money I made outside of the country, I was spending here in France! So what was the point of bringing a statement when there is no bread in the account? They didn't understand this and they continued giving me their shit until one day the lady saw that I was not going to move out from in front of that desk. I created so much trouble in there that the real boss called me into her office. I told her, "Look, I make money in the States, I make money in London, I travel and bring money back here. Now I want to go out to play in Switzerland, so I need to have my carte de séjour." She said, "But you never brought your bank statement in, so there's no proof of how you live." I told her that I had been living and I've never made any problems in France and that they were depriving me of my income. Then she asked me where the proof was that I had really been to London and all of those places, as I was claiming. I handed my passport to her, and she opened the pages and saw that the stamps were all recent. In fact, I had just come back from New York, where I was collecting money from Jean Caracos of Celluloid, because they had released *N.E.P.A.* in the States. I had also been to London to collect my royalties from PRS, a British publishing agency. That was for my old royalties from my old Africa 70 recordings.

Once I even went into the office with Sylvie's sister. And she asked them, "What is the problem? This guy has a son with my sister!" Toyin had already been born at that time. She narrated everything, because at that time I didn't speak one word of French. But the woman told us that having a son does not mean anything because I wasn't married, and I could disappear at any time. She told me that she was gonna give me two more months. Not even three months! And that anytime I came back there, I must make sure I came back with a bank statement. I told her, "Thank you very much. But if you ever see my feet in this office again, cut them off completely!" It was a Yoruba parable, whether she understood or not. Fucking hell! I was dying to kill her, you know?

That was a very bad day, because I saw an African guy right in front of me that this same woman was dealing with. He had almost the same situation as me. They started to argue, and the next thing I saw was this guy in handcuffs! She called the police and they took the guy right out! So I left. When I arrived back home, I was facing a decision, man. Sylvie asked me, "What is the result?" And I said, "The result is that we have to get married for sure, and we have to do it within two months!" Sylvie agreed, but when you start processing marriage here in France, it's not that fast. You have to be under valid paper when you register for that. And even after that, you have to leave another twenty days open for anyone who will contest it. Anyway, we did all the processing and it happened. Within two months it was done. We were officially married on December 19, 1987. And on our marriage day, just a few days were remaining on my séjour!

There were no hard feelings with Ibilola when I left Nigeria and got married to Sylvie. If we are talking about a marriage certificate, I never got that back home in Nigeria, because whether you get married or not, if you are living with a woman who has kids for you and the kids are bearing your name, it's automatically like marriage for us. Ibilola and I never went and said, "Let us document it," and went to the registry or to the judge or to the court. Even if we had got the certificate, it only means so much in Nigeria. So it was just a matter of continuing to maintain the mother of my kids, and working in Europe helped me to do that more easily. The first time I actually got married with a certificate was in France.

At that time, Sylvie and I were still living in Paris. So I went back to the authorities to tell them that my séjour had expired and that they should extend it. But they looked at my marriage papers and told me that my situation was changed from now on and that I didn't need this paper anymore. Actually, they already knew, because the computer showed everything. They told me that I should go back to the mairie to get the new type of extension, which was for five months. And I needed that extension because I wanted to travel to Nigeria for the burial of my father, who passed away around March of 1988. He was seventy-four at that time. So I went to Lagos for three weeks.

My father's burial was a big deal, man. The house was full up — my family from my mother's side, my family from my father's side. Full up. And my friends and my brothers, their colleagues, their wives and their wives' family, and so on. You know that Fela was the neighbor of my father, because of that property that my father sold to him on Gbemisola Street in Ikeja. So Fela's house is right next door to where we had the ceremony. And I remember that on the funeral day, the only person that came to the burial from Fela's people was his photographer, Femi Foto, to take pictures. My father was buried in Ikoyi. And then we came back home, for the reception. We were right next door to Fela's house. Fela was there in his house, but he never came down to pay his respects.

There was a live band, and the party was going and food was going. The place was full up and people were dancing. But it was on a Friday night and Fela had to go play at the Shrine. Well, somebody came back from the Shrine while the party was going on to say that Fela announced to everyone that he was stopping the show because somebody that was very important for him, that made him have his own abode, is dead and they are celebrating, so he had to stop. And he announced that the person was Tony Allen's father. He announced that and he came back to the party to pay his respects, but the body was gone already. The body had been buried by then.

With all my family seeing Fela at the party, they thought he would have given me a good present, moneywise, which is our tradition. All my brothers and sisters thought that yes, it's normal that I would have got a good "envelope," as we say. Fela and his wives came and enjoyed the party, and when they were going home, Fela asked for extra food and drink to take back. So my people prepared the food and everything along with a bottle of whisky and a bottle of wine. And that was it. They left.

But later Fela's good friend JK came back to my house before I left to come back to Paris. JK came to my house and asked me that day at the party, how much did Fela give to me? I said, "He never gave me nothing." Well, JK was just looking at me like "Don't make a joke, man. Don't joke. He must have given you some envelope." I told JK, "He never gave me no envelope, never gave me nothing, whether you believe it or not. He's there in his house, so go and ask him if you don't believe me." JK didn't believe me, so he went to meet Fela and he asked him, "Is it true that you never gave Allenko any envelope that day?" And JK came back to tell me that Fela said, "Give Allenko money, give him envelope? How can I? How can I give envelope to Allenko that lives in Europe and has the hard currency?"

Luckily for me I didn't need to focus on these ridiculous things, because when I arrived back from Lagos, a letter was waiting for me from the immigration authorities, saying that I should bring back the five-month extension. When I arrived there, everything was done—my ten-year *carte de residence*—this time, in a plastic card. And the law said I had the right to become a national in two years. But I didn't do it until the ten years expired. I know it sounds crazy, but I wanted to keep myself open because at that time in Nigeria, if you took the nationality of any other place you automatically lost your Nigerian citizenship. And that would mean that whenever I was going to Lagos, I would have to queue up for a visa. That would be a nightmare! I didn't want to pass through something like this. Because the Nigerian embassy is one of the worst places in the world, man. They will treat you badly and suck you dry, because they know you are coming from Europe. So I decided not to go for the French citizenship immediately. I left it as is. And then five years later, President Babangida said that we could have triple nationality, not even just dual!

Another reason I waited is that when you start to go for your citizenship in France, you have to get a police clearance from your country saying that you've never been to jail before. The police clearance in Nigeria is coming from the Alagbon, the central police station where everybody's records are. If you've been in prison at home, they are not going to accept that in France — they don't want any criminals! Well, I had been caught up in some stuff with Fela, but I was never prosecuted. I never faced any judge at any time to defend myself. I passed through police interrogation, yes, but no convictions. Still, I had to make sure. One could pay for that, you know. It's a racket there in Nigeria, for the police to make some funny money. I did it through a friend of mine. His wife is a judge and his son used to stay with me here in France for a while. They did it for me and eventually I became a citizen of France. I was really there solidly from 1988, but the official date that I became a citizen of France was June 3, 1998. And that's when my struggling really started!

PARIS BLUES

9 Now that my papers were official in France, I wanted to keep gigging, but I knew that to have more gigs, I needed to have a new record out. I was receiving so much praise for my music, but I never had a full-length album out since I did *No Discrimination* back in 1979. So I got a loan from Sylvie's father to do a record called *Afrobeat Express*. I got Victor Addis and the other guys from Addis Ababa studio in London, where we did *N.E.P.A.* We got the basic tracks done, and they sounded fantastic! The problem was that we couldn't finish it up completely, because Sylvie and I had to use some of the loan money to live on.

So I went to my publisher, who was Emmanuel de Burtel. He was later the head of Virgin. I hadn't received any publishing money in a long time, and I asked Emmanuel for a budget to go back and finish this production in London. But he proposed that instead of giving me the money, he could finish the album up here in Paris for me. That means we were gonna be fifty-fifty owning it and he was gonna be part of the business now. He booked a studio in Paris called Antenna, and he brought in his own engineers — one guy called Pascal Koziarek, who's dead now, and another guy named Martin Ingle. I'm sure Emmanuel thought he was being nice to give me the studio here in France to finish it up, but that's where the whole album was fucked up! Pascal was a nice guy, but he was really a freak for computers and electronics, and they killed the music with it. By the end of that production, it was not my music anymore. They did the same shit like on *Too Many Prisoners*—they used the original tracks to trigger their computers, and then they erased many things out of the original tape. The engineer was saying that the levels of the original tracks were not high enough, telling me all kinds of bullshit to make me think that I had to go with their electronic tricks. But at the end I asked them, "Where are my drums, man?" The whole thing was originally done with drum set, from beginning to end. But they took that off and replaced it with machines, and it sounded terrible now. The one thing you cannot hear on there is the drum set—on a Tony Allen record!

I would never have gone to Emmanuel if I knew that they were gonna fuck my album up like that! If I knew what the result would be, I would have just gone back to London to bargain with the people at Addis Ababa studio so that we could finish it there. It would have even cost me less and I would have come out with the production I wanted. Then when the album came out on a label called Cobalt, it wasn't really promoted. Cobalt was run by a guy named Phil Conrath, and he was recording eight artists at the same time—eight artists! I didn't know what he was trying to do—how did he expect to promote eight artists at the same time? Impossible!

After this, the whole situation fell apart. Emmanuel de Burtel dropped everything, because he wasn't getting along with the record company, which was Cobalt. He didn't like my manager, Joe Pando. The record company also didn't like Joe Pando, and Pando didn't like the record company. And me—I was the middle of the sandwich, being squeezed in between everyone. So at the end of the day, I was the one that got the blow, because it was my money lost. That's the way I looked at it.

This electronics thing also made me to see how difficult it was to be an African drummer in Europe, because it was like one extreme or the other. Either you have to do the electronics thing, or they want to force you to do some kind of traditional thing. Even before I arrived in Europe, Fela used to talk about the African musicians coming to Europe. They would ask the guy what instrument he played, and if the guy told them he was a drum set player, they always say, "Oh, you play *tambour*?" You know, like hand drums, *jembe* or something. They never considered that any African guy would be able to sit down on the trap drums and play them to the extent that they will be able to respect. It seems they always want to force the African drum set players to go down to that level of jembe or talking drum because that's what the Europeans expect of him as an African.

Check how many of us that were trap drummers in Africa that arrived in Europe or America and maintained it. Very, very rare, man. When they arrive here, most of them change to hand drums.

Look at Remi Kabaka, for instance — a wicked drum set player, man! You need to hear him, man. He's thunder! But now that he's in the States, no more trap drums. I was challenging him last time I saw him. I asked him, "Why did you leave trap drums? You should be playing trap drums, just even if it's highlife you have to play! Just maintain something African and do it on these drums for them. Why are you playing talking drum now? You never played this instrument back home!" For me, I will not accept it as a job. If it is hand percussion that you want me to play, I prefer you give that style to another drummer that can do that style. It's not because I don't know how to play that style, but I don't want to play anything that will make me leave my drum set. I detest that completely. The point is — why can't we maintain what we came here with? That's why Fela himself was not really convinced when any African guy was going to Europe as a musician. He always asked them, "What are you going to do there?"

This time was hard for me, man. It was a lot of frustration. Even when I was in Africa, I was still playing. But in France I was having a lot of problems playing my music. I knew many musicians, it's true. And people were always proposing things. But 90 percent of what musicians talk about backstage after concerts is bullshit: "Man, we got to get together to do this, we got to do that!" Ninety percent of that stuff never happens, and I got sick of waiting. I started to realize that I was in the house more times than not. It got to the point that I had to sometimes ask myself, "What the fuck are you doing in this country, man?" I was just sitting and waiting for things to happen, and that's dangerous, man. A lot of times, that's where the trouble comes in — sitting and waiting. And it was because of this boredom and frustration that I slipped into some shit that took me four years to get out of.

A drug is a drug. Either you use it for curative measures, or you are using it for kicks. Either way, it has something to do with the mind. In the end, it's the mind that wants this thing. Me, I don't believe in that — like feeling a headache and taking aspirin, and when the headache is gone you still want more aspirin. That's what people are doing to themselves with this addiction thing, and they want it harder every time. They want it stronger every time. Impossible—the body has got enough at a certain point! So see-ing these things made me say "Fuck it" when it came to hard drugs, man.

The only heavy thing I touched in Africa was freebasing cocaine. But you see, I can be in the middle of people taking this shit, and I see the way they are behaving, and from there I will be asking myself, "Would I want to behave like this?" So it's something that I could say, "No, stop." That was my own way of dealing with that shit. So forget about cocaine. Coke is a rich man's game anyway. You want to get high, your pocket must be okay. But heroin, you can get it quicker, and the quantity you need is not as much as coke.

I had never tried heroin myself. But in the 1980s before I left Nigeria, heroin became something that was flowing too much. It was so common there, you could even get it faster than grass, because they were trans-porting it through there. A lot of people were taking it in Nigeria, but they had the money to follow up their habit, so you wouldn't know. But those ones that didn't have the bread to follow up the habit, you could see them all the time. They were just strung out, they became nothing, and their lives were ruined. This is what it was like in the '80s, before I left Lagos. I was seeing the lesson right in front of me every day. People that I knew before that were up, I saw them go down through this shit. Heroin ruined many people in Nigeria, man. So wasn't that lesson enough to learn from? Did I want to be like that? Especially after what I saw with Frank Butler back in Los Angeles, I never thought that I myself would end up dealing with this shit. It was the only drug that I thought, "Never."

I never touched it in Africa, because living is too hard there. I never touched it when I was in England. Even after I came to France, it took me a long time to touch heroin. But eventually I took it, and right away I could see that taking this shit is like ruining your life. As soon as this thing enters your body—oh God, I just pray for those that are in it. Be-cause first of all the high is fantastic, so one gets pulled in easily. And afterwards, every motherfucking day when you are getting up from your bed, it's the first thing you have to put in your body to be able to face the day. Whatever kind of work you are doing—whether you are a bank man-ager or the director of a business—when you are into this shit you have to maintain it. Maintenance means maybe you have to have a lot of it at home, to fix yourself every day.

Me, I never tried to inject anything into my body. Needle business, I never tried it in my life. Maybe if I'm sick in the hospital, and the doc-tor injects me, okay. That's the only way any injection has ever entered my body. Not through wanting to get high. Even sniffing it came later, just a few times. I didn't like sniffing, because I looked at it like the sister of shooting. That was just something I just passed through quickly and I stopped. Because you never know what they cut it with. I never "chased the dragon." That means putting the heroin on a piece of tin foil and then burning it from under and smoking it. I hate it whenever I see them doing that. It's the look on their faces that I hate.

So what I did was to put the heroin in my cigarette. If I had to take it, I took it when I smoked. I always took it this way. Because even then, if there's any other shit inside that they have cut it with, it has been burned off through the fire. But the truth is that whether you smoke it, sniff it, or shoot it, something's gonna happen to you—you're gonna be hooked and it's the same fucking sickness you're gonna get. Just one week of constant taking, and *boom*—you're in! The next week, if you don't have it, you're miserable. It's going to be as if you're dead. Even for that one cigarette that I was taking daily. You'll be sick, and nothing can cure the sickness. That's what happened with me. I smoked it every day for a week and then I smoked it every day for four years.

I was able to maintain my habit during this time because some people brought me the stuff from Nigeria. So I could sell it off and make their money back for them, because I had some musicians around me who used to take the stuff. And this way I could take a few grams for myself. So instead of me spending money buying, I maintained my habit through selling a little bit. But I had to come off of heroin, because this sickness is not a joke, man. It's not any sickness that you can compare with others. No, it's fuckery. Pure fuckery. Besides that, I didn't like the way people were dealing with me. They were shipping a lot of heroin through Nigeria at that time, and I was beginning to be known in Lagos as someone that the drug people back there could use to sell their stuff in France. And my reputation was suffering here in Paris because I was beginning to be known more for selling this shit than for my drumming. I really had to ask myself what I was doing. What was happening to my music?

When one is hooked to that, it's really something to try and come off of it. But finally I did come off of it, with the help of some tablets that they have here in France. Sylvie's father is a doctor, and he gave me a prescription for the pills because he knew what was happening. When you take these pills, they make you not feel like having the heroin. It kills your appetite for it. They told me to start with four tablets, drop it to two the next day, and then drop it to one for the last two days. So I followed up the instructions, and kicked it from home. Because when I wanted to quit this shit, I wanted to be on my feet, not in bed. Not hospitalized. Not going through any goddamn thing in some hospital in front of the government in France that they could use against me. It was tough, but I did it. I was never hospitalized to help me get out of this shit. I knew the first three days were going to be a bit hectic, but I had the pills to soften it.

As long as you can stand a whole week without relapsing, you have gone out of it. Because it's in your mind. You wanted to do it. No amount of curative measures can help you if you are not ready to stop. And you know what? After those three days when you see the outside, even though it's the same sun you see every day, it's going to seem like another kind of brightness—something you were really missing. And you ask yourself, "Was I missing all of this brightness?" I was jubilating, and I never want to miss that brightness again! You also begin to get back some of your power. When you stop the shit, you also start having abnormal erections, that you don't even need! The thing is just jumping down there! That's because your life force is coming back, and that's when Sylvie got pregnant again with our second son, Baptiste, who is also called Babatunde. Baptiste was born in July of 1990. Then in 1995, we had our youngest son, Rémi, who is also called Oluwaremilekun. He was born in April.

So I was finally off the stuff, but I was still smoking grass. That's one thing I never stopped. Even that could be complicated sometimes, because I was traveling a lot. I'll tell you a funny story about that. I remember once when my band arrived at the Helsinki airport, in Finland. Everybody was waiting at the carousel for their bags, and all of a sudden I saw my sound engineer being taken aside by the border police, because the drug-sniffing dogs had come to him. The next person was my bass player, Cesar, who doesn't smoke anything—he doesn't even smoke cigarettes, but the dog went for him anyway! So now I saw that the two of them had been taken aside, and I myself I had just a small stash of some grass that I had hidden in my underpants. When I saw these actions of the dogs, I quickly took the grass out and I held it underneath my three small fingers. Before I knew it, the dog had come to me. And the border police told me that since the dog came to me, I must follow them after I picked up my bags. My bags came and I followed the police into their office. Once we were in there they opened up my bag, and two different people searched it. Meanwhile two other people took me inside a room and told me to put my hands up in the air while they searched my body and patted me down. Then they asked me, open up your trousers. I still had the stuff under my three fingers. So I took my trousers down, and then they asked me to take off my underpants as well. I did and they said I should bend over. Finally they said, "Okay—put your clothes back on." As soon as I was pulling my underpants back up, I coolly dropped the stuff back in there. They never saw it and I walked out of the airport. They never even thought to look under my fingers! They never thought that it could be there, that somebody could play this type of game with them. Probably because they were looking for quantity. But that was my lucky day!

While I was going through all of these changes, I was also engaged by Martin Meissonnier on the project of his wife, who is a French Tunisian singer named Amina. The recording lasted about eighteen months from 1992 into 1993, and the tour went on until about 1994 or 1995. We gigged all around the whole of Europe with Amina, and it was great. Martin is my good friend and he was trying to help me all the time. He understood my situation from day one, going all the way back to Nigeria. And he knew what I was facing here in France. It was just the follow-up which was the problem sometimes. So when the tour with Amina ended, it was time for me to try and stand on my own two feet again.

I kept my own band going through all of this. Around 1995, I put a new band together because I was still getting some small jobs. But I cut down to a quintet. I had a few of the people from before, like Claude Dibson, who is a guitarist, and Caesar Anot or sometimes Hilaire Penda on bass. I was just shuffling between small gigs around Paris, café gigs and things like that. I wasn't getting many gigs around this time. Joe Pando was out because nobody could get along with him. Sylvie was managing me around this time, while we were doing the café thing. The café gigs were sometimes good money, but also badly handled sometimes. It all depended on the place. And it was on-and-off like this until I started to do a gig at a club called La Citea, which was on rue Oberkampf near Menilmontant in the 11th arrondissement. That's where I met Eric Trossét around 1996. Eric was already a fan of my music, and he wanted to work with me. He became my manager, and the first thing we did was a production called *Live in Citea*. It wasn't me alone; it was a live compilation of the artists that were playing at the club. So it was from there that he started having the idea of doing the *Ariya* EP that was released on vinyl. Eric wanted me to work with Doctor L., who is a big electronics guy. Doctor L.'s real name is Liam Farrell. It was a big argument between us from the beginning because Eric and Doctor L. were telling me I needed to be more electronic, and I was still bitter about that shit of *Afrobeat Express*. Here I was facing the same road again, and I asked myself, "When will I be able to do my music properly, and do it my way?" Most of those guys in the business who have been calling the shots told me that I should leave it that way and that I shouldn't contest what they have done with the electronics. So I told them, okay—in that case, let us do one straight mix so that the public will know what is happening. That way they can hear Doctor L.'s contribution and they can hear my contribution. So that's what we've done on that one, because the EP has two versions of the track there. When the record came out, some critics said it was good, some said it was bad. But it did good enough so that Eric could follow up with a full album deal. That's when we did *Black Voices*, and that's when Eric started his label Comet Records, with a guy named Manu Bouble. This was around 1997. Eric had his assistants come in, and we all started to write again. Plus, I got a couple of the singers from Parliament-Funkadelic who were living in France at that time. Gary "Mudbone" Cooper was on there, and so was Michael "Clip" Payne. Actually, Mudbone still lives here. But the first time I met him was with Bootsy Collins, because he sings with Bootsy's band when Bootsy comes to Europe. Then I ran into him again when we were working at a small home studio near Republique called Corduroy, and Mudbone and Clip were friends with the owner, who was a French-Algerian guy. A little after that, I also worked with Mudbone on his own project, which was called *Funky Juju*. It was really a good time back then, working with Mudbone. He's a great singer and it's nice to work with him.

That's where we got everything together, right there in Corduroy. We had the electronics, but it didn't overpower the Afrobeat. With *Afrobeat Express*, it was too heavy on the electronics side. But now with *Black Voices*, we were starting to get it more balanced. What I was hearing on *Black Voices* was Afrobeat mixed with dub again, but deeper dub than what we did on *N.E.P.A.* The dub spaces it out a little bit. You don't want to put too much space so that the music is not interlocked properly. It depends on who is doing the dub. If I'm doing the dub, I know how to connect it with the music properly. You know, you must have a good groove to make good dub. The groove must be rolling down there correctly.

I was trying to make a fusion using some things that are happening right now, but I didn't want to go off my root, which is Afrobeat. We started to blend the electronics with the band, in the studio. We wanted things to sound live, like we were all altogether, but at the same time, it sounded cleaner if we overdubbed and avoided all of the sounds bleeding into each other. It was a small studio anyway, and there was no room for all of us to play together. I went in and laid down the basic rhythm tracks. Then my keyboardist, Fixi, came in. Fixi's real name is Jean-Francois Bossard. We wrote the music together, and Mudbone and Clip were passing by from time to time and singing. Then we overdubbed the horns. But we were still in the spirit of the live band because when the horns did their overdubs, they were hearing the band behind them while they were playing. Then Doctor L. came in and did the production, and he helped to finish the whole thing. Doctor L. was really the guy who helped to bring that electronic sound into the Afrobeat, and I have to give that credit to him because that is his speciality. He's known for that. It was like an experiment. If you listen to the raw Afrobeat of Fela in the Africa 70 days, it was clean — no effects. *Black Voices* was different. I was trying to play Afrobeat the way I heard it, but adding some things, and the album came out of that mixture. That album was released in 1999. People liked the album, and because of that, I took my band to the States in 2000, for the first time.

It wasn't easy playing that music onstage. The problem was to reproduce this music live as it sounds on the record, because of the role the electronics were playing in it. Even with Doctor L. on the stage, it was a very different thing. Onstage, if you are not careful, there's no discipline with the electronics. I tried to control it and make it appear professional to the audience, but it was getting completely out of hand because Doctor L. was doing crazy things that were not supposed to be there. You know, the electronics is a different trip, so it was kind of difficult for me. That is why later I knocked off all those extra gadgets and put the emphasis on the keyboards. The keyboard too has many sounds, but it was more musical. The sounds were *in* the music now, instead of *on top of* it. So there you can get the best of both worlds in a way.

It was during that US trip that we composed the music on the tour bus for *Psycho on Da Bus*. That was Afrobeat patterns, and we were still trying to push the electronics into it. And later I gave some of my drum tracks to different producers to put their own feel on it, and we came up with the *Allenko Brotherhood* album. I just gave them the tracks and said, "Do what you want!" That's why we called it the "Brotherhood." It was still Afrobeat. But it was a very different type of Afrobeat than what I had done with Fela.

Fela himself was supposed to do a show in Paris in the summer of 1997 at the Elysée Mont-martre. And for that show, it was the heaviest publicity he ever had in France, with big posters everywhere. Everybody was waiting for him to come. And his son Femi came before him, earlier in the summer. Femi was playing with his own band at a club called Trabendo. I went to the show, and there was one boy there named Segun Damisa that played percussion for Femi. So after their show, I just happened to say to him, "Fela will be coming next, after you people have left." But Segun told me no — he didn't think Fela was going to come, because he was very sick. But I didn't understand the gravity of the sickness, because it was five years since I had seen Fela. Since I came to France, I had been visiting Lagos every year until '92, when I stopped for a while.

Then I remembered the last time I had seen Fela. I went to Nigeria back in the spring of '92 and I saw him in his house and at the Shrine. And then he came here to Paris that same summer. I went to his gig here at the Elysée Montmartre and it was a full house. He was lodging down at Chatelet with some of his people at the Hotel Ibis. It was summer, and it was fucking hot that day — Paris was on fire! I was waiting for Fela there in the sitting room, and first of all, he had made the hotel people turn the heat on in the suite! I was only wearing a cut-off T-shirt, and I was really suffering in there. And then when he came out, he was wearing a big fur coat! I asked him, "Why are you putting on a fur coat in the summer — it's fucking hot out there, man!" And he just said to me, "Oh, but Allenko — don't you know that I'm sick?" I didn't know that he was sick. I noticed he was kind of thin, but I didn't want to start thinking any negative thoughts. Fela had always been a thin guy anyway. Anyway, about one month after he was supposed to be in Paris in '97 was when Fela died. It took me some time to believe that he was really dead. I couldn't believe that he was gone. For one month, I was not myself. I just stayed in my house feeling fucked up, because in my heart, I always thought that one day we would get back together and make some more great music.

But the question was, why should Fela die like that? It wasn't because he was old. No, it was this spiritual stuff he was into, because he didn't look at it properly. He was dabbling into things that he didn't really have any knowledge of. You see, these Yoruba herbalists — they call them *babalawos* — they work with herbs for healing, but they are also into some black magic stuff, and that's what Fela got into. He never separated them out from each other. He wanted everything to be real rootsy and African, and he didn't believe in any orthodox Western medicine anymore. In fact, he completely detested Western medicine, to the point that if something was wrong with him, he would only accept African traditional medicine. But that traditional medicine cannot cure everything. And the things it can cure, sometimes it works very slowly. They said that Fela was suffering from AIDS, but even lesser things like syphilis and gonorrhea—the traditional people will be running to the penicillin for that! Because if you try to cure them the traditional way, with herbs, it takes a long time and you will still be suffering and spreading this stuff around in the meantime.

I couldn't go to Fela's funeral, because to go to Lagos means I would have to spend some thousands and I wasn't able to do that. But did you see how many people buried Fela? Nobody else in the country would ever get that kind of burial. There were millions there, man! I saw it on TV, because they showed the whole thing here in France. Fela was a guy that was loved by the people. And when he disappeared was when everything he sang about started happening. In the end, I look at Fela as kind of a spirit being that passed through Earth, who was sent to do many beautiful things and some ugly things too. He had a lot of power—there's no two ways about that. It was a spiritual power. A lot of it came out in his music, but he also had the power to lead people directly. He was a person who could make people follow him, and I'm sure he was born that way. It was a built-in power. Look at my own example—I was not jobless when I met Fela. And I was the type of person that left bands very easily, if I got bored or if some small thing went wrong. The most time I ever spent with any band before Fela was one year. But when I met this guy, I ended up staying for fifteen years, and putting up with a lot more!

So I think that Fela was a natural leader of people. He had to be, because even with all of his crazy doings, people were still following him. He wanted to be president and all that, but he was not meant to be a head of state. He was meant to be a militant—someone that can agitate and make a whole country go crazy against their government. He could do that, and he did it. For me personally, I wouldn't say that I was able to believe in everything he was doing at the time. Because some of those people, they were misled by his philosophy. Even when you are a leader, you have a choice. You can choose to lead people the sane way, with good ideas, or you can choose to have them follow you like zombies into a lot of craziness. Fela chose the radical way. What I believed in was his music. He still remained Fela, and the respect that I must give to him is as a musician; he was a genius composer to his very last day. Even when he was facing his blues at the end, he was still writing some mind-blowing music, man! His way of thinking about music was very different. You cannot copy his music. Nobody should try to copy his music, or his lifestyle, because he was one of a kind.

I know that Fela respected me until the end. Not only musically. Some of his friends came and told me that Fela told them that when I left the band back in 1978, it was the best thing that I could have done for my own life. So deep down, he knew. Whenever he came to Paris, he would always call me, and I would go visit him with my wife. He was treating me extra nicely. In fact, the last time I saw him was the first time I saw him yell at his wives on my behalf—"Get your ass up and let this man sit down! Don't you know that this is Tony?" So I have no hard feelings or regrets, because at least I had one person pass through my life that I was able to achieve greatness with.

But it wasn't until after this guy died that his music was properly exposed! I never thought it would happen that way! I never thought that when Fela passed away, it was finally going to happen. The way I looked at was, why now? It should have happened years ago. Because people are now wanting to listen to Afrobeat, but when this thing was stronger, back in the '70s, nobody really recognized it. It was recognized in a way back then that, yeah, somebody's there doing something different there in Nigeria, but they never really brought it to light. But there was probably a reason for that. Maybe the characters involved, like those record companies that were dealing with Fela in the 1960s, thought it was a difficult situation. First off, they knew what this guy was like before, when he didn't smoke. But after he started to take things, he became kind of weird. And maybe they felt that to go into business with this type of character might not be really positive for them. Either way it would be a gamble. Because this is also a guy who has problems with his government, and nobody's going to come do business with somebody that has problems with his own government. I'm sure that none of them wanted to get involved in all these things, and that's why they stayed away.

So then the kind of people that came around him later had the attitude that they didn't care about whatever kind of person this guy is, they just wanted to sell this music. And I think that if these kinds of people had been around back in the 1970s, it would have happened then. But at the end of the day, those people that were in business with him at the end and who are now handling his music after his death, it's also like they have foreseen the end of this guy and prepared for it. They knew that at a certain time he was going to be gone and then they would have room to use his music as they wanted, because he wouldn't let them use it the way they wanted when he was alive. That's the way this thing appears to me at the end of the day, and I don't want to be part of this way of thinking. That's why when these journalists ask me about that period after Fela died, when everybody was talking about Afrobeat, I just tell them that I wasn't jubilating, because it should have happened the longest time ago. The reason I say that was because it was only after Fela passed away that people in the business started to do things like expose me to the US, which they never really did before. I always thought that when I arrived here in France in the '80s, they would have handled me like I am being handled now. They should have done business with me coolly. But they didn't do it then, because it would have been competing with Fela, and nobody wanted to put anybody else across Fela's way. Then he had a son that sprang up at the end of his life, which was Femi, and that too cooled my own side down a bit. It's like Bob Marley's story. You can see that nobody can jump in the way of Bob Marley's children because they cannot sell that person, whereas they can always sell the children quickly as the son of this legend. It's the same with Fela. That's the music business, you know? So I just stayed clear. I was here, and I'd been doing my thing my way for a long time already. I've been playing since the '60s, and I just kept treading on. I knew that eventually I would get somewhere, because there is no end to business, and I still had a lot of music in me!

NO END TO BUSINESS

10 It was really moving to France that made me start to work with many different musicians. To play with them live, that never happened too much because I've always had my own band going. My goal was always to have my own band. I never said I wouldn't work with anybody, but my priority was my own band. But I've recorded with many people. For example, Ernest Ranglin is a great guitarist, and a great composer too. I really liked working with him. When we got to the studio and he was handing the music out, he told me, "Just be yourself," and I created my own way of working according to his music. We spent about five days getting the music together, and the people at Palm Pictures really liked the album when it was finished. There was another artist in France, named Sebastian Telier. He's a guitarist, and his music is so weird—he's a weird composer. But I was able to put rhythm behind it on the recording and it worked. I recorded two times with Air, the rock band. Everything they put in front of me, I played and they were happy with it. Recently, I've also been touring with Joseph "Amp" Fiddler, who is coming from George Clinton and Parliament-Funkadelic. Amp is a great keyboardist and really a genius, man. He's one of my favorite people to play with in the world!

Actually, it was my dream to make some fusions with the rock bands, the funk bands, or any band in Europe or in the States. It was my aim to cowrite with them, to fuse things together. I didn't know how it was going to happen, but I was trying. And it was a string of events. The first guy that almost gave me a chance was Dave Stewart of the Eurythmics. But I don't know what happened at the end of the day. I played live with him one time, in 2000. That was me and Mudbone, live in London. Later I went to his house in the countryside and recorded with him, but nothing never happened. He was going to open a club called the Marquee in London, and his intention was to have me play there once a month. But the Marquee was only open for three months before it closed. Well, Dave told me one time that he didn't look at me like somebody to be going about playing drums everywhere. His intention was just to give me a job as producer for his label of African music, kind of like doing A&R. But it never happened, so I continued just doing my own thing. I did a session with Jimmy Cliff, in the studio. That was recorded and released on Jimmy Cliff's album called *Black Magic*.

When all those projects were finished, it was around 2001 and my own project was coming up, called *Home Cooking*. When I had finished all the tracks, I wanted some guests—hip-hop, blues, whatever. That means I've written those tracks for everybody. Keziah Jones was supposed to sing the first track on the album. He's a singer from Nigeria who is popular here in Europe. But at the last minute, he couldn't do it. So there was a group called Unsung Heroes, who had been on the *Brotherhood* album, and they suggested that I should meet Damon Albarn. Damon was coming from a British group called Blur. He was a complete discovery for me. The guys from Unsung Heroes suggested Damon because they used go to his parties when he was deejaying, and one of the records he always played was "Tony Allen Makes Me Dance"—that was the title of one of his own songs, even before we met! They played me some of his music, and I decided that I wanted him to come and sing on my album. So then they went to talk to him, and he was open to it.

We met at a bar there in London, and Damon was shelling us with drinks—you know, they say "shelling" in England, like in war. Even after the deal was made, we went to the studio to sing, and Damon came with two cases of champagne, about twelve bottles. We were all enjoying ourselves so much that we couldn't work that day, because everybody was drunk! So he told me that he would take the music to his studio and deliver it later. Damon is a good writer, man. He's a good lyrics writer, and he's a good musician. You need to see him at work in the studio and you'll know he's a genius. When he came back with the track—fucking hell, man, it was my best track on my album! It's called "Every Season," it's the first track on *Home Cooking*. That album came out in 2002.

After Damon got a taste from *Home Cooking* and "Every Season," he wanted to try for a bit of Afrobeat style in his own music. And I told him that I was looking forward to the day when we can work up something together from the beginning, and maybe even do it in Nigeria. And he actually followed it up a year later, because we went twice to record in Nigeria. Nigeria's not an easy place to work, but Damon is a rugged guy and he loves Lagos! He knows what is good there and what is bad. He and his guys go out in Lagos on their own, without anybody guiding them, and they manage. He gets on fine with the musicians there, and they get on fine with him too. He gave them a lot, things that they would never dream of in their life. We did two CDs of material with Damon, but afterwards he couldn't release all of it because he decided that it wasn't going to be easy for him to go in concert with this sound. It was going to divert him from his own identity of being a British pop singer. Also, he felt that if we put the album out this way, we would need a big band to tour, and most of the musicians were in Nigeria. That means a lot of problems with visas and all that. But he told me that I should come to London so that we could keep writing new material together. That's why we eventually did another record that they released as *The Good, the Bad and the Queen*. That one is a better mixture. Damon had to think about it properly because anything he touches turns to gold, man! Look at the Gorillaz project—they sold millions with that, and all of them are already millionaires now. Even their sound engineer had a hit single which went to number one. And Gorillaz is even bringing in more money in the States now. Meanwhile, I used the bread I made from *The Good, the Bad and the Queen* to finance *Secret Agent*, which came out in 2009 on World Circuit. I financed the whole thing, recorded it, and then I leased it to them. Everyone said it was a great album, so I felt good about that. Now we're getting ready to do another project with Damon, myself, and Flea, the bass player from the Red Hot Chili Peppers. Flea himself loves Afrobeat and I'm sure it's gonna be great, man! The way Damon came into my life, it was kind of like it had been written. He turned out to be the most important one for me among all these projects. Meeting him was like meeting another Fela for me; it was really that important because not only did this guy make a big difference in my career, but we are also very good friends.

Since then, I've been traveling all around the world with my band. Traveling is an experience, and it made me discover different places that I would have never even dreamt of just taking a flight to. If I didn't have anything doing in all those places, I might not even think of them, you know. I'm not going to these places like a tourist. Anytime I go to play somewhere, I might stay one week, maximum. Usually, I don't have fun trying to go and discover things, or see historical things. I never get time to really see the place. It's always that I have to go directly from Paris to the sound check in that other city. Directly to the sound check, and then stay at the sound check because there's no time to go back to the hotel. So you stay and perform the concert and then go back to the hotel and jump in your bed! It's very tiring and you don't get to see many things. But a few places I remember because we got to see a few things, and they really made an impression on me.

Brazil was one of them. When we played there it was in Bahia during their carnival, and I gave a master class there. And I saw many drummers and drum makers, and heard a lot of drumming too. And I took part in it. We did a real big jam session with them before the concert. That was fantastic, man! Bahia, you know, that's really where the Yorubas are. They worship all those old gods — Olodumare, Babaluaye, Ogun, Yemaya, and all the others. I even went to where they worshipped and I filmed them. That was an experience, man! It was different from the Yorubas in Nigeria. The Brazilian one is kind of polished — they polished the traditional thing. They used a lot of flowers, and you don't see blood flowing everywhere like in Nigeria. They have a cooler way of doing things.

The foods are too similar! They have something like what we call *fufu* (pounded yam), and I think they call it fufu, too. They use *gari* (grated cassava) and palm oil, and sometimes they mix it with dried meat in balls, or dried fish. What they call *akara* is really like our own akara in Nigeria. It's made from bean paste, like what we call *moi-moi*. They slice it into sandwiches and put some shrimp in the middle of it. That was the main thing to eat when we were hungry. When you eat two of those and drink water, you're okay, man. You don't need to eat it with anything.

We also went to La Reunion, just on the East of Madagascar near South Africa. I gave a master class there for the drummers, and to me it was like a little France down there. They speak broken French there, like, Creole. Apart from that, it's like you never really left France! But it's so beautiful, it's like a paradise in the middle of the sea. In a way it's strange, because you see big jungles, but there are no animals in there. If you go into the jungle expecting to see animals like monkeys or tigers, they don't have that. The only thing that they have are birds. Dangerous beaches, though, because they have sharks, and some other fishes that they call stonefish. When you are swimming, you get attacked by them and they give you marks everywhere. So they always tell you to watch it while you are swimming. They eat a lot of fish and it's good, man. Seafood business, mixed with French stuff that you can get in their Creole restaurants. It's tasty—almost like the way we cook stew and mix it together in African cooking. It's kind of the same style but with the French influence.

One trip I'll never forget is when we went to Israel to play in Jerusalem and Tel Aviv for three or four concerts. I remember that the last concert was in the afternoon and we had some time to kill. So we all said, "Let's go and discover Jerusalem!" Our tour manager took us in a minibus and we all went to Jerusalem. We looked around at the mosque there, and then we wanted to cross to the Jewish side near the wall where people go to write their wishes. And the police told us that we could go to the wall but we couldn't put any writing there because of the Sabbath. They said no pictures, no filming, and that we should just make our wishes in our minds. So we went to the wall and touched it, and then went into a church nearby. We wanted to go to the Christian side, but the police told us that it wasn't the same gate. It was like we were in the airport, with all the security! Police everywhere, and all of our bags and everything had to pass under the scanner. So we went to another gate and that checkpoint, to get to the Christian side.

We went into all the churches there, the tour guy gave us the story of the church. In the Bible, that's the church where Jesus Christ sent off those sellers, you know. Then we went to where he was laid to rest first, before they put him into the tomb. I took a picture there. After that I wanted to see the tomb too, but the queue was too long and we had to travel back to Tel Aviv to play. So we had to leave. But if I was a tourist, I would have queued to enter the place. And even the taxi driver was telling us that we should have gone to Bethlehem. Like I said, if I had been a tourist, I would have jumped on that opportunity, man. But unfortunately, we didn't have the time. So we had to leave the Christian side.

But what is the Christian side? What is the Jewish side, or the Muslim side? I didn't see any difference; you just cross through a gate, and you're still in the same land. There is a big market there, and you see Israelis and Palestinians mixing. And I could not tell the difference between them. That's why, watching the news and seeing all this business of Palestinians and the Israelis—I can't understand what is happening! Because to me they are like the same people! Same thing with the Christians there—they're all the same to me, they all have the same look.

I've gone to Japan twice already and every time I've been to Japan it was always successful, man, because the Japanese are very inquisitive people. They want to know all about what this Afrobeat thing is—especially the musicians. There was even an all-women Afrobeat band that gave me their CD, with them singing and playing Afrobeat. A five-piece band—drummer, bassist, guitarist, keyboards, and horn. We played a few gigs in Tokyo and a few other places and they were completely packed—about one-quarter of the people couldn't enter the club. It was so full with people that I myself and the band were stuck! We couldn't move. When we were finally able to enter the stage, we were stuck there, so when we finished, it was impossible to come off that stage. We had to wait until everyone left! And their food—I love it so much, man. I cannot stop eating sushi. When it's in front of me, only God knows when I will stop eating!

There is no time I've ever played, anywhere in the world, when the audience has moved from the place we were playing. I don't care where it is, but I know that no audience will ever move when I'm playing. They will never leave! When I'm onstage, I'm not there to joke with nobody. I don't come there to disappoint them. I want them to go back home and say, "We have heard something that we wouldn't even have imagined if we were not there!" That's what I put in the mind of my audience every time. Every time we go play somewhere, we always take them by surprise. Because they see that our own is different from what the others are playing as Afrobeat. They always come back to say that this one is something else. We're playing with a quintet or maximum a sextet, which you cannot compare with an eighteen-piece band. But still, we wrung them out so much because my music is easy to dance to.

For my own side, I won't say that it's necessarily political. Fela was able to use Afrobeat for his own messages because he was politically inclined, but he was not in the government where he could say things, or in the university where he could lecture and publish things. So he had his own platform to deliver what he felt about the government and what he wanted them to do. Afrobeat was Fela's power. But you can use music for any message you want to deliver, politically or whatever. You can deliver love songs and people can trip with that, too. Look at the Koola Lobitos time, when we were playing love songs like "Olufemi," "Yese," and all those things. It didn't have anything to do with politics or any roughness at that time. It was simply music for enjoyment. So my music touches on many different things, and that's why I could play with many different artists.

All these projects with other artists and with the electronics were completely different from what I had been doing in the past. But at least they put me on the road and made people think about Tony Allen. If I hadn't had that back catalog, it would have been difficult to work. These records and touring exposed me physically to people, and at that point I was being written up everywhere. Some people just came and watched for curiosity, to see the Tony Allen that they had heard so much about. But then sometimes other musicians would invite me for something like sessions or collaborations, so it was also a discovery. I presented myself in different forms for them to know that I can cope with whatever they bring my way. I said the longest time ago, "Put Chinese music in front of me, I will deal with it. Put Japanese music in front of me, anything. Just don't tell me to play as it used to be." I will play it and I'm sure you will never say it's bad, because it will relate to the music. And I think it worked. I have been here in Europe for fifteen years already, and I have been getting the big festivals, and touring all over. I'm rarely at home for more than one week at a time these days, man.

Even though I was finally having a lot of success in Europe, I wanted to find a way to bring my music back home to Nigeria, to open up some chances for the people there. That's why I did my album called *Lagos No Shaking*, which really means "No problems in Lagos." And that's why I wanted to go to Lagos to produce the album. Except for me living in France, everybody on that album was from Lagos. I even invited the juju singer Fatayi Rolling Dollar for my album. I had never worked with him before, but he's a guy that I used to know from a very early stage because he used to play at the Plaza Hotel near Mosholasi. At that time, Ebenezer Obey was playing percussion for him, before he started to play guitar and sing himself. The only limitation on *Lagos No Shaking* was the production, because I could get a certain kind of perfection from a studio here in France, but in Lagos you must deal with the machines they have there. I got the best I could get from them there, despite those limits. But all the critics loved it because that time, I went down to the real root! Working with Damon was what led me to do that album, because that album came out on Honest Jon's label, which he is involved in. For them to have helped me release that one was great for me, because at that time everybody was complaining that with all the electronics, I was running away from the original Afrobeat that I used to do before.

Even with all of the traveling that I have done in my life, I will say that Lagos is number one for me—I still love it so much. Lagos is my home. But Nigeria is fucking corrupt, man. I understand what those young ones are going through there. You can imagine some of them doing all these criminal things— they went to school and everything, and came out with some kind of certificate, at least for work. But they can't work. It's very hard to get employment there. Most places, they will tell you that you have to pay a certain bribe amount to get a particular job. But even then it's hard to get work if you don't have a "godfather." A godfather is someone that will look out for you and bring you in and get you a job instead of you having to pay a bribe. Even if there's no job there, they could create one for you! If you don't have a godfather, you don't get nothing. You must have a god-father. These kids have no one to look out for them and help them. And that's why I myself decided not to blame all these robbers. I would blame them if everything was okay in the country, there was no corruption and unemployment was zero. Then I would think it was crazy for them to do these things and I would prosecute it. But I cannot fully say that it's not proper, because things are not right in that country, man. It's not easy for any ordinary person to live coolly in that environment. You will go crazy there just trying to survive. The rich are always becoming richer, and it seems like they want to make sure that they clean out everything and completely bury the rest of us. It can't always be like that! When people see their colleague on the street with mansions, they ask themselves, "Why can't it be me too? Does that guy have two heads? No!" So when they react, the reaction is extreme and the thing is spreading. It's all be-cause of inequality. And this shit is coming from the top, from all of this North/South business, the problems between the North and the South in Nigeria. I am not a politician, so I am not an expert on the causes, but I am just watching.

It was the oil that made everything go haywire in the country. The oil money was supposed to be for the good of the people, and the gov-ernment itself was supposed to be for the good of the people. But then, our own government didn't turn out to be any better than the British. So much stealing and corruption, man! Believe me, if Lagos could have been left to develop naturally from where it was back in the '60s, it would have been something else by now. It doesn't mean that there wouldn't be any ghettos around — ghettos are everywhere in the world. But at least you would see that this type of ghetto is from the country that has oil. I mean, a higher standard of ghetto! But the way things are today, the whole country is fucked up. I blame the leadership in Africa for that. And I also blame Europe and America. Just go back and check for yourself; check what's happening in all those countries they call the "Third World." Check who was there before colonizing, and who is there now. Check who were the handlers before, and who the handlers are now. It's the same people, plus the Americans are a part of it now. It's like you have to dance to their tune, man — even after independence! Let's say you are a black guy in Africa and you know your own abilities properly. You see your counterpart — a white guy from Europe or America — and you both have the same qualifications and you are doing the same job. Usually the Western guy just knows it from the book, whereas the African guy, he knows it from the book and from the practical side as well. So who is the best? But the Western guy has a certificate, and even though he's working in your own country, you can never see the two guys being treated equally. The white guy is making double or triple what the African guy is making. You understand what I mean? So who's conducting the show?

The African leaders always pretend that their countries are standing on their own feet, but behind, on their phones, they're calling their former colonial masters. That's where all the bullshit is, man. The independence they gave to us — not even Nigeria alone, but to every African country that got independence — it's a tactic of giving the goat while hanging onto the string around the neck of the goat. We have a proverb in Yoruba — they say, "Olokun lo l'eron," meaning, "The one that has the string is the owner of the goat." If it was really independence, the Europeans would have to let go of the goat along with the string, which never happened. So who is the ringleader of the whole show? And how can that stop? Sometimes it appears that it can never stop. For example, what are they doing in Iraq? Saddam Hussein, he's only one guy. With all the technology the Americans have, Saddam could be taken single-handedly, without killing anybody there. And then the next morning when the Iraqis wake up, it's in the newspaper — Saddam is gone! But the Westerners don't want that. They don't care nothing about Saddam. The type of democracy they want to implement there now is just colonialism, so they can snatch the oil of those people there. Since how many years has Iraq got its independence? Many years back, man! But what are they facing now? And it's now the same shit in Libya, with Gaddafi. It doesn't have anything to do with democracy, man. It's all because of oil! In Nigeria, we were lucky that when the British gave us independence in 1960, they didn't really know about all the oil we had. If they had known, I bet we wouldn't have got it. But the British had just left, and it was after that when the oil started to show its face.

All the big heads in Nigeria—the smart ones that are supposed to stay and develop the country—are leaving. They cannot stay, because their talents are wasted there because of no opportunities. So they go and make use of what they know somewhere where it's appreciated. It's the same thing like my own case. I had to leave to make a life for myself in another country. Maybe in another century, someone will come and try to make a little bit of improvement. Like, one-quarter of improvement. Twenty-five percent better. I think that's all we can hope for. You will never get all, man. But even it if it were only that much, I would go back. Nigeria is a good country. So I'm praying that they'll be able to turn it around. I'm praying so that my own kids and their own kids will not think that Europe or America are the only places that one can exist. Even if a country is not perfect, it doesn't have to be that kind of chaos like what we have back home.

I always say that maybe it will take one of my own children to decide that he wants to play the drums. I have three kids here in France, and I have six in Africa. It might take one of them to be able to have my tricks. Because these tricks, I can't teach anybody. I cannot even teach my own children. I will just show them the basics. But when it comes to techniques, they have to develop it themselves. They have to have it in their blood, so they'll be able to develop it. They will know that their father had a kind of style to his thing, and this thing will grow up inside them. But really, it could be anyone. That's why I'm trying to do this DVD of lessons, so that there's a legacy to leave behind for people. Whoever wants to play like Tony Allen, get the stuff and study it, lesson by lesson. It's a discipline, you know—when you finish one lesson, you go to the next one. And after you can start to put them all together, and you have your own head to start working for you, to develop your own style from those techniques.

In the meantime, like I say, there's no end to this business. I have been playing music for fifty years, and wherever I play, the people always come and bow to me. I think people are happy to see a guy that's associated with a legend doing his own thing and doing it strongly. I still challenge myself every time with my playing. I still want to play something impossible, something that I never played before. That's what I'm after and it will be established. I have to do it like that. I couldn't do it any less because it's a big competition out there—I have to keep Afrobeat going and I must not relent at all! If anyone would try to count how many reggae bands exist, or how many jazz bands, or rock bands, they couldn't—it would be impossible. With Afrobeat, we can still count it, but it's coming up and I'm happy to see it growing. Everywhere I go around the world, I see Afrobeat bands forming. I know that it will take some years to reach the level of the others, but it's growing and I feel great about that because I know I participated in the creation of this thing.

I was looking to be something in life, and I achieved it. I took some risks, but if I hadn't taken any risks, there would be no way to achieve. Way back in the beginning when I decided to go for it, I left my parents' house and I told myself that I wasn't going to come back—I was just going to face it, whatever it was. And along the way I got so good that everybody around me could bear with me through all my ups and downs and the fact that I decided to put myself in shit more than security. I just kept on doing my thing because I believed that it was going to happen. If people were not ready to listen at a certain time, I was sure that there was gonna be a time when they would listen. And look at me today—I have reached a climax and I will never want to go and do any other job. The money might come big sometimes, and sometimes it might be just enough for living. I just need enough to feed my family, to make everybody around me happy, and to make sure nobody's lacking anything. That's all I'm after, and that is what I have. So I'm content, man. I think it's beautiful for me like this.

selected references

BOOKS AND ARTICLES

Allman, Jean. *Fashioning Africa: Power and the Politics of Dress.* Bloomington: Indiana University Press, 2004.

Apter, Andrew. *The Pan-African Nation: Oil and the Spectacle of Culture in Nigeria.* Chicago: University of Chicago Press, 2005.

Arogundade, Fola. "Why I'm No Longer Guy Warren" (interview with Kofi Ghanaba). *Punch*, May 12, 1979.

Babcock, Jay. "Bootsy Collins on Fela Kuti." *Mean*, October 1999. Reprinted at *Arthur Magazine Archive*, http://www.arthurmag.com/2009/11/02/bootsy-collins/.

Baker, Ginger. *Hellraiser: The Story of the World's Greatest Drummer.* London: John Blake, 2010.

Barber, Karin, ed., with Mary-Jo Arnoldi, Frederick Cooper, Donald Cosentino, and Bennetta Jules-Rosette. "Popular Arts in Africa." *African Studies Review* 30, no. 3 (September 1987): 1–78.

Bender, Wolfgang. *Sweet Mother: Modern African Music.* Chicago: University of Chicago Press, 1991.

———. *Der nigerianische Highlife.* Wuppertal: Peter Hammer Verlag, 2007.

ben-Jochanan, Yosef. *Black Man of the Nile and His Family.* Baltimore: Black Classic Press, 1996.

Biobaku, Saburi Oladeni. *The Egba and Their Neighbors, 1842–1872.* Oxford: Clarendon, 1965.

Chadbourne, Eugene. "Frank Butler." http://www.allmusic.com/artist/p6215/biography. Accessed May 21, 2012.

Charry, Eric. *Mande Music.* Chicago: University of Chicago Press, 2000.

Chernoff, John Miller. *African Rhythm and African Sensibility.* Chicago: University of Chicago Press, 1979.

Collins, John. *Music Makers of West Africa.* Washington, DC: Three Continents, 1985.

———. "Jazz Feedback to Africa." *American Music*, Summer 1987.

———. *West African Pop Roots.* Philadelphia: Temple University Press, 1992.

―――. *Highlife Time*. Accra: Anansesem, 1996.

―――. *Kalakuta Notes*. Amsterdam: KIT, 2009.

Darnton, John. "Nigeria's Dissident Superstar." *New York Times*, July 24, 1977.

Davis, Angela. *Angela Davis: An Autobiography*. New York: Random House, 1974.

Diawara, Manthia. *We Won't Budge*. New York: Basic Civitas, 2004.

Dibango, Manu. *Three Kilos of Coffee*. Chicago: University of Chicago Press, 1994.

Euba, Akin. "Islamic Musical Culture among the Yoruba: A Preliminary Survey." In *Essays on Music in Africa*, ed. Klaus Wachsmann. Evanston: University of Illinois Press, 1967.

―――. *Yoruba Drumming: The Dundun Tradition*. Bayreuth: E. Breitinger, 1990.

Ewens, Graeme. *Congo Colossus: The Life and Legacy of Franco and OK Jazz*. Norfolk, UK: Buku Press, 1994.

Feld, Steven. *Jazz Cosmopolitanism in Accra: Five Musical Years in Ghana*. Durham, NC: Duke University Press, 2012.

Graham, Ronnie. *The Da Capo Guide to African Music*. New York: Da Capo, 1988.

Idowu, Mabinuori Kayode. *Fela le combatant*. Paris: Le Castor Astral, 2002.

Jacobs, Dan. *The Brutality of Nations*. New York: Knopf, 1987.

Johnson, Rotimi. "The Language and Content of Nigerian Popular Music." In *Perspectives on African Music*, ed. Wolfgang Bender. Bayreuth: African Studies Series, 1985.

Kelley, Robin D. G. *Africa Speaks, America Answers: Modern Jazz in Revolutionary Times*. Cambridge, MA: Harvard University Press, 2012.

Kilby, Jak. "Master of Afrobeat." *West Africa*, January 28, 1985.

Korall, Burt. *Drummin' Men: The Heartbeat of Jazz: The Bebop Years*. London: Oxford University Press, 2002.

Locke, David. *Drum Gahu: An Introduction to African Rhythm*. Tempe: White Cliffs, 1998.

Makeba, Miriam, with James Hall. *Makeba: My Story*. New York: New American Library, 1987.

Masekela, Hugh, and D. Michael Cheers. *Still Grazing: The Musical Journey of Hugh Masekela*. New York: Crown, 2004.

Mattingly, Rick. *The Drummer's Time: Conversations with the Great Drummers of Jazz*. New York: Modern Drummer, 1999.

Monson, Ingrid. *Saying Something: Jazz Improvisation and Interaction*. Chicago: University of Chicago Press, 1996.

―――. *Freedom Sounds: Civil Rights Call Out to Jazz and Africa*. Oxford: Oxford University Press, 2007.

Moore, Carlos. *Fela, Fela: This Bitch of a Life*. Chicago: Lawrence Hill, 1982.

Olaniyan, Tejumola. *"Arrest the Music": Fela and His Rebel Art and Politics*. Bloomington: University of Indiana Press, 2004.

Olorunyomi, Sola. *Fela and the Imagined Continent*. Trenton: Africa World Press, 2003.

Oroh, Abdul. "I'm Still Scratching the Surface." *African Guardian*, October 17, 1988.

Oti, Sonny. *Highlife Music in West Africa*. Oxford: Malthouse, 2009.

Payne, Jim. *Give the Drummers Some! The Great Drummers of R&B, Funk and Soul*. New York: Manhattan Music, 1996.

Schoonmaker, Trevor. *The Black President: The Art and Legacy of Fela Anikulapo-Kuti*. New York: New Museum of Contemporary Art, 2003.

————. *Fela: From West Africa to West Broadway*. New York: Palgrave, 2003.

Seck, Nago. *Les musiciens du beat Africaine*. Paris: Bordas, 1993.

Seck, Nago, and Sylvie Clerfeuille. *Musiciens Africains des annes 80*. Paris: L'Harmattan, 1986.

Shapiro, Peter. "Tony Allen: Talking Drums." *Wire*, July 1999.

Slutsky, Allan, and Chuck Silverman. *The Funkmasters: The Great James Brown Rhythm Sections, 1960–1973*. New York: Manhattan Music, 1997.

Smith, C. C. "Tony Allen—The Soul of Afrobeat." *The Beat*, December 1984.

Stapleton, Chris, and Chris May. *African Rock: The Pop Music of a Continent*. New York: Obelisk, 1990.

Thomas, T. Ajayi. *The History of Juju Music*. New York: Thomas, 1992.

Thress, Dan. "African Drummers in Paris." *Drum!*, June 2001.

Veal, Michael. *Fela: The Life and Times of an African Musical Icon*. Philadelphia: Temple University Press, 2000.

von Essen, Penny M. *Satchmo Blows Up the World: Jazz Ambassadors Play the Cold War*. Cambridge, MA: Harvard University Press, 2006.

Warren, Guy. *I Have a Story to Tell*. Accra: Guinea Press, 1962.

Waterman, Christopher. *Juju: A Social History and Ethnography of an African Popular Music*. Chicago: University of Chicago Press, 1990.

Wilson, Olly. "The Significance of the Relationship between Afro-American Music and West African Music." *Black Perspective in Music* 2 (Spring 1974): 3–22.

Winders, James. *Paris Africain: Rhythms of the African Diaspora*. New York: Palgrave Macmillan, 2006.

SELECTED DISCOGRAPHY

I. TONY ALLEN: SOLO RECORDINGS

Note: Recordings in this section are listed chronologically.

Jealousy (with Africa 70). Soundworkshop. 1975.

Progress (with Africa 70). Phonogram. 1977.

No Accommodation for Lagos (with Africa 70). Phonogram. 1979.

No Discrimination. Shanu-Olu. 1979.

Never Expect Power Always (N.E.P.A.). Moving Target. 1985.

Too Many Prisoners. Barclay. 1987.

Afrobeat Express. Justin. 1989.

Ariya. Comet. 1998.

Black Voices. Comet. 1999.

Black Voices Remixed. Comet. 2000.

Allenko Brotherhood Ensemble. Comet. 2000.

Home Cooking. Wrasse. 2002.

Eager Hands and Restless Feet. Wrasse. 2002.

Live. Comet. 2004.

Lagos No Shaking. Astralwerks. 2006.

Secret Agent. World Circuit. 2009.

Inspiration Information (w/Jimi Tenor). Strut. 2009.

II. TONY ALLEN: RECORDINGS WITH
FELA ANIKULAPO-KUTI (NÉE RANSOME-KUTI)

Ransome-Kuti, Fela, and His Koola Lobitos. *Highlife-Jazz and Afro-Soul: 1963–1969.* P-Vine. 1960s.

Note: The following recordings are listed chronologically. As of 2008, all of them have been reissued on the Knitting Factory label, unless otherwise noted.

Anikulapo-Kuti (née Ransome-Kuti), Fela. *Fela's London Scene.* 1970.
————. *Fela Ransome and the Africa 70 Live with Ginger Baker.* 1971.
————. *Open and Close.* 1971.
————. *Music of Fela: Roforofo Fight.* 1972.
————. *Afrodisiac.* 1973.
————. *Gentleman.* 1973.
————. *Confusion.* 1974.
————. *He Miss Road.* 1974.
————. *Alagbon Close.* 1975.
————. *Everything Scatter.* 1975.
————. *Excuse-O.* 1975.
————. *Expensive Shit.* 1975.
————. *Before I Jump Like Monkey Give Me Banana.* 1975.
————. *Noise for Vendor Mouth.* 1975.
————. *Ikoyi Blindness.* 1976.
————. *Kalakuta Show.* 1976.
————. *Na Poi.* 1976.
————. *Unnecessary Begging.* 1976.
————. *Upside Down.* 1976.
————. *Yellow Fever.* 1976.
————. *Fear Not for Man.* 1977.
————. *J.J.D. (Johnny Just Drop).* 1977.
————. *No Agreement.* 1977.
————. *Opposite People.* 1977.
————. *Sorrow, Tears and Blood.* 1977.
————. *Stalemate.* 1977.
————. *Zombie.* 1977.
————. *Shuffering and Shmiling.* 1978.
————. *V.I.P. (Vagabonds in Power).* 1979.
————. *Music of Many Colors.* 1980.
————. *I Go Shout Plenty.* 1986.
————. *Anthology, Volume 2.* Indie Europe/Zoom. 2010.

III. TONY ALLEN: RECORDINGS WITH OTHER ARTISTS

Ade, King Sunny. *Aura.* Island ILPS 9746. 1984.
Air. *Pocket Symphony.* CDV302. 2007.
Annabi, Amina. *Wa di yé.* Philips 512 697–1. 1992.
Common. *Like Water for Chocolate.* MCA 088 111 970–2. 2000.

Dibango, Manu. *Wakafrica*. FNAC 592137. 1994.

Gainsbourg, Charlotte. *5:55*. Because PRO16134. 2006.

The Good, the Bad and the Queen. *The Good, the Bad and the Queen*. Parlophone 00946-3-73067-2-7. 2007.

Jones, Grace. *Hurricane*. Wall of Sound WOS050CD. 2008.

Lema, Ray. *Medicine*. Celluloid. 1985.

Psycho on Da Bus. *Psycho on Da Bus*. Comet. 2001.

Raman, Susheela. *Love Trap*. Narada 724359006703. 2003.

Ranglin, Ernest. *Modern Answers to Old Problems*. Telarc. 2000.

Raphael. *Je Sais Que La Terre Est Plate*. Delabel 5099952010507. 2008.

Soul Ascendants. *Variations*. Nuphonic NUX134CD. 1999.

Tellier, Sebastian. *Politics*. Virgin 137243594283214. 2004.

Ty. *Upwards*. Big Dada BDCD057. 2003.

Various Artists. *Red Hot & Riot: A Tribute to Fela*. MCA MCAR-25898-1. 2002.

Zap Mama. *Supermoon*. Heads Up International HUCD3132. 2007.

IV. OTHER SELECTED RECORDINGS

Note: Multiple recordings by the same artist are listed chronologically.

Ade, King Sunny. *Syncro System—Movement*. African Songs. 1976.

———. *Juju Music*. Mango. 1981.

———. *Ajoo*. Sunny Alade. 1982.

———. *Synchro System*. Island. 1983.

———. *Aura*. Island. 1984.

Akinsanya, Adeolu, and His Rio Lindo Orchestra. *Those Days in Nigeria: Juju Roots*. Evergreen. 2011.

Baker, Ginger. *Stratavarious*. Atco SD 7013. 1972.

Blakey, Art. *Moanin'*. Blue Note BST 84003. 1959.

———. *A Night in Tunisia*. Blue Note BLP 4049. 1960.

———. *The African Beat*. Blue Note BLP 4097. 1962.

Blur. *Music Is My Radar*. Food CDFOODS135. 2000.

Brown, James. *Star Time*. Polydor 331. 1991.

Butler, Frank. *The Stepper*. Xanadu 152. 1977.

———. *Wheelin' and Dealin'*. Xanadu 169. 1978.

Checker, Chubby. *The Best of Chubby Checker 1959–1963*. Abkco 9225. 2005.

Coltrane, John. *Kulu Sé Mama*. Impulse A 9106. 1965.

———. *The Classic Quartet: The Complete Impulse! Recordings*. Impulse IMPD 8–280. 1998.

Davis, Miles. *Seven Steps to Heaven*. Columbia 65341. 1963.

———. *The Complete Studio Recordings of the Miles Davis Quintet 1965–1968*. Columbia/Legacy C6K 67398. 1998.

Edwards, Jackie. *Best of Jackie Edwards*. Island 936. 1966.

Ghetto Blaster. *People*. Moving Target MT 012. 1985.

Goodman, Benny. *Live at Carnegie Hall*. Columbia G2K 40244. 1938.

Ishola, Haruna. *Apala Messenger*. Indigedisc 495–002. 2001.

Julius (Ekemode), Orlando. *Dance Afro-Beat*. Shanachie 43029. 1985.

———. *Super Afro Soul*. Afro Strut STRUTACD 002. 2000.

———. *Orlando's Afro Ideas.* Eko Sound/Soundway 001. 2003.

———. *Orlando Julius and His Afro Sounders.* Voodoo Funk VFCD01. 2011.

Lawson, Cardinal Rex Jim. *The Classics, Volume 1.* Premier Music KMCD 006. 2004(?).

———. *The Classics, Volume 2.* Premier Music KMCD 009. 2004(?).

Masekela, Hugh. *Introducing Hedzoleh Soundz.* Blue Thumb BTS62. 1973.

Mensah, E. T. *All for You.* RetroAfric Retro1XCD. 1998.

———. *Day by Day.* RetroAfric Retro3CD. 2003.

Olaiya, Victor. *Three Decades of Highlife: The Best of Dr. Victor Olaiya.* Premier. 2003.

Parker, Charlie. *The Genius of Charlie Parker #3: Now's the Time.* Verve MGV 8005. 1953.

Pino, Geraldo, and the Heartbeats. *Heavy Heavy Heavy.* Retro Afric 20. 2005.

Ramblers Dance Band. *The Hit Sound of the Ramblers Dance Band.* Flame Tree FLTRCD 526. 1975.

Rollins, Sonny. *Saxophone Colossus.* Prestige PRLP 7079. 1956.

Silver, Horace. *Song for My Father.* Blue Note BLP 4185. 1964.

Small, Millicent. *My Boy Lollipop.* Smash 1893. 1964.

Various Artists. *Juju Roots: 1930s–1950s.* Rounder 5017. 1985.

———. *Giants of Dance Band Highlife 1950s–1970s.* Original Music OMCD 011. 1990s.

———. *Azagas and Archibogs: The Sixties Sounds of Lagos Highlife.* Original Music OMCD 014. 1990s.

———. *Yoruba Street Percussion.* Original Music OMCD 016. 1990s.

———. *Money No Be Sand.* Original Music OMCD 016. 1990s.

———. *Afro-Baby: The Evolution of the Afro-Sound in Nigeria.* Soundway SNDWCD002. 2004.

———. *Lagos All Routes.* HJRCD17. 2005.

———. *Lagos Chop-Up.* HJRCD15. 2005.

———. *Out of Cuba: Latin American Music Takes Africa by Storm.* Topic TSCD927. 2005.

———. *Àwon Ojísé Olorun: Popular Music in Yorubaland, 1931–1952.* Savannahphone AFCD 010. 2006.

———. *Ghana Special: Modern Highlife, Afro-Sounds and Ghanaian Blues 1968–81.* Soundway SNDWCD016. 2009.

———. *Nigeria 70: The Definitive Story of 1970s Funky Lagos.* Strut 044CD. 2009.

———. *Nigeria Afrobeat Special: The New Explosive Sound in 1970s Nigeria.* Soundway SNDW LP021. 2010.

———. *Nigeria Special, Volume 2: Modern Highlife, Afro Sounds, and Nigerian Blues 1970–1976.* SNDW LP020. 2010.

Warren, Guy (Kofi Ghanaba). *Themes for African Drums.* RCA-Victor LSP-1864. 1959.

———. *Ghanaba: The Divine Drummer.* RetroAfric Retro 16CD. 2002.

Williams, Tunde. *Mr. Big Mouth.* Honest Jons CD 101/2. 1977.

index

Wallace, Leroy "Horsemouth," 1, 10
Warren, Guy. *See* Ghanaba, Kofi
Washington, Morris, 70–71, 72, 78
"Water No Get Enemy," 9
Weather Report, 147–48
Wendell, Mr. (friend), 73–74, 85
Wesley, Fred, 12
Western Toppers, the, 44–45, 49, 50,
    52–54, 54, 126
Weston, Randy, 113
"When One Road Close, Another One
    Opens," 151
Williams, Rex, 44
Williams, Tony, 1, 4, 50
Williams, Tunde, 54, 76, 88, 132–33, 135
Williams, Y.D., 117, 132–33
Willington, Yomi, 81

Wokoma, Charles, 42–43
Wonder, Stevie, 113
Wright, Richard, 14

Yar'Adua, Shehu, 87
"Yellow Fever," 9
"Yese," 54, 180
Yoruba: Allen's heritage, 2, 8, 21–23, 24;
    conflict with Hausas, 48; culture, 2, 6,
    23, 26, 141, 178; language, 22, 45; music,
    27–29, 89, 130–31; proverbs, 158, 183;
    traditional medicine, 137, 171–72
Yusuf, M. D., 86

Zawinul, Joe, 147
"Zombie," 87, 114